THE  TIMES
GUIDE TO
THE
ENVIRONMENT

First published by Times Books,
16, Golden Square
London W1R 4BN

© Times Books, London 1990
Reprinted with revisions 1990

British Library Cataloguing in Publication Data
Simpson, Struan
The Times Guide to The Environment : a comprehensive
handbook to Green issues.
1. Environment. Conservation
I. Title
333.72

ISBN 0-7230-0347-5

Typeset by Rowland Phototypesetting Limited,
Bury St Edmunds, Suffolk

Printed in Great Britain by
Richard Clay Limited, St Ives plc
Bungay, Suffolk

THE TIMES GUIDE TO THE ENVIRONMENT

A COMPREHENSIVE HANDBOOK TO GREEN ISSUES

STRUAN SIMPSON

TIMES BOOKS

About the author

Struan Simpson advises on the international regulation of safety and the environment and has wider interests in Third World development and the opportunities for disabled people in recreation and employment. In the 1960s and 1970s Struan spent several years in West Africa organizing family planning programmes for The Ford Foundation and was awarded a Fellowship to the University of California at Berkeley in recognition of his work on infant feeding in Nigeria. Until recently, when he began to take a close interest in ecology, Struan worked as an independent consultant to the offshore oil industry, contributing to the development of an international basis for comparing accident data and representing the industry at the International Maritime Organization.

Apart from writing this book, in the past year he has worked on projects for the Nature Conservancy Council and the Sports Council as well as producing a guide to UK nature reserves for the Country Landowners Association and RADAR. Struan Simpson is fifty-three years old, was educated at Kingston Grammar School and lives with his wife Jean and two children in Westminster.

Publisher's note: The paper in this book is manufactured from wood derived from an economically sustainable forest.

CONTENTS

APPENDICES

PREFACE

Most, if not all, pollution problems in developed countries are tractable though not necessarily economically expedient. Sustainable economic growth generally and the problems of developing countries in particular require adjustments to economic perspectives and a longer-term view than is normally characteristic of market philosophy. Nuclear power, global warming and biodiversity are three key issues which are subject to both ethical and scientific evaluation, and raise fundamental questions on the socio-economic organization of the means of wealth creation.

Nuclear war and atmospheric pollution

The Scientific Committee on the Problems of the Environment (SCOPE) has defined the risks of a large-scale nuclear war overshadowing all other threats to humanity and how they pose the ultimate hazard to life on this planet. Smoke and dust resulting from fires generated by thermonuclear explosions would reduce the intensity of sunlight and change the chemical composition of the atmosphere. Large-scale weather disruptions and far-reaching biological consequences would follow. Immediate death for up to one billion people and subsequent death, disease and famine are realistically calculated to affect 4 billion people.

The sun, whose surface temperature is 6000°C, warms the Earth from a distance of 150 million km. Thermal energy released from nuclear explosions is of the same order of magnitude, but from a distance of 4.15–14 km above the Earth's surface.

The 1988 Toronto Conference on the 'Changing Atmosphere: Implications for Global Security' described man-made air pollution as an 'unintended, uncontrolled, globally pervasive experiment whose ultimate consequences could be second only to a global nuclear war'.

While undoubtedly the worst consequences of global warming would have the most severe effects upon the world's population, the extent to which man-made air pollution can affect climate is still conjecture. The principles for control of industrial emissions are nevertheless in urgent need of a more widespread endorsement than that given by Mrs Thatcher following the May 1990 UNEP Report and the IPCC meeting. Comparing the consequences of a nuclear holocaust to the potential effects of atmospheric pollution raises the question of whether a diversion of military expenditures may be a more effective approach. The political choice is security or stability, goals which appear to have become synonymous only by an accident of semantics.

Conservation, pollution control and industrial society

Much of the scientific background to our perceptions and understanding of the industrial effects on the biosphere, global ecology, the environment and development comes from US academic and scientific institutions. US research budgets are large; up to $1.0 billion is likely to be voted for climate studies alone. Research budgets available to the scientific community outside the USA, enabling other nations to contribute fully to the understanding of global environmental problems, are very low in real and comparative terms, restricting the ability of policymakers to take rational decisions which would balance environmental and economic criteria.

The findings and propositions of US research carry considerable weight in the formulation of government and industry attitudes outside the USA towards domestic and foreign policy and consumer behaviour. Nevertheless, other national programmes for scientific discovery of the relationship between energy production and the natural forces that shape the destiny of mankind, involving the world's major scientific institutions, are under way. These are either independent or part of international programmes initiated by intergovernmental agencies and the non-governmental international scientific community.

Europe and its institutions are becoming a major influence upon the global attitudes through the environmental component of its economic policies and their relations with the Third World. The implementation and success of global initiatives by regional institutions, not only in Europe but also in Asia and Africa, will depend upon the changing role and responsibilities of the USA, as producers and consumers and as the centre of many multinational operations, to ameliorate the environmental problems facing industrial societies and to improve the economic status of Third World countries.

The US contribution to global pollution can be attributed to high industrial intensity and the greater levels of personal consumption of its 246 million inhabitants. Five per cent of the world's population consumes nearly 30% of total world primary energy, and produces effluents and waste at a level that probably will never be matched at a per capita level anywhere else. Western Europe, representing 7%, requires half as much energy as the USA. The USSR, with 6%, consumes a percentage point more than Western Europe. Western Europe and the USSR, with two-and-a-third times the population of the USA, uses approximately the same volume of energy. Together, Western Europe, the USA and the USSR (total population: 870 million) consume 60% of the world's energy supply, while the balance is unevenly divided among the remaining 4.2 billion in other industrialized countries and the developing countries of the Third World.

Global patterns of energy consumption, effluent and waste and the problems of improving living standards in the Third World are the factors which undermine the very foundations and credibility of politics, law, economics, trade, industry and secular religion.

There has been recent discussion in the press concerning the role and future of the United Nations. It is difficult to shed any new light on the general debate as to whether a badly organized system is better than no system at all. Accepting the strengths and weaknesses of the UN in its role of maintaining global security, some of its present problems undoubtedly stem from the difficulties facing large, bureaucratic and politically imbalanced organizations to respond appropriately to purposes for which they were not originally set up and which cannot be coped with unilaterally by member governments. The problems of AIDS, drug abuse, world terrorism and Third World poverty are major examples. In terms of the environment, UN agencies have both set the agenda and supported the involvement of non-governmental scientific and conservation organizations since the early 1950s. The UN system provides the framework for co-operation with its existing range of international agreements and conventions on the environment as well as the fora in which non-governmental interests can be represented.

Global environmental management requires a more intimate alignment between natural science, economics and international politics and research and programme funding to make such an alignment possible and productive. Otherwise, the propositions contained in theoretical models are likely to overtake industrial societies and the goals of sustainable development in the Third World will prove to be unattainable.

This preface is intended to be neither blunt nor bleak, even though it may appear to be both. The author is riven by internal conflict, between natural personal optimism at the expansion of public and scientific awareness of the need to change our ways and awe at the idea of instilling post-development ideals among billions of people of whom the only option is to consume finite resources to meet their day-to-day needs.

Demography offers some clues to the tendency of populations to make natural adjustments to ensure their survival. In the Third World, having more babies is a micro-insurance policy in the absence of social and economic supports. Fewer babies result when there is education, employment, improved standards of living and prospects of family stability.

Environmental stability and population stability are interdependent. While developed countries can make conscious adjustments to reduce pollution, conserve resources and protect the environment, global stability will come about only when Third World governments promote agricultural and industrial policies which allow families, in the aggregate, to be more confident about their survival and their future.

Struan Simpson, October 1990

ACKNOWLEDGEMENTS

The author would like to thank the following organizations for supplying the information and advice upon which much of this book is based.

International Council of Scientific Unions (ICSU)
United Nations Environment Programme (UNEP)
National Aeronautics and Space Administration (NASA)
Natural Environment Research Council (NERC)
Organization of Economic and Cultural Development (OECD)
Commission of the European Communities (CEC)
Council of Europe (COE)
Institute of European Environment Policy (IEEP)
European Free Trade Association (EFTA)
North Atlantic Treaty Organization (NATO)
British Antarctic Survey (BAS)
The International Union for the Conservation of Nature and Natural Resources (IUCN)
UK Department of the Environment
UN Scientific Committee on the Effects of Atomic Radiation (UNSCEAR)
National Radiological Protection Board (NRPB)
Nature Conservancy Council (NCC)
Countryside Commission
UN Food and Agriculture Organization (FAO)
Overseas Development Administration (ODA)
Friends of the Earth (FOE)

Thanks are gratefully due to James Shepherd, who edited this book, to Mike McCarthy, Environmental Correspondent of *The Times*, and to the staff of Times Books for all their invaluable help.

The views expressed are entirely those of the author. It is hoped that they are in consonance with fact and will provide a useful perspective.

INTRODUCTION

This book outlines the manner in which nature conservation and pollution control have become important factors of political and economic policy, in international and regional relations and in those between government, industry and the consumer. Most environmental propositions rely upon the interdependent theories of ecology, economics and demography, where cause and effect are frequently unclear (except sometimes in retrospect) and are subject to the unpredictability of human behaviour. Put another way, human societies tend to be more flexible than theoretical models suggest (however intellectually rigorous they may be). This may also be true of the relationship between species and ecological systems, the maintenance of which is a crucial issue in nature conservation strategy.

The terms 'environment' and 'ecology' are related rather than synonymous. That is, the environment is the habitat for living species comprising the atmosphere, *terra firma*, the oceans and seas, river and lake systems and the built environment for human societies. The word 'ecology' was first noted in 1873 (*Oxford English Dictionary*). In its biological context it deals with the mutual relationship between organisms and their environment and sociologically with the spatial distribution of populations in relation to materials and to social cause and effect. The relationship between living species and their habitats represent ecology and its basis as a biological science. Geographically, ecology defines the interrelationship between the four main physical zones of the Earth's system: biosphere, atmosphere, hydrosphere and lithosphere. 'Environment' and 'ecology' are intimately related concepts, impinging upon the public and private sectors of politics, economics and social engineering, within a complex web of defined and undefined interdependence.

This book reviews some of the key evidence of man's effects on the four zones and how industrial and economic activities are undermining the natural ecological balances between species and their habitats. These balances are not fully understood, but evidence suggests that they may be seriously perturbed by reductions in biological variation. These are caused by the systematic destruction of vegetation and life-supporting organisms by industrial and agricultural encroachments and by the output of their effluents.

There is an immense array of scientific programmes of research and investigation concerning the global environmental impact of these influences, under way since 1972 and earlier. In one way or another, they have led to actual and proposed instruments for international co-operation, regional programmes and national controls to manage the effects of industrial, agricultural and social activities.

Nuclear war is identified as the most serious threat to man's survival on Earth (SCOPE). Otherwise, environmental issues can be summarized quite simply. The world population is so large that the quantity of its organic wastes, the amount and toxicity of its industrial effluents and its declining natural resources urgently require new technology, new management practices to share this technology and modified patterns of consumption in order to maintain the prosperity of developed countries and to arrest the spread of poverty and disease in the Third World.

Ecology takes on board these economic and demographic problems, and puts them into the context of their effects upon the natural order, wherein mankind's own survival is no longer determined by natural selection but by cultural, economic and medical factors. Nevertheless, the attrition of man's demands upon the Earth and upon other living species will impose severe constraints upon his abilities for technological adaptation.

The information, research and policy roles of international and regional intergovernmental agencies, the United Nations Economic and Social Council (UN-ECOSOC), United Nations organizations, the Council of Europe, the Commission of the European Communities (CEC) and the Organization for Economic and Cultural Development (OECD) encourage and foster international co-operation on pollution control and nature conservation. From the global scientific 'ecological' angle we make many references to the multi-disciplinary scientific research activities of the independent, authoritative non-governmental International Council of Scientific Unions (ICSU) and its national academic and scientific member institutions (for example, the French Academie des Sciences, the Royal Society in the UK, the Swedish Academy of Sciences, the National Academy of Sciences in the USA, the Academy of Sciences of the USSR). ICSU co-ordinates the principal international multi-disciplinary research work in the Antarctic on climate change, biodiversity, chemical and energy exchanges and information systems, as the primary source of scientific consensus to international and national policy making. At the national level, the Natural Environment Research Council in the UK provides an outstanding example of international scientific partnership.

We also note that politics, economics and trade considerations take precedence over the potential for pollution control. While there is every evidence that the environment and conservation are adding a new dimension to the manner in which these policies are being developed, there does not appear to be much enthusiasm, in the UK and the USA specifically, to reduce power station emissions to healthier levels, even though these are higher than in most European countries.

Habitat and species protection, with some exceptions, is somewhat better served than pollution, because of the well-established influence of active wildlife and naturalists' trusts, in Europe and in the USA, and indeed throughout the world. Pollution control and waste management are characterized by confrontation between industry, local authorities, government and representative environmental groups, and the dilemma between central controls and the operation of the free market in the face of large investments.

These problems in the USA and Europe are by no means intractable. Political will and compliance by industry stimulated by public pressure are anticipated to set targets for the 1990s over the range of issues presented here. There appears to be a need, however, outside the areas of nature conservation, for environmental pressure groups to become more specialized and co-ordinated in their aims and objectives.

In developing countries, the problems are more fundamental, dealing with hunger and poverty, the relationship of people to the land, the management of water and sanitation, deforestation and economic growth. The environmental problems of Western societies (OECD member nations) and developing countries would be equally serious were it not for the fact that OECD members have it in their power to act. Developing countries need assistance with fiscal infrastructure, less exploitative trade arrangements and investment in appropriate technology.

It would not be helpful to present these issues as a litany of an ecological apocalypse even though they may turn out to be such. It is clear, nevertheless, that some extremely damaging modifications to the atmosphere have been made. Natural resources are diminishing, the number and variety of plants, wildlife and other organisms are declining, solutions to the disposal of toxic and radioactive wastes are urgently needed, and the growing populations in the Third World need to be fed, housed, clothed and employed. A new economic understanding between the North and the South needs to evolve, and consumers, particularly in the USA, must appreciate that less often means more. This is the magnitude of the political and economic tasks ahead.

The recent environmental genesis

The environment, demography, political and industrial accountability as related contemporary issues came to prominence during the 1960s, when the wisdom and judgement of the Establishment and the effects of industrialization were being increasingly questioned. The 1960s, of course, was also the period of the Beatles, the contraceptive pill, anti-Vietnam war sentiment, consumerism and 'Nader's raiders' in pursuit of product safety.

Ecology, the 'subversive science' (Sears, 1964), was then frequently regarded by those outside the academic and scientific communities as being the agitprop of dissidents and alarmists bent upon the discomfiture of government and industry. The beginnings of several of today's acute problems were observed and the evidence well documented. Rapid population growth following the end of the Second World War, acid rain (first documented in 1954), increased radiation levels from atmospheric testing of nuclear weapons and the problems of persistent chemicals (PCBs and DDT, to name but two) were already showing most disturbing effects throughout the world.

The emerging uncomfortable issue of industrial accountability was wider than the typically adversarial struggle recorded from Roman antiquity between a factory operator, producing a useful product and providing employment, yet giving off noisome effluents, and a complaining neighbour living downstream or downwind with recourse to common law for remedy. It had implications for new and broadened responsibility and extended liability for pollution beyond local boundaries, extending common law doctrines of pollution abatement into the international arena. At the same time, the viability of a resource base which relied upon the exploitation and consumption of easily acquired, non-renewable resources was in serious doubt but was not universally accepted by economists and politicians.

The hypotheses upon which the science of ecology were based had all the signs of endangering the traditional assumptions and practices adopted by modern societies. Nevertheless, as a populist movement in the USA and Europe, concerned with the conservation of nature, related pollution issues and the salvation of Planet Earth, it has gained momentum and achieved unprecedented recognition, reinforced by the flow of hard scientific and economic evidence, particularly in the last decade. This confirmed the early caveats about the finite nature of Earth's resources and the essential fragility of ecosystems.

The economic challenge embodied in the notion of environmentally secure economic growth was described within the principles of sustainable development (World Conservation Strategy, 1980) as 'development that meets the needs of the present without compromising the ability of future generations to meet them'. The implied scale of economic and social adjustment to meet this challenge, redirections of investment, re-orientation of technological development and institutional changes to organize the use of resources taking into account their environmental impact is, on the face of it, somewhat daunting. However, thoughtful evaluation suggests that the innate flexibility of a market-based economy would allow the adoption of pollution control and conservation objectives without structural changes, but at a financial cost which incumbent governments are not prepared to meet.

Nevertheless, national policies towards sustainable economic growth could be determined by scientific and technological developments and by the commercial possibilities offered by pollution control and conservation. Politics and economics could ensure that these are compatible with the needs and aspirations of Third World countries to rapidly improve their asset base and income. Ecological health will be determined by the levels of co-operation that can be established between industrialized and non-industrialized countries.

Unless industrial and commercial interests are wrought by principles of sustainable economic growth, pollution and industrial effluents will destroy the quality of life in the developed nations. The Third World will be unable to support its growing populations and more serious political issues than those presently faced will emerge.

Before outlining the environmental agenda it is convenient to briefly review the significant features of the historic unfolding of man's impact on the environment, up to Darwin and then to the present.

The environment in an historical perspective

Man's impact on his environment must first have been apparent with his discovery of the use of fire some 500,000 years ago. The havoc wreaked to the local flora and fauna in the early millennia of its discovery can only be surmised, but the time scale from friction to fission, from *Homo erectus* to Neanderthal and thence to civilized man, may be said to be of an evolutionary order of magnitude.

From the earliest cave drawings to the archaeological artefacts of the ancient Egyptians and the scrolls of Greeks and Roman antiquity, nature in all its manifestations provided the deities and focus of social organization. The relationship between the solar system, wind, fire, earth and water, and agriculture were self-evident to primitive, pagan and pastorialist societies. The Judeo-Christian ethic elevated the status of mankind as inheritors of the Earth to be outwith natural laws.

The transition of man from hunter and gatherer to cultivator in the late Neolithic period led eventually to the emergence of the first cities in Mesopotamia about 6,000 years ago and the beginnings of civilization. While these grew in size and importance as seats of government and centres for trade over the next seven and a half millennia, their rise and the increase in world population remained gradual. From the time of the first cities to around 1830, population had grown from some 10 million to 750 million in a world based upon a more or less stable relationship between agriculture and commerce.

Thomas Malthus (1766–1834), in his *Essay on the Principle of Population*, proposed that human populations increase up to the limit set by the availability of food, determined by the physical resources of agriculture. Malthus recognized the contribution of improved agricultural practices as a mitigating factor, but he also believed that rates of food production would always be less than the capacity for human beings to reproduce themselves. The present potential for food production exceeds predicted population growth, but calorie distribution remains inequitable, and the marginal and semi-arid lands which support nearly one fifth of the total world population are productively fragile, subject to drought or flooding and vulnerable to the effects of population instability.

The nineteenth century witnessed both the European industrial revolution and the publication in 1859 of Charles Darwin's *On the Origin of Species*, which provided the intellectual framework in which to analyse and assess man's relationship with his environment in a biogenetic context. Darwin put mankind back within the natural order as an evolved species and not one which had been created. Thus, in his view, mankind had indeed been subject to the process of natural selection and to the survival of the fittest.

The modern theory of organic evolution (as opposed to the evolution of the cosmos) presents natural selection as a two-step process. The first is genetic variability engendered by recombination, mutation and chance events. Genetic variability is random, and unrelated to the needs of the organism or to the nature of the environment. The second step is the ordering of genetic variability by natural selection.

Biological systems are highly individualistic and display innumerable variabilities which can adapt in improbable ways to almost any set of environmental circumstances. The leap from evolutionary theory to industrial pollution and the environment is therefore not too distant. To attribute pollution to being a factor in the evolutionary process, however, would be incorrect. Evolution is not a deterministic process; it does not consist of sudden changes but is gradual and continuous.

Pollution is an external factor introduced by man's economic activities, intervening often to destroy or modify the natural order. That it can cause mutational or other effects abhorrent to nature is indisputable, but we do not know what the longer-term effects will be. Nevertheless, pollution is an option of man's social organization.

Growth of conservation societies

It is interesting to note that several naturalist and wildlife societies had their origins in the late nineteenth century. The Royal Society for the Protection of Birds (RSPB) was founded in 1889. The National Trust (created in 1895) acquired Wicken Fen in Cambridgeshire in 1899 as the first nature reserve. The Royal Society for the Conservation of Nature (UK) was formed in 1912. Other societies emerged over the years to promote environmental study, to protect wildlife and their habitats from the encroachment of industry and urbanization and to act as pressure groups in the interests of species conservation and the protection of the rural environment. The acquisition of natural habitats and nature reserves has grown considerably over the years, and their conservation has become a factor in commercial, industrial and economic planning throughout the world.

Not only have environmental societies proliferated in Europe and the USA in recent years, the number of paid-up members in the UK (some 5 million) is reportedly higher than the membership of trade union organizations. Moreover, perceptions of the importance of the environment are continuing to grow and the 'green movement' is raising political consciousness of the influence of the green voter.

Scientific and public awareness of ecology

Taking a broad view of the disciplines that give us an understanding of the way in which the natural order operates, we can draw threads from every progenitor of original thought, through Archimedes to Newton's law of classical physics to Einstein, and from the discoveries and observations of geographers, biologists, naturalists, zoologists, palaeontologists and mathematicians who have provided a particular insight into an area of speciality. Thus, most of the phenomena that we are now faced with have been established in principles formulated by philosophers and scientists over many centuries. The magnitude of the eco-political task is to synthesize the breadth of this information and data generated into a rubric that redefines economic and social behaviour along more sustainable lines. Without dwelling on this, a few recent milestones are outlined below.

Svante Arrhenius, a Swedish physical chemist, published a paper in 1896 ('The influence of carbonic acid in the air upon the temperature of the ground'), which noted that the Earth and its atmosphere formed a natural greenhouse. In 1929 the Russian minerologist Vernadskiy published a treatise, entitled *La Biosphere*, dealing with the relationships between natural and man-made systems. The term 'ecosystem', proposed by Tansley, a contemporary biologist, appeared in 1935. The International Council of Scientific Unions (ICSU) was established in 1931 to encourage international scientific co-operation along non-political lines, in the earth, life and physical sciences to serve mankind. In 1948, The International Union for the Conservation of Nature (IUCN) was founded to deal with such specific topics as the preservation of flora and fauna and act as an exchange for international data.

The 1950s and 1960s witnessed focused scientific study and observation of man's ecological significance. This period now can be regarded as seminal. Rachel Carson's *Silent Spring*, published in 1963, aroused scientific and public consciousness of the effects upon human health and of the threat of ecological imbalance brought about through the destruction of wildlife by the uncontrolled application of insecticides, herbicides and fungicides containing highly toxic chlorinated hydrocarbons. While Dr Carson's work concentrated upon the ecological implications of persistent chemicals in the USA and the Third World, similar effects were noticed in the UK where, in the late 1950s and 1960s, tens of thousands of birds and other wild creatures perished from ingesting benzene hexachloride, mercury, heptachloride and Dieldrin.

Several observations were made in this period concerning the cumulative effects of chemicals and their toxic persistence in the food chain affecting wildlife and human health. Adaptive resistance of insects and lower organisms resulted in greater chemical concentrations being applied with decreasing efficacy. In the UK, the evidence, while clear, was more a cause of discomfort to agricultural planners and the chemical industry, but it led at least to an initial voluntary ban, thanks to parliamentary protests and to the interventions of the RSPB and the British Ornithological Society, before the decisions to establish permitted exposure levels to these and other persistent chemicals were made.

The dilemma posed by fertilizers and pesticides is that in the developed world, food production would be less efficient to a marked degree, while in the Third World many millions of hectares would remain unproductive. Having said this, the over-reliance on chemicals at the expense of naturally organic substances and more traditional farming practices have created soil and water imbalances that are in urgent need of correction.

The desideratum for a chemical pesticide is toxic efficiency. Bio-genetically engineered alternatives to pest control, such as the 'sterile insect technique' (EC/EFTA), are still in development. Successful field trials or viral controls on soybean crop pests have been conducted in Nicaragua (NERC). In general, the principles of integrated chemical and organic methods are well under way and the possibilities for biotechnology are considerable. Overuse of fertilizers exhausts the soil and de-oxygenates freshwater and coastal systems, causing eutrophication and habitat depletion.

The effects of population growth and the transformation of ecosystems to meet exponentially rising demands for energy, food, urban habitation, transport and recreation, the destruction of other living species and an unstable realignment of natural processes are to be found in the earlier predictions of the Huxleys and their contemporary naturalists, biologists, chemists and social scientists.

Anti-nuclear power groups metamorphosed from the old anti-war groups, such as the Campaign for Nuclear Disarmament (CND), following the Kennedy–Khrushchev decision in 1963 (inspired by Jawaharlal Nehru's appeal in 1955), which had even more profound implications for human health and the ecology, to adopt the Partial Test Ban Treaty. This brought atmospheric nuclear testing virtually to an end. These groups represent a substantial, concerned and active minority opposing nuclear power on four main grounds:

The potential role of reactors in the proliferation of nuclear weapons among trustworthy and untrustworthy parties;
Safety, particularly of light-water reactors;
Disposal of nuclear waste;
Lack of candour among government and industry concerning the effects of radiation and decisions being made on political rather than scientifically sound judgements.

Much of the public antipathy towards nuclear power stems less from the destructive capability of bombs than from the long-term effects of persistent radiation and distrust which has been generated by governments and industry through their uninformed reassurances, lack of candour and apparent outright deception on nuclear issues and management. The nuclear reprocessing plant at Sellafield (formerly Windscale) in Cumbria is a case in point. The original plant was built hurriedly by the Attlee government in order to establish a nuclear deterrent independently of the USA. Following a fire in 1957, information of the subsequent plutonium escape was witheld from the Medical Research Council and from the National Radiation Protection Board as late as 1982. Moreover, the operators of the plant, British Nuclear Fuels, continued to discharge low-level radioactive waste and debris into the Irish Sea until 1987.

Most nuclear testing went underground in 1963 with the adoption of the Treaty, by which time atmospheric testing had added up to 7.0% to natural levels of radiation. Since 1963, this has fallen to 1.0%, maintained by a series of smaller-scale atmospheric tests carried out by China and France until 1980. In the meantime, the Scientific Committee on Problems of the Environment (SCOPE), formed in 1969 as an adjunct to the International Council of Scientific Unions (ICSU), provided an important focus for the scientific study of the issues which were already under international scrutiny, including key work on the climatic effects of nuclear war.

Family planning was being extensively promoted on an international scale during the 1960s and the 1970s to tackle population growth in developing countries, led by agencies in the USA (the US Agency for International Development and the Ford and Rockefeller Foundations, among others).

International programmes

Several international programmes encouraging scientific study on a range of conservation and biological issues began in the 1950s and onwards, including the management of arid zones, biological productivity and use of natural resources. These were principally under the management of Unesco as an intergovernmental agency and the ICSU as an independent non-government liaison of scientists and scientific bodies. The Arid Zone Programme (Unesco, 1951–64), the Upper Mantle Project (ICSU, 1961–70), the International Biological Programme (ICSU, 1964–74), the 'Man and the Biosphere' Programme (Unesco, launched in 1971), and the current International Geosphere–Biosphere Programme (ICSU, 1990s) study the interactions between the chemical, physical and anthropogenic agents of global change (Global Change Programme). The ICSU's International Geophysical Year (1957–8) and subsequently the International Antarctic Glaciological Project (from 1969) produced considerable data relating to the hitherto little-known nature of Antarctic ice (thickness, extent, flows, etc.), providing much material for the assessment of atmospheric pollution. The

1972 UN Stockholm Conference on the Human Environment established an infrastructure for intergovernmental co-operation in research, education and programme development to address the issues identified during this period.

The United Nations Environment Programme (UNEP) was set up as an outcome of the conference with the task of identifying research needs and stimulating environmental programmes among United Nations organizations and agencies, including Unesco, the World Health Organization (WHO), the Food and Agriculture Organization (FAO), the International Atomic Energy Agency (IAEA) and the World Meteorological Organization (WMO), as well as other agencies and regional affiliations such as the European Commission and the Council of Europe.

The principal UNEP conferences since 1972 were the 1976 Vancouver Conference on Human Settlements ('Habitat') and the 1977 Nairobi Conference on Desertification. The next main conference is scheduled for 1992, in Brazil, to consider the issues of environment and development.

It is worth making a brief comment that the events of 1972 led to an increase in the ranks of international, government, industry, academic, consumer and voluntary non-governmental organizations (NGOs), to address environmental issues for scientific, partisan or pressure group motives. Also, of course, they resulted in the 'green movement'.

International influences

From its scientific roots, environmental awareness and concern is generally well established in international political circles. Intergovernmental agencies gather information and make proposals in conference and convention for national action. National governments set the agendas for international conferences. Treaties and agreements which emerge from these activities tend to promote minimum standards for universal application, usually above those which most developed nations have already met. Instruments of agreement usually take several years to agree and ratify, and even longer before their provisions are drafted into national statutes.

The intervals between international meetings are somewhat protracted, which explains the long gestation period of most conventions. It can often take several years to consider evidence, find common ground upon which to define problems and haggle over national performance standards and the timetables to meet them.

The recent international agreement to phase out the production and uses of chlorofluorocarbons (CFCs) and related halon gases which directly affect climate and atmosphere followed ten years of proving the theoretical basis for ozone depletion and a period of considerable disquiet among manufacturers and governments concerning the future of commercially valuable, non-toxic and otherwise apparently safe chemicals. The 1985 Vienna Convention on the Protection of the Ozone Layer was seen in this light.

The hole in the ozone layer above Antarctica first appeared in 1975. From 1975 to 1985 ozone levels above Antarctica decreased by about 50%, and other losses were observed in the higher latitudes of the Northern Hemisphere. Although the changing composition of the atmosphere resulting from the widespread use of CFCs had been suggested (Molina and Rowland, 1974), it was not until 1986 that the deep hole in the ozone layer was first observed. In 1987 the 1985 Montreal Protocol to the Vienna Convention was signed, and CFC production is to be reduced in phases to 50% of 1986 levels by 1998.

No other environmental issue has been given such prompt endorsement even where scientific proof has been unassailable. Yet it must be remembered that Canada, Norway, Sweden and the USA banned the use of CFCs in non-essential aerosols as early as 1978 (though not for other uses), and in 1980 the EC adopted similar measures.

UN organizations and specialized agencies traditionally deal with multinational operations, shipping, maritime aspects of offshore exploration and production, technical co-operation, labour relations, trading agreements, Third World industrial development, etc. Their main task is to gather and interpret scientific and economic data for agreeing international safety and pollution standards as well as economic behaviour. The WHO, FAO and IAEA, together with numerous scientific support agencies, exert similar influences in the fields of health, agriculture, nuclear and conventional energy, which have a direct (through national legislation) or indirect (through regional or national specialist agencies) bearing on the manner in which scientific information determines public policy.

Even though there may be general agreement and ratification of UN conventions, there is no UN tribunal to enforce compliance. This raises interesting questions concerning the control of trans-boundary pollution. In these cases the effectiveness of regional agreements has been demonstrated within the framework of marine safety and pollution treaties and in establishing the precedent for agreements on air pollution. The 1987 Single European Act also cut across traditional notions of sovereignty in EC regulations and directives which, from 1992, will be binding on member states.

The role of UNEP has been to catalyse and co-ordinate the research and other environmental activities of UN organizations and agencies. With the growth of information technology, which fortunately has coincided with the need to process huge amounts of data already generated, UNEP is now contemplating an enlarged monitoring and auditing role of national environmental performance and is developing its existing scientific data and information-gathering systems. Its activities in the environmental aspects of tourism and road transport are also expected to expand.

One of the problems, which was touched upon earlier, is that of funding. Funding for scientific environmental research in the USA is of orders of magnitude greater than the total funding of national science budgets or of international programmes such as UNEP, struggling on a $30 million budget. Given that the intellectual strength of international science depends upon the level of national commitment, and that the solution to environmental problems will depend upon international co-operation, national science funding to allow for participation in the range of international investigations envisaged by UNEP and ICSU, for example, should be accorded a high place on the environmental agenda.

Environmental management

Environmental management is to do with the conservation of economic and natural resources, as defined and clarified in this book, which also refers to public health and accidents. Deliberate reference to these issues is made for a number of reasons, the main one being that the human race is a resource, and it may be argued that most would not seek to protect the environment for its own sake but to arrive at a more equitable relationship with nature in order to sustain the human race.

Analogous to the presently inequitable balance between man and nature is the human cost in death and injury in the interests of economic and industrial development. Although people are not actually invited to sacrifice their lives to the greater economic good, many are exposed to higher risks than are necessary in order to achieve commercial profitability. The point is that the human cost of industrial activity is too high, as is the cost that we exact from nature.

Public opinion polls (OECD, 1982 and 1984) suggest that in Europe and the USA the majority of people (some 60%) would accept restrictions in economic growth in order to protect the environment. Similar results were obtained in a more recent *New York Times*/CBS survey.

Conserving resources for sustainable economic growth, on the one hand, should be based upon the fundamental industry principles of health, safety and the environment and on the other, in the knowledge that efforts by government and industry in this direction would be supported by the electorate. A laggard government and a reluctant industry will result in fewer votes and reduced sales.

Putting strategy before objectives for the moment, the main issues of sustainable development are fuel efficiency (energy conservation), waste control, effluent reduction, accident prevention, the protection of nature, education, incentives and penalties. The objectives of environmental management are to maintain economic growth through the husbanding and equitable distribution of natural resources and the development of new and alternative technology aimed at energy efficiency. At the same time, the destructive effects of industrial and human effluents must be minimized by reducing the output of some pollutants and eliminating others.

Biological transformation (photosynthesis, respiration, decomposition) by the atmosphere, the oceans, soils, vegetation and fresh-water systems effectively absorbs large volumes of effluent, particularly of carbon dioxide. For many organic or naturally reducing substances it is unclear how large these volumes can be without overloading chemical balance and energy fluxes. For persistent substances, toxic chemicals, heavy metals and gases, whose effects are acutely severe, long-lived and predictable, human health and ecological benefits far outweigh any economic arguments for release. Permitted levels of these substances are hotly contested between government, industry and conservation societies.

The elimination of all forms of pollution is unrealistic in economical and practical terms. Yet the extreme of ecological argument demands the elimination of all known poisons and contaminants, at least to levels not exceeding those produced by nature. Such demands assert that all substances which are not part of the natural ecological background in which living species have adapted are intrinsically harmful. Moreover, naturally occurring biologically active substances should not be increased beyond the levels which already appear in nature.

However, while an objective to meet such criteria would remove a heavy burden from economists and politicians in that agreements regarding 'acceptable' levels of pollution would no longer be necessary and the repeated upgrading of regulations to take into account new scientific evidence would be avoided, the motives for such demands could be regarded as being wholly unrealistic. Meeting such demands is patently impossible. While the development and application of new technology would be given a compelling impetus, the reduction and containment of known contaminants can more realistically be accommodated given rigorous toxicological testing.

A progressively demanding programme of international agreements and controls to phase out existing pollutants and to avoid the introduction of new waste-producing substances is the challenge which the environment presents to industry. It is likely that the consumer will exert more influence upon industry, particularly in Europe and the USA, than legal constraints, although the latter are necessary to sharpen the focus.

Environmental management is a general framework in which to consider living space and relationships between one species and another, taking into account the political imperatives to balance economic and social needs of growing human populations against finite natural resources and the availability of present technology.

1 THE ENVIRONMENTAL AGENDA

Scientific, political and industrial

The 1980s was the decade in which protection and preservation of the global environment became a central preoccupation of Western societies. The validation of certain scientific propositions during this period, the growth of the 'green movement', the emergence of the green consumer, broader media coverage, new legislation, the further decline of many African countries and the rising industrial output of India, South Korea, Taiwan and other countries of the Pacific Rim, major industrial accidents and serious pollution incidents, all have created a climate in which philosophy should now give way to the search for and implementation of solutions. This apparently ideal development is, however, still subject to global research, international conferences and facing up to the dilemmas of national politics concerning the relationship between the environment and economic growth.

The research agenda for the next decade is virtually established in ongoing and new scientific studies into atmosphere and climate and the operational aspects of sustainable economic growth and agriculture, which can be summarized as follows:

Sustainable development (economic and agricultural)
Chemistry of the global atmosphere (regulating factors; role of
    terrestrial processes in producing and consuming trace gases)
Ocean biogeochemical cycles (influence on and response to climate
    change)
Global change and ecosystems (interaction between vegetation and
    physical processes in the hydrological cycle; effect of climate
    change upon terrestrial ecosystems)
Health and ecotoxicology (chemicals in the environment)

The environmental agenda is very clearly a matter of striking the correct balance between science and politics. There is enough information available, on the one hand, to support the time-bomb scenario, but not enough to support policy and planning beyond the clear priorities to manage waste and reduce effluents. The scientific programme is directed towards the management of sustainable growth. It is only too apparent that exponential consumption, waste and effluence is not an option. While this, in any event, would be unlikely in Western societies, industrial growth in Third World countries will impose considerable strain on global ecological balance.

The conflict between environmentalists and policymakers can be reduced to the level of 'man proposes and God disposes'. The question is whether environmental man has offered enough data to support his propositions. Policymakers are calling for more data and proof beyond a shadow of doubt, which buys time but also continues the experiment. Government requirements for hard evidence need more scientific funding than is presently allocated for national research and development programmes and international scientific co-operation.

The scientific agenda

The major areas for scientific study of the environment are summarized in Table 1.1. The scientific study of man's influence on the Earth during the coming decade and beyond, as proposed, will need considerable political commitment to both its conduct and to the management of change to political and economic systems which undoubtedly is going to emerge.

An unprecedented worldwide scientific research effort to study the functioning of the Earth's system, and to understand how this system is changing, is being co-ordinated by ICSU within the International Geosphere–Biosphere Programme (IGBP), which is expected to continue for the next ten to fifteen years. The IGBP international scientific network operates through 34 national committees, co-ordinated by a special committee on which the UK is represented by NERC, whose own programme comprises many of the topics set out in Table 1.1. Core projects have already been established to study global and climatic changes via atmospheric chemistry, ocean flux, earth history and past global variations through the glacial and interglacial cycles in the Late Quaternary. New core projects are proposed for coastal-zone studies and hydrological cycle and terrestrial ecosystems, including agriculture and forestry and biogeochemical cycles. The US Global Change Research Program, with a total expected budget of $1.0 billion in the 1991 fiscal year, will initiate the development of the NASA Earth Observing System, which will be an integrated international satellite programme for monitoring global change and providing comprehensive data and information. The Program incorporates the broad range of issues embraced within the IGBP on the basis of multi-disciplinary development and international co-operation.

Many measures need not await the results of scientific research before their implementation. The phasing out of sulphur and nitrogen oxides and CFCs, the management and disposal of toxic and hazardous wastes, groundwater pollution, oil discharges and contingency planning measures are pragmatic management issues, where co-operation between industry, government and consumers is most relevant. Carbon dioxide controls present the greatest dilemma, since carbon flux is an inescapable aspect of energy production and consumption, and bears directly upon the fundamental aspects of energy and transport policy.

Co-operation is the key to progress in all these issues, from multi-

Table 1.1 Scientific study of the environment

Topic	Focus of study
Agriculture and the environment	Social impact of changing land use from reduced food production Sustainable agriculture
Aquatic ecotoxicology	Chemical contaminants and effects on biota
Arctic research	Meteorology, sea ice and Arctic ecosystems
Climate and climate change	Land, sea and atmospheric components Quaternary geology and record Orbital forcing on the hydrosphere, atmosphere and cryosphere Antarctic ice sheet Arctic meteorology Global atmospheric modelling Land surface/climate interactions Land/atmosphere interactions Land/aquatic ecosystems Biogeochemical ocean fluxes Changes in sea level Health effects
Environmental geochemistry	Natural ecosystems, wildlife nutriton and pollution pathways
Environmental microbiology	Behaviour of micro-organisms in the environment
Fisheries	Ecology; oil and gas impacts; marine predator–prey relations; benthic and pelagic populations
Forests and woodlands	Conservation and land use; biology and physiology of tree improvement
Health and ecotoxicology	Chemical safety
Marine mammals	Seals and whales
Ocean circulation	World Ocean Circulation Experiment
The populations of biological species	Terrestrial and freshwater ecology; biodiversity
Shelf seas, coastal waters and estuaries	Sediment particles and contaminants; effects on biological systems
Tropospheric chemistry	Transport, transformation and removal of atmospheric pollutants
Water quality and groundwater modelling	River ecosystem dynamics; nitrate and pesticide pollution
Waste disposal and environmental health	Geological studies for site locations

disciplinary scientific activities already established through ICSU to economic co-operation at micro and macro levels. In the latter, economic benefits may be derived from efficient environmental management in developed countries as well as from co-operative programmes with the Third World.

The general message that we wish to convey is that there are areas of uncertainty in the data that are available on the effects of climatic change, biodiversity and ecosystem functioning, radiation, biogeochemical cycles, ecotoxicology and their interrelationships, all of which are subject to long-term scientific programmes. The other matters to be dealt with, hazardous and toxic waste management and water quality, which have a significant impact upon human and ecological health, are not contentious issues (except nuclear waste), and can be handled within the normal legislative framework.

It is evident from reviewing the considerable environmental bibliography and present media coverage that a new order of good housekeeping is urgently required.

The political agenda

Table 1.2 outlines the objectives and strategies for the political management of the environment. Objectives and strategies are not generally well defined simply because the management of most agenda items require major collaboration between natural and life sciences, economists and politicians. Effective management will rely heavily upon advocating a cadre of multi-disciplinary planners and policymakers.

Table 1.2

Objectives	Strategies	Plans
1. Climate and atmosphere	International co-operation National legislation Incentives and penalties	Emission controls (CO_2, CFCs, SO_x, NO_x, etc.) LNWT/energy efficiency Research Energy conservation
2. Water and sanitation River and lake systems Groundwater	National programmes Regional co-operation Agricultural policy Urban planning	Sewage treatment Chemical controls Toxic wastes Fertilizers and pesticides
3. Forests and woodlands Tropical rainforests	National land management Agricultural policy International co-operation	Reafforestation Economic assistance Trade agreements
4. Oceans and coastal areas Wetlands	National programmes International co-operation	Sewage treatment Oil spills Industrial effluents
5. Public health	National programmes Research	Chemical controls Emission controls Water and sanitation
6. Sustainable development	National programmes International co-operation Agricultural policy Conservation Environmental accounting	Renewable energy LNWT Fuel efficiency
7. Biodiversity River and lake systems Oceans and coastal areas	National programmes International co-operation Financial incentives Research	Chemical controls Agriculture and forestry Habitat creation and protection
8. Third World development and population	Sustainable economic growth Technology sharing Free-market planning National programmes International co-operation Agricultural policy Institutional change	Industry Agriculture Family planning Education Appropriate technology

Table 1.2 gives some idea of the systemic nature of environmental issues. Emission control, for example, would be a national plan to achieve atmospheric balance from internationally agreed standards. Improved public health is an important objective of emission control. Economic use of energy is a strategy to conserve fossil fuel and reduce atmospheric emissions. Reduction of waste is a means of conserving energy. Proper waste disposal protects water and soils. Without labouring the point, objectives and strategies need to be defined qualitatively and quantitively in order to provide a much-needed focus on roles and responsibilities of governments, local authorities, industry and the consumer.

The ranking of environmental issues is neither necessary nor practical, given their general interdependence. They have different priorities, according to the economic status and aspirations of the countries involved. Moreover, while each is important (given the constraints of manpower and other resources in developing countries, for example), to put nature before human welfare is clearly wrong. To rush in with green money to save a forest without a concomitant effort to sustain the local rural population and its economic infrastructure would be short-sighted.

Industry, conservation and related issues

Effluent and waste pollute the hydrological cycle and just about everything else. Industry is an inseparable and motivating factor of social cohesion, wealth creation and progress, and exists both to serve and to exploit the consumer. In the latter respect, industry has a life of its own which, in common with any organization, is also self-protecting. Rising consumer influence has led in recent years to the development of a more balanced relationship between supplier and consumer, where higher standards of health, safety and environmental protection are being demanded and, up to a point, met. That there is resistance to these demands is evident from the accidents which occur, leading to loss of life and serious pollution incidents. These can frequently be attributed to lack of corporate commitment on the grounds of profitability, inertia or in defiance of the laws of probability.

Nevertheless, much of today's pollution remains, due to the costs and difficulties of modernizing old plant, methods and attitudes. Even state-of-the-art industries, such as chemicals and oil, are faced with these problems, which are exacerbated by ever-emerging evidence of environmental impact and the prospect of premature obsolescence of new plant when unanticipated standards are introduced.

While a book of this nature cannot fully explore the complex interactions between living species and the physical environment (even if there were a consensus concerning causes and effects), an outline of the principal environmental issues and the manner in which they are being tackled can only reinforce the concepts of universal personal responsibility. In the final analysis, major environmental impacts and their remedies will continue to be industry driven, subject to scientific discoveries, national policies and the economics of supply and demand, with consumers in Western societies imposing a significant supply determinant.

It would be wrong to imagine that industry is not responding to environmental issues, but there is a great deal of difference between the abilities of small firms, large national companies and multinationals to manage the environmental challenge. The Confederation of British Industry (CBI) recognizes the difficulty in monitoring the performance of companies who cannot perceive the environment as being to their commercial advantage.

Traditionally, industry has been defensive and reactive to intiatives (principally health, safety and the environment) that are likely to increase operating costs, leaning heavily on the argument of the law of diminishing returns and cost benefit. Industry's statements of concern for the environment are qualified by economic considerations.

It is difficult to fault the realism of such an approach when faced with environmental conjecture and a lack of hard evidence. Yet the ability of industry to recoup and adapt to the environmental onslaught and to absorb costs without affecting income or profitability is quite remarkable. In the same way, national claims that environmental costs would be inflationary or an obstacle to economic growth must be treated with the same suspicion as any model based upon econometrics, demography or expediency.

In establishing environmental priorities there are two points to bear in mind. First, the more responsible multinational corporations perceive considerable economic value in having a clean environmental performance. The importance of the 'green consumer' and of enlightened purchasing behaviour cannot therefore be over-emphasized.

Second, the largest contributors to atmospheric pollution (oil- and coal-burning heavy industry and power generation) will become more amenable to market pressures provided that these are applied. Although price determines fuel options and pollution is more directly related to the availability of cleaner-burning low-sulphur fuels, the installation of clean-up technology and direct legislation are both readily available.

Environmental directions in Western societies

Pollution control and conservation are national responsibilities. Government and industry have considerable data from biological and medical research concerning the detrimental effects of atmospheric pollution upon human health and, more recently from other research, of its likely long-term effects on climate.

A principal constraint to introducing national pollution control standards, as well as the more stringent application of safety controls, is the question of trade competitiveness. If the development and application of controls costs money and no-one else is doing it, then why bother, if in the process, one country or company loses a competitive edge and the global situation remains unchanged?

For example, cleaner power generation means more expensive electricity. The costs of other goods and services increases and return on investment is slower. The hidden downside of this approach, increased human morbidity and mortality, lower productivity, greater absenteeism, dead fish, dirty water, etc., are not costs that industry has had to take into account in its balance sheets. Notionally, these are huge costs which accrue to the taxpayer but which are difficult to identify. Yet if it were possible to equate macro-economics with the quality of life, investment in pollution control would be even more compelling. It seems that the cost of pollution and its control must be put into a larger equation in which nature's resources and health are quantified in cash terms, if any real progress is to be made in the dialogue between government, industry and the consumer in the development of public policy over pollution, conservation and sustainable economic growth.

Industrial pollution

Industrial pollution arises from public and private sector organization of the means of production and energy utilization; the design and implementation of agricultural policies; urbanization and provision of social amenities such as roads, transport and public health (water supply and sewage-disposal) systems. Where there are symptoms of environmental degradation (and these are plainly evident in waste-disposal malpractices, unrestored redundant industrial sites, urban decay and uncontrolled effluents) they cannot be traced through the conventional paths of cause and effect determined by prosperity or poverty, growth or decline. The environment has not been relevant in either set of circumstances. It has suffered, though, at the hands of local planners, industrial and commercial developers, and has been both hostage and sacrifice to rising and lowering standards of living, investment decisions for optimum profitability, lack of awareness or concern for environmental and ecological impact, support and subsidies for dubiously useful enterprises, unrealistic costing of natural resources and unequal distribution of the means of production and wealth. Thankfully, Western societies have now reached a state of relative economic and political maturity, and have an awareness of environmental issues such that solutions to the grosser forms of pollution could be found, particularly in respect to land and water.

Industry's appreciation of the effects of pollution is growing while its assumption of reponsibility is tempered by the prospects of large (though not unaffordable) investments, and appears to some to be laggard. This may be an unfair view, particularly of companies that rely upon consumer sales for their livelihoods, but expenditures on health, safety and the environment are among the first cuts to be made when economic sentiment is gloomy. These items are accounted as costs rather than as investments. 'Greenness', nevertheless, is acquiring an economic status with a potential for delivering tangible benefits.

The tendency of industry is also to take a 'wait and see' position in the absence of hard data, legislation or consumer pressure. The Industrial Society in the UK predicts that industrial environmental consciousness may well be reinforced by employees as participants in the emergence of the 'green consumer'. Extending this thought, it would be helpful if it did not appear that industry, the consumer, governments and scientists were in conflict almost, it may be said, as different species, each having its own discrete environment. In terms of short-term profitability or political gain this is often the case. This is why a common identification with environmental goals can bring about cohesive social policies.

Industry and nature conservation

The relationship between industrial and commercial companies and conservation societies is already well established. There are many examples of support for habitat restoration (Shell's 'Better Britain' Campaign or the Heinz Guardians of the Countryside Programme, for example) or to fund more broad-based international programmes (IBM and UNEP: see Chapter 14).

As an aside, in the USA the first major task of the Bird Rescue Co-ordination Centre at Berkeley, originally funded by Mobil in 1985, was to assist in the clean-up of Prince William Sound following the *Exxon Valdez* incident in 1988.

Industrial and commercial support for conservation societies comes from the power-generating, coal and construction industries, textile manufacturers, commercial laboratories, banks and finance houses, retailers, etc. Wildlife is also a motif of much consumer marketing material. Corporate contributions, amounting to £1.6 million, accounted for nearly 20% of the Worldwide Fund for Nature income in 1987, almost equal to that derived from membership subscriptions.

Site restoration is a traditional aspect of conservation for several industries, mostly oil and construction, returning gravel pits and mining sites back to nature. In the UK, the Groundwork Trust movement provides an example of an alliance between industry and conservation societies for these purposes as well as to clean up the detritus of previous industrial activity.

Broadly speaking, many of the solutions to the problems of pollution and nature conservation lie in management education and the assumption of corporate responsibility. Consumer influence, taxation and legislation have their places, but it would appear that much proselytism at the non-scientific levels of management needs to be undertaken. In the UK, the Nature Conservancy Council is promoting the establishment of industry and conservation associations (INCAs), as a community-based liaison system between industry and its local environment. The system is similar in the UK to the Farming and Wildlife Advisory Groups (FWAGs), which extend the opportunities of conservation bodies in environmental awareness programmes.

Industry self-regulation and the role of multinational corporations

Industries that operate internationally can be granted non-governmental status by agencies such as the UN, CEC and OECD for the purpose of contributing technical and other information which can have considerable influence on the drafting of environmental policy and legislation. Industry seeks practical and cost-effective compromises to often politically motivated initiatives, which meet the spirit of environmental concerns without damaging commercial viability or competitiveness.

Stringent regulations do not harm industry provided that they are universally applied and are not used as an instrument to obtain or achieve national competitive advantages. For example, if European standards are more stringent than those of the Third World, their exports to industrialized countries may price locally produced goods out of the market. It is interesting that EFTA standards tend to be more stringent than EC or international ones, particularly in maritime affairs. Aiming at a *status quo*, Norway, for example, would seek to introduce higher international standards in order to protect its own competitiveness in world markets.

Differences in environmental and safety performance between sectors of industry are difficult to judge at the international level in view of different operating methods. Also, since multinational corporations are better able to cope with emerging regulation and control than smaller industries (which are also more difficult to monitor), international negotiations seek to protect the interests of national industries as a whole.

Multinationals generally wish to protect their position as being self-regulating, and seek therefore to establish international operating principles rather than detailed controls. On the whole, this tends to work quite well, particularly among those industries which contribute to the international dialogue. Unlike the oil and petrochemical industries, it has been noted that chemical companies do not participate as an international representative industry association in the development of international standards and codes of practice.

Industry is particularly sensitive to measures which would require the publication of proprietary confidential information. In the case of labelling chemicals, for example, the identification of active substances could assist competitors.

A more serious aspect of sharing information concerns the causes and consequences of industrial accidents, including those which affect the environment, where information and data which may have implications for accident prevention are withheld on account of potential lawsuits and claims for damages. This aspect of the law is a serious obstacle to the prevention of future accidents where cause and fault could be attributed.

In Europe and the USA consumer influence on safety, quality and product pricing has grown since the 1960s with public environmental awareness, leading to demands for greater industrial accountability and openness. Industry now faces the challenge of reconciling profitability with the new consumer and stockholder demands for responsible environmental behaviour in the production and marketing of goods and services.

Costs, profitability and politics nevertheless act as constraints to technological and managerial solutions to some major polluting factors. Successful resistance by industry in the USA to reducing levels of nitrogen oxide emissions provides an example of trade-off lobbying, where car exhausts will be subject to increasing controls but emissions from power plants, which contribute much higher levels of nitrogen oxide, will be permitted to increase.

International aspects of industry and the environment

Multinational corporations exert considerable influence on the work of intergovernmental organizations and agencies, at the United Nations and the European Commission, either as industry-specific groupings or through the International Chamber of Commerce (ICC). Intergovernmental organizations seek to establish harmonized health, safety, environmental protection and trading standards among their member countries. Multinationals, principally the petroleum and shipping industries, have a voice at these organizations as non-governmental organizations (NGOs), and are represented at the International Labour Organization (ILO), International Maritime Organization (IMO), the World Health Organization (WHO) and at the United Nations Environment Programme (UNEP). They provide technical background in the development of conventions, codes of practice and standards. Interests of national industries are also promoted through their member-government delegations.

UNEP, since its inception following the Stockholm Conference in 1972, has the main responsibility of organizing industry's technical contribution to the environmental programmes of UN organizations. However, because UNEP's activities did not extend far enough into the relationship between the environment and Third World economic development, in 1983 a World Commission on Environment and Development (WCED) was set up as an independent body to report to the UN General Assembly on the relationship between the environment and economic development. This was due to the non-sustainable economic development patterns which were being promoted by organizations such as UNCTAD-GATT. WCED thus set out to propose 'an alternative agenda' to that of UNEP.

WCED worked with UNEP through a committee chaired by Mrs Gro Harlem Brundtland, then prime minister of Norway. In 1984, a World Industry Conference on Environmental Management (WICEM) involving UNEP, the International Chamber of Commerce (ICC) and WCED was held at Versailles as a forum for intergovernmental bodies, a broad cross-section of industry and non-governmental environment agencies. The main item on its agenda was the question of reconciling economic growth with continued improvement in the quality of the environment. WCED presented its report, entitled *Our Common Future*, in 1987 (the Brundtland Report). It examined the basic principles of sustainable economic growth (and would have been more accessible if its contents had been indexed).

It is trite to say that public concern for the environment presents industry, commerce and the legislature with major challenges. It is truer to state that responsibilities for the current state of the environment can be allocated to government, local authorities, primary energy producers, raw-materials suppliers, manufacturing industry and the consumer.

Environmental concern has spread from the scientific community, through the aggressive and frequently constructive tactics of environmental pressure groups, to the consumer and thence to local and central government. Industry and commerce have taken up the marketing challenge. Environmental friendliness has replaced 'new' and 'free' as the main consumer inducement.

The market approach is somewhat trivial when we consider that long-term consumer behaviour in Western societies is part of the key to restoring environmental stability. In the shorter term, it is the responsibility of energy producers and their suppliers to reduce industrial effluents, manage waste disposal, conserve resources and remit energy savings to lowering prices. Regulations and tax incentives, as well as penalties, may encourage industry to invest, and the consumer will benefit in improved health and fuel-efficient energy.

International co-operation

The UN and other intergovernmental agencies provide useful fora for multinationals to contribute technical data supplementing the input from scientific institutions. Such organizations act as a catalyst to the formation of regional affiliations to tackle regional problems (e.g. UNEP's Oceans and Coastal Areas Programme). The Commission of the European Communities has close formal links with the UN system and it is clear from the EC programmes that political, economic and technical solutions to pollution are more readily identified among economically dependent regional groupings. For this reason, regional affiliations outside Europe may need to be either formed or strengthened with the objectives of integrating environmental issues into political and economic agendas (for example, OPEC and ASEAN).

Industry has a leading and constructive role to play in providing information and technical data to intergovernmental and other international agencies. Indeed, it has a number of representative associations to co-ordinate data and respond to intergovernment initiatives. The International Chamber of Commerce has a general role in this area on behalf of multinational corporations, while sectoral interests such as oil and shipping have their own individual affiliations.

Environmental directions in the Third World

Many Third World countries lack the resources for the enactment, implementation and enforcement of environmental laws. Moreover, they have not reached the fairly mature levels of environmental awareness of Western industrial societies. Thus the Third World is not under the same public pressure as the developed countries to contain pollution. Environmental considerations are perceived, if at all, as imposing a brake on economic growth. Safety and environmental standards adopted at international conventions take into account the levels that Third World economies can more readily meet. Hence, the principles of 'minimum standards' characterize drafting criteria, applying equally to the host country as well as to foreign companies operating there. Regional standards, such as those adopted by EC member states, are more stringent than those of United Nations agencies as appropriate to richer countries. Standards adopted by the European Free Trade Association (EFTA) countries tend to be more stringent than either.

While industrialized nations reduce pollution, in the Third World it will increase. Apart from multinational companies applying standards to overseas operations similar to those at home (a practice observed among multinational oil and chemical operators), it is unreasonable to expect that effective national controls will be introduced without economic incentive or penalty, even though extremely severe accidents and pollution incidents could otherwise be avoided.

Pollution problems in the Third World are the most serious, as they relate to the direct result on public health of untreated sewage and contaminated water. Third World countries are faced with water and air pollution, severely depleted croplands and rainforests and a range of infrastructural problems which are both the cause and consequences of poverty. Such problems have universal economic, political and ecological significance, and their solutions can be found only in fundamental changes in the style of national economic management (i.e. less direct government control) and the development of appropriate technology and investment strategies which allow the Third World to increase its asset base.

Western society is shifting perceptibly towards a service rather than a manufacturing economy. In the medium to long term, primary production in the Third World will serve the needs of the Western consumer, a trend already established in trading relationships with Taiwan, South Korea and the Philippines, accounting for their exemplary economic performance.

International co-operation

Possibly, with global warming and depletion of the ozone layer and of tropical rainforests as unifying factors, the 1990s will be the decade of intergovernmental co-operation. Of these three issues, unilateral national action (for example, to reduce carbon dioxide emissions) would be comparable to unilateral disarmament, and considerably more expensive. Co-operation would be manifest in agreements to support the necessary scientific research, to agree on desired minimum levels of global effluents, to develop alternative strategies to deforestation, to assist in Third World development by strengthened regional alliances and to dissuade governments from exploitative whaling and fishing and other natural resource-depleting activities.

Government and industry

Traditionally, 'health, safety and the environment' has been a middle-management function. Notwithstanding Cabinet or corporate statements of concern, in lean times, this is where cuts are made. In the USA, the Environmental Protection Agency has been elevated to departmental level. The UK is embarked upon the first real environmental legislation since the Control of Pollution Act 1978. The Department of the Environment now has a 'Global Pollution Division' and industry has been entrusted with the task of monitoring the UK's obligations to the Montreal Protocol and preparing for the Second World Climate Conference, scheduled for November 1990.

In industry, with notable exceptions, multinational corporations do not have health, safety or environmental vice-presidents. This is also true in Europe, where responsibility for the environment has not reached many boards. Following the *Exxon Valdez* incident, it is interesting to note that the Exxon Corporation now has an environmental vice-president.

The Introduction has indicated that there is a considerable amount of authoritative data on environmental issues, a well-established regional infrastructure and a body of national legislation to tackle pollution and protect nature. There is a long way to go, particularly in the development of an environment–economic–political matrix, and much effort and commitment will be needed.

National anti-pollution priorities are control of hazardous waste, clean water, conservation and recycling, the encouragement of green consumerism and faith in the market system to find new avenues of investment and profitability in a cleaner environment.

Non-governmental environment groups

In US terminology, the environment has become as respectable as 'motherhood and apple pie'. However, outside the scientific community there appears to be little focus and no concert. The issues appear to be so numerous that their presentation all at once, as it were, tends to lead to considerable confusion in the public mind and an overwhelming sense of despair. The fact that practically everything can be classified as environmental or ecological does not help matters very much. The value of an ecological approach, nevertheless, provides the necessary perspective on cause and effect for government, industry and individuals to consider.

The present fragmentation and apparent lack of cohesion in the way that environmental issues are presented to the public by different pressure groups attests to the environment being a grassroots movement. Its transition to the upper levels of power broking has yet to occur, even though the influence of, for example, Friends of the Earth and the Worldwide Fund for Nature will continue to ensure that they are not to be discounted.

There appears to be a need for a specialized institutional focus upon specific issues in order to properly evaluate intergovernmental and non-governmental research, and to use this for more directionalized lobbying and educational purposes.

The Greens

The 'green movement' is well established. It has popular electoral support throughout Europe and has extended the social influence of environmental pressure groups at the national and local levels, not to mention their political influence as non-governmental observers and spokesmen at national and intergovernmental deliberations. The socio-economic profile of the green political parties are young, middle class, educated and tending

Table 1.3 The European green parties

Country	Party name	National status and comments
Belgium	Agalev (Flemish) Ecolo (Walloon)	Radical Christian-lifestyle movement Disorganized
France	les Verts	Weak programme
Germany (FRG)	Grunen	Vociferous, quite influential, but split between factions
Holland	Groenen	Radically political
Ireland	Comhaontas Glas	Success in recent elections but unorganized; anti-1992
Italy	Federazione delle Liste Verde	Eco-feminist, minority rights and anti-nuclear
Sweden	Miljopartiet de Grona	Local council strength; may expect up to 10% national support
Switzerland	Grune partie	Nine out of the 200-seat National chamber; strongest in French-speaking Switzerland
	POCH (Left Alliance)	Not so influential
United Kingdom	Green Party	Popular, but disorganized and without coherence; may achieve 8–9% of the vote (2.0 million at last General Election)

towards the left in political philosophy, and historically comparable to the anti-'military–industrial complex' sentiments of the 1960s and 1970s.

Given the all-embracing nature of ecology, it would be understandable that the British Green Party might wish to take an holistic approach to treating the body politic and economic. The Green platform is anti-pollution, 'population reduction', an end to nuclear power, cancelling Third World debt repayments and redistribution of wealth and more parental influence in education, but cohesion, coherence and leadership are weak. The first green party was founded in New Zealand in 1972, and European green parties are shown in Table 1.3

It would appear that the Swedish and Swiss 'greens' are the most influential of the European eco-politicians. It is interesting that neither of these countries is in the EC, and both are within the environmentally conscious EFTA alliance.

The following chapters provide background information to the main environmental concerns with which we are confronted, in relation to practical issues and the causes and consequences of the main types of industrial pollution in a political, scientific and economic context.

2 NUCLEAR RADIATION
Man-made and in nature

Public policy is often determined by the way society perceives risk of damage, injury, death and ill-health. People are prepared to accept higher actuarial or statistical risks for economic and personal expediency than might otherwise be considered prudent, and to reject low risk on what might appear to be irrational grounds. Acceptance or rejection is frequently associated with the availability of alternative courses of action or options and whether the risks are voluntary or imposed.

Although probability is, by its very nature, uncertain, we may quite confidently expect a given number of events among a given population associated with certain known actions within a given time period. Even in these terms, since the role in nature of radiation from radioactive material (ionizing radiation) at natural levels is unclear and the effects of variable additional low levels of exposure on the human body are uncertain, the attitudes to nuclear power among the general public range from wary acceptance to outright hostility.

The presentation of some aspects of nuclear power and radiation is not an attempt to influence views on nuclear power one way or another. The subject is highly complex, and the situation is not helped by the fact that there is considerable uncertainty concerning the effects of radiation at low levels. Public perceptions are served neither by strident alarmism nor by bland reassurance, but nuclear power and radiation are relevant to the environmental debate because of their health implications and the future contribution that nuclear power can make to energy consumption and conservation.

The history of nuclear power holds a key to the understanding of public attitudes, where political and bureaucratic lack of candour in the information provided to the public on safety factors and health risks created considerable distrust in the UK and the USA following the Windscale and Three Mile Island accidents and, more recently, in the USSR after Chernobyl. In addition, on a global scale, the association between the peaceful uses of nuclear power and the proliferation of nuclear weapons engenders anxiety.

This chapter describes some aspects of the nature of radiation, the effects upon the human body from combined natural and anthropogenic sources, levels of public exposure to radiation from natural sources and from releases to the environment from nuclear fission processes, the consequences and implications of the three recorded nuclear power accidents and the management of nuclear wastes.

Ionizing radiation

Ionization of human cells and other matter is caused by irradiation resulting from the deposition of radioactive energy. The principal type of radiation with which we are concerned is ionizing radiation emitted during the decay of unstable isotopes (radionuclides) of uranium used in the nuclear fuel cycle. Radionuclides are unstable isotopes of any element, and radioactivity is emitted mainly in the form of alpha and beta particles and gamma rays. Naturally occurring ionizing radiations, accounting for the background of human exposure to radiation, originate in cosmic rays and from a number of terrestrial sources such as radon and thorium.

Radioactivity is ever present in the natural environment and pervades the cosmos. All living tissue contains radioactive substances; energy (nuclear power) and health (X-rays, radiation therapy, radio-isotope analysis, etc.) derive their benefits from controlled use of radiation. The potential for harmful effects are thus the result of radiation of both natural and artificial origin but, in terms of nuclear power anxieties, centre upon the longevity of radionuclides in materials used in the nuclear fuel cycle, which includes the disposal of radioactive waste.

Effects of ionizing radiation

The interaction of ionizing radiation with body tissues can result in cells that carry DNA abnormalities and hence a predisposition to cancer and hereditary defects. It is assumed that there is no threshold level below which cancers and hereditary effects do not occur and that there is a linear relationship between radiation received by populations and individuals and the risk of harm. The linearity of known and assumed risks of radiation effects according to dose is illustrated in Table 2.1.

A sievert is a weighted factor which takes into account the potential damage to a human body exposed to alpha, beta or gamma radiation. Alpha radiation is more potentially damaging than beta radiation by a factor of twenty. One sievert (Sv) is the dose equivalent from 1 gray (Gy) of radiation from beta particles, gamma and X-rays; the absorbed dose from 1 Gy of alpha radiation is equivalent to 20 Sv.

The risks of radiation doses above 1 Sv are documented from observations of the effects of radiation on the survivors of the atom bombs dropped on Hiroshima and Nagasaki. The effects of exposure levels below 1 Sv are based largely upon a linear hypothesis of somatic and hereditary defects by inference from studies of mice. However, no conclusive evidence of hereditary defects, attributable to exposure from either natural or artificial radiation, has been found in human offspring.

The calculation of the risks to individuals and populations from high and low levels of radiation (linearity) assumes a risk of one latent cancer appearing over a period of 30–40 years following 20 man-sieverts exposure. There is, in addition, an emerging theory of supralinearity, which suggests that risk of cancer death per millisievert increases as the dose

Table 2.1 Linear effects of ionizing radiation per gram of body tissue

Dose (sieverts)	Consequence	Affecting
100	Death (certain)	Central nervous system
3	Death (50% probability)	Bone marrow damage
1–3	Probable radiation injury	
1	5% linear risk of cancer per sievert	
0.0028 (2.8 mSv)	Natural radiation (global average)	
0.001–0.050 (1–50 mSv)	Recommended exposure limits for the public and radiation workers	

Source: UNSCEAR

Radiation dose units (gray): The quantity of energy imparted to a unit mass by ionizing radiation (alpha, beta and gamma). One gray is equivalent to 1 joule per kilogram

Radiation dose equivalent (sievert): The quantity obtained by multiplying the absorbed dose of radiation in the human body, weighted according to its damage potential. One sievert is also equivalent to 1 joule per kilogram

Collective dose (man-sievert): The collective is total radiation exposure divided by the population, expressed as an average. One millisievert (mSv) = 1/1,000 if a sievert

Radiation activity (becquerel): One disintegration per second of any radionuclide = 1Bq.

decreases. Stated another way, the response to radiation rises more rapidly at lower levels of exposure. An alternative hypothesis suggests that the risk is less for the same dose delivered over longer periods.

The health effects of human exposure to low levels of man-made radiation are difficult to evaluate not only because of the lack of direct evidence, but also because of other social and environmental factors which can compound or compensate for such radiation effects. Negative factors include smoking and vehicle emissions, while mitigating ones can be climate, altitude and latitude. The basic assumption of UNSCEAR and others working in the field is that any increase in human exposure will result in a rise in the incidence of cancer, however small.

Nevertheless, the likely effects of radiation on the human body at higher levels (1 Sv and above) are better understood than the effects of chemicals and air pollutants, food additives or pesticides, since human response to radiation is measured and monitored directly. Reasonably reliable estimates of the maximum effects of various levels of radiation on the human body are available not only from the Hiroshima and Nagasaki studies but from patients with chronic conditions exposed to medically prescribed doses, X-rays and occupational radiation.

It is evident from the levels of natural radiation to which individuals and populations are exposed that the body's natural immune system is able to withstand moderate doses of radiation from natural and man-made sources. There is, however, no clear correlation between illness and variations in exposure to natural radiation levels, or at levels below 100 mSv. The interpretation of risks illustrates, nevertheless, the different requirements for proof among scientific and non-scientific communities.

Table 2.2 Annual risk of death from selected causes (actuarial and estimated)

Risk type	Annual probability of death (per million population)
Actuarial risks	12,000
Smoking (10 cigarettes a day)	5,000
From natural causes, 40 years old	1,400
Accidents in the home	100
Accidents on the road	100
Accidents at work (among working population)	20
Spontaneous leukaemia	67
All other causes and conditions	5,477
Estimated and notional risks of death from radiation exposure	
Notional cancer risk from lifetime exposure to background radiation (natural and man-made)	39–126
Individuals most exposed to nuclear effluents (estimated)	14
Leukaemia after 40 years' natural radiation	8
Estimated cancers following whole body high-dose gamma-exposure to 1 Gy radiation	70,000–110,000
Estimated cancers following whole body low-dose gamma-exposure to 1 Gy radiation	14,000–45,000

Sources: UNSCEAR; NRPB

Statisticians are fond of reminding us that there is only one certainty in life. Most of us live in the hope that this certainty will not be overtaken by intervening events over which we have no control. At the same time, it is fair to say that most people do not dwell upon possible events which have a low probability of occurrence. The management of man-made radiation is certainly attended by risks of accidental exposure of workers and the public, but there are still no data that can confirm the effects of radiation in the general population below relatively high doses which may be delivered to those immediately affected by accidental occurrences. It would appear from scientific evidence that the risks and benefits of nuclear power can be more objectively weighed.

Global radiation (i.e. average exposure of the world population to man-made sources in addition to natural background radiation) is of the order of 14 million man-sieverts a year, equivalent to an average dose of 0.0028 Sv, or 2.8 mSv per person (5 billion global population) per year. Natural sources are cosmic and galactic gamma rays, radon gases in rocks, soils, groundwater and building materials and radioactive potassium in human tissues. UNSCEAR estimates that background levels of natural radiation exposure from all sources, revising previous estimates of radon and its

Table 2.3 Sources of human exposure to natural, artificial and average annual doses in the population (mSv)

Source	UK (1988)	USA (1987)	Global (1988)
Natural			
Radon and thoron (background and household)	1.3	2.0	2.4
Gamma rays, other terrestrial, cosmic and misc. sources	0.9	1.03	
Artificial			
X-rays, etc.	0.3	0.53	0.4
Radioactive fallout	0.01	0.0006	0.01
Occupational exposure	0.005	0.009	0.002
Radioactive discharges (nuclear installations)	0.001	0.0005	0.0002
Total (rounded)	2.5	3.6	2.8

Sources: UNSCEAR; *UK Social Trends*

daughter radionuclides, increased from 2.0 mSv in 1977 to 2.4 mSv in 1988. Average exposure to man-made sources of radiation appears to have remained at a level of approximately 0.4 mSv per year (Table 2.3).

Radon in the home is the main source of human exposure to ionizing radiation. This is a naturally occurring radioactive gas produced by radium decay in rocks and soils. Lack of ventilation in energy-efficient or unventilated homes traps radon and increases the potential for developing lung cancer in individuals later in life from irradiation by alpha particles. Radon is easy to detect and relatively inexpensive to reduce. In the UK, the National Radiological Protection Board has established an 'action level' of 10 mSv a year in existing homes against an existing average of 1 mSv. The US Environmental Protection Agency, in a study of 20,000 homes in 17 states, found 25% to contain higher than normal radon levels (which in the USA would typically average the equivalent of 2 mSv). This partly explains the generally higher levels of natural radiation to which US citizens are exposed. In certain European countries, background levels in existing homes range from an average of 1 mSv (range 0.25–250 mSv) in the UK to up to an average of 5 mSv in Finland, Norway and Sweden.

Between 1963 and 1980, 3.6 million man-sieverts of radioactive fallout from nuclear weapons had been delivered (12% of the total effective dose equivalent of 30.0 million man-sieverts). 500,000 man-sieverts at ground level were delivered in 1980 and in 1986 fallout continued at the rate of 50,000 man-sieverts, an average dose equivalent to 0.01 mSv.

IRCP recommends that for members of the public, annual average exposure to man-made radiation should not exceed 1 mSv (excluding medical applications), which is substantially less than the natural levels to which individuals and populations are normally exposed, with no more than 50 mSv for the most exposed workers. Although some annual variations are permissible within these limits, the annual average exposure within a lifetime for members of the public should not exceed 1 mSv. The UK National Radiological Protection Board, however, recommends that time-averaged restriction on individual occupation exposure should be 15 mSv and 0.5 mSv from a single nuclear power station site to members of the public. Higher limits of occupational exposure are deemed to be acceptable on the grounds of voluntary risks taken by workers versus involuntary risks to which members of the public should not be gratuitously exposed. It appears that average annual doses in the range of 0.2–0.4 mSv of workers in the UK nuclear industry have been typical in recent years, with an average annual dose of 2 mSv a year compared to an average of 1.1 mSv among all occupations, reflecting a continuing emphasis in the nuclear industry upon optimizing radiation protection (Table 2.8).

The point about nuclear energy is that the background risks from well-designed and efficient operation can be demonstrated to be very low. While this is true for Europe and the USA, the same cannot confidently be said of the design and operation of reactors in Eastern Europe and the USSR. The three recorded accidents which have thus far occurred, causing measurable exposures of the public to radiation, were the result of poor design (Windscale and Chernobyl) and operational negligence (Three Mile Island and Chernobyl). Before discussing the implications of these accidents in detail, the basic types and characteristics of nuclear reactors are shown in Table 2.4. (See pages 98–99).

Table 2.4 Basic operating characteristics of nuclear reactors

Reactor type	Characteristics and distribution
Pressurized water and boiling water reactors	These are the most common types. Water is used for both coolant and steam generation; safety depends upon the reliability of engineered systems (pumps, generators, etc.)
Gas cooled (CO_2 and graphite-moderated helium)	Systems relying on 'passive' safety measures; less power than water-cooled systems
Heavy water	Canada, India
Light-water cooled, graphite moderated	USSR only
Fast breeder reactors	New generation (France, UK, USA)

The quantities of radioactive materials used in nuclear power plants vary from type to type and according to different design specifications. Emissions generally have tended to decrease on account of technological improvements and stricter controls. While the Three Mile Island incident demonstrated the inherent technical safety of water-cooled nuclear reactors, it highlighted the vulnerability of systems designed in such a way that they demand prompt human intervention in low-probability events (Table 2.5).

Table 2.5 Emissions of ionizing radiation from three nuclear incidents and exposure of local populations

	Total man-sieverts to local population	Average individual exposure (sieverts)	Total radiation (terabequerels)
Windscale (Sellafield), 1957	150	0.009	13,000
Three Mile Island, 1979	16–53	0.08	310,000
Chernobyl, 1986	17,000	0.1	2,500,000

Sources: UNSCEAR; NRPB

Human operational error is at the root of the great majority of accidents. It is also true that human intervention often mitigates the worst effects. In the nuclear context, it would appear that deliberate acts would have more severe consequences than accidental events.

Radioactivity (total radiation) from these incidents, measured in terabecquerels (million × million bequerels) were of orders of magnitude greater at Three Mile Island and Chernobyl than at Windscale. Human exposure, and thus health effects, measured in man-sieverts delivered to local inhabitants was greater at Windscale and Chernobyl than at Three Mile Island. The main pathways of exposure to man from Windscale was via iodine-131 in milk and inhalation of polonium-210. Releases from Three Mile Island consisted mostly of radioactive noble gases, principally the relatively short-lived xenon-133. From Chernobyl, local residents at Chelyabinsk were exposed to milk contaminated with strontium-90 and external irradiation. In addition, widespread contamination in the western part of the USSR and other European countries resulted from gamma emitters deposited in the soils and from caesium-137 in dairy and meat products. Outside the immediate area, first-year effective radiation dose equivalents ranged from 7.5 mSv in Bulgaria to 0.3 mSv in the UK to slightly above 0 mSv in Canada and the USA.

The design of the Three Mile Island facility actually contained the radioactivity that might have been released. This was not the case at Chernobyl, and efforts to contain the effects of the accident led to fatalities among the reactor operators, fireman and emergency workers. Chernobyl caused 32 immediate deaths and, out of 299 people admitted to hospital, 203 had been exposed to more than 1 Sv of radiation.

Press reports suggest that in the short-term aftermath, the Byelo-russian population experienced outbreaks of tyroid cancer and that a number of freak animal births also resulted. These effects were largely discounted in early Russian reports, but they may now appear to be more serious. Press reports have also suggested that thyroid cancer among children is widespread and that the incidence of congenital defects in children and infant mortality levels have risen significantly. While the evidence thus far is anecdotal, one reason for an untoward pattern of disease and mortality could be inadequate lack of treatment or management of people exposed to radiation at the time of the accident or subsequently, although 135,000 people were immediately evacuated and treated. At the same time, Byelorussia lies within an area of endemic goitre, a result of iodine deficiency, which could well confuse assessments of the general health of the population. The lack of hard data from the Russian authorities and of opportunities for international monitoring does not assist in objective scientific evaluation of the Chernobyl disaster.

It is too soon to assess the extent of radiation effects from Chernobyl in terms of increased cancer deaths in the USSR and neighbouring countries. Monitoring and documentation is under way at UNSCEAR in association with the US Department of Energy, the US National Cancer Institute, the UK National Radiological Protection Board, the Institute of Biophysics in Moscow, the Italian National Committee for the Research and Development of Nuclear Energy and Alternative Energies and the Monitoring and Assessment Research Centre (of UNEP/GEMS) in London.

Post-nuclear accident monitoring and management

Victims of Hiroshima and Nagasaki have been subject to lifetime monitoring and treatment, which should also to be the case for the estimated 696,000 people exposed to radiation from Chernobyl. Chernobyl presents an invaluable opportunity for post-accident monitoring, the measurement of dose-response and the development of contingency planning measures in the event of future accidents. As it is, effects upon cattle, wildlife and soil already impose a continuing task of monitoring and assessment not only in the USSR but throughout the areas of Europe exposed to the fallout.

For European countries affected by Chernobyl, NRPB suggests that there is a theoretical risk of 3,000 cancer deaths resulting from the Chernobyl accident over the next 50 years in addition to the expected 20 million cancers from all other causes (an additional 0.015%). In an epidemiological context, it would be very difficult to distinguish these cancers from those of other causes.

The Windscale fire

Windscale was constructed in the late 1940s and early 1950s in order to produce plutonium for the UK's first atomic bomb, which was detonated in 1952, the same year as the first US hydrogen bomb. In 1957, following a fire, the piles were shut down and sealed. In 1962 an Advanced Gas-Cooled (AGR) demonstration reactor was commissioned at Windscale and subsequently shut down at the end of its fuel development programme in 1981.

Windscale now comprises Sellafield, renamed in 1982 by British Nuclear Fuels and operated as a nuclear fuel reprocessing and waste-management unit, and UKAEA Windscale, which is developing decommissioning techniques based upon and applied to the original AGR and to UK reactors that have reached the end of their design lives. Calder Hall, the UK's first nuclear power reactor (Magnox gas-cooled), also on the Sellafield site, was the world's first nuclear power connection to a national grid, in 1956.

The first and only significant nuclear accident in the UK occurred at Windscale in 1957, when some of the graphite moderator overheated and caught fire. The consequences of the radioiodine and polonium releases from the fire were expected to give rise to a small number of additional cases of thyroid cancer in the local Cumbrian population, supplementing the number which would normally occur from other causes.

Radioactive effluents and discharges from Sellafield

The discussions, claims and counterclaims concerning observations of the rise of lymphoid leukaemia among children in the area is quite complex, for in the event, the incidence of leukaemia fatalities in the period 1955–84 was one in 52 (seven fatalities in 1068 births), which is ten times more than the national expectation of an average of one additional case per 50,000 births postulated from these releases.

The discrepancy remains unexplained. One theory suggested that if leukaemia is caused by a yet-unsuspected virus, then the influx of new populations into hitherto isolated communities could account for the increased incidence. However, recent research by the University of Southampton suggests a link between childhood leukaemia and occupational exposure of fathers at the plant during the pre-conception period. It would appear that workers were exposed to levels which were less than those deemed to comply with ICRP radiation dose limits, and thus lower than levels at which harm might be expected. The level of exposure of the fathers of the affected children were up to 100 mSv.

Current radiobiological knowledge does not suggest a causal link between occupational exposures at these levels and the incidence of leukaemia in offspring. However, UNSCEAR stresses that there are still no direct data in man of the induction by radiation of hereditary diseases, and that numerical estimates of genetic risks are based upon assumption rather than observation. Moreover, recently published data of the distribution of leukaemia and related diseases in different counties in England and Wales does not indicate that there is evidence of non-random acute lymphatic leukaemia (ALL) at Sellafield (Leukaemia Research Fund).

Historically, from 1975 to 1979 radioactive discharges into the sea, levels of occupational exposure (almost equivalent to underground uranium workers) and collective effective dose equivalents to the local population per gigawatt year of produced electricity were higher from Sellafield than from its sister reprocessing plant at La Hague in France. Similarly, collective doses per unit of electrical energy to which nuclear research and development workers have been exposed were higher in the UK than, for example, in Japan or Switzerland. In this period Sellafield radiation workers were receiving an average of approximately 10 mSv, within the ICRP recommended exposure limits of 50 mSv.

On the question of the effect of Sellafield discharges on marine life and contamination of the adjacent Irish Sea, the principal evidence is that while concentrations of artificial radionuclides in seafoods, seaweed and sea-water are elevated, but human exposures have been within the dose limits recommended by the ICRP. In any event, discharges of both alpha and beta wastes were reduced from the equivalent of 90 terabecquerels (alpha) and 9,000 terabequerels (beta) in 1975 to 2.1 and 81, respectively, in 1989. Discharges of beta emitting radionuclides are currently less than the levels presently discharged at La Hague.

Disposal of nuclear wastes

The time that it takes 50% of the particles of a radioactive element to decay is termed its 'half-life' (Table 2.6). Exponential decay occurs randomly at each subsequent half-life of any atom at a constant 50%. As an example, 50% of uranium-238 radionuclides decay within 4.7 billion years, turning into thorium-234 and eventually to stability in the form of lead-206.

Table 2.6 Example of radionuclide decay: uranium-238

	Nuclide	Half-life (years)		Nuclide	Half-life
A	Uranium-238	4.47 billion			
			B	Thorium-234	24.1 days
			B	Protactinium-234	1.17 minutes
A	Uranium-234	245,000			
A	Thorium-230	8,000			
A	Radium-226	1,600			
			A	Radon-222	3.8 days
			A	Polonium-218	3.05 minutes
			B	Lead-214	26.8 minutes
			B	Bismuth-214	19.7 minutes
			A	Polonium-214	0.0002 seconds
B	Lead-210	22.3			
			B	Bismuth-210	5.0 days
			A	Polonium-210	138.4 days
				Lead-206	Stable

Source: UNSCEAR
A and B are alpha and beta emitters, respectively

In view of the long-lived nature of uranium, particularly as nuclear fuel, the problems of managing high-level waste (HLW) disposal is that predictions of potential accidents leading to release need to be made over periods ranging from 1,000 to 10,000 years, taking into account geological, hydrological, atmospheric and human factors.

Natural uranium contains 99.2% uranium-238 and 0.7% pure uranium-235. Fuel for nuclear power generation is either natural uranium (for example, in UK Magnox reactors) or enriched uranium containing up to about 3% uranium-235. In either case, spent fuel is removed from the reactor and stored for several months to allow isotopes with a short radioactive half-life to decay. Following storage, one option is to recover uranium and plutonium from the spent fuel for reprocessing into new fuel. The residual high-level wastes are made up of fission products and isotopes of neptunium, americium and curium with small amounts of unseparated uranium and plutonium, and are stored for disposal (Table 2.7).

Globally, one tenth of the irradiated fuel is reprocessed to remove uranium and plutonium for re-use. Most fuel for reprocessing originates from Europe and Japan, but spent fuel from the US nuclear industry is discarded as waste. At present, there are three reprocessing plants, at Sellafield in the UK, and at La Hague, and Marcoule in France.

Table 2.7 Projected volumes of waste from nuclear power plants, worldwide (000s m³)

Waste type	1988	1990	1995	2005
Low level (LLW)	335	375	405	520
Intermediate level (ILW)	23	27	31	38
High level (HLW)	3.25	3.5	3.8	5.1
Spent fuel volume	15	16	19	29

Sources: Nuclear Energy Agency (OECD); IAEA

A 1,000-megawatt nuclear reactor produces about a two cubic metre volume of radioactive waste annually, but the problem is where to put it. The UK Atomic Energy Authority (UKEA) estimates that the UK generates some 50 m³ of high-level nuclear waste annually, arising from the fuel cycle and including the reprocessing of spent fuel. A further 5,000 m³ are of intermediate-level waste (resins and chemical sludges from nuclear power) and 40,000 m³ of low-level waste, made up generally of radiation-contaminated disposable items.

National strategies to dispose of low- and intermediate-level wastes include incineration, treatment, packaging and storing in shallow land, landfill and coastal site repositories. Prior to 1983 some 40 sites in the Atlantic and Pacific oceans had been used for sea dumping but no known sea dumping of intermediate-level wastes has occurred since then, in compliance with the extended moratorium on sea dumping adopted at the 1985 tenth consultative meeting of the signatories to the 1975 London Dumping Convention.

A European Commission project, PACOMA (Performance Assessments of Confinement of Medium Active wastes), is currently under way to assess disposal in different types of geological formation, but essentially the search for suitable sites is characterized by delay, with apparently no technical advantages in the continued storage of these wastes. In the UK several possible sites have been under review for several years by UK Nirex Ltd (Billingham, Bradwell, Dounreay, Elstow, Fulbeck, Killingholme and Sellafield). No disposal of high-level radioactive wastes from nuclear power stations or nuclear weapons plants has yet taken place, although 24 IAEA member states are developing strategies based upon geological disposal combined with either domestic or foreign reprocessing of spent fuels.

The disposal problem is one of the several objections raised to the expansion of the nuclear programme in the UK and in the USA, and in many countries the future and continued use is contingent on acceptable solutions for waste management and disposal. Plausible scientific options, such as burial in deep geological formations, have been available since 1957 (US National Academy of Sciences) and a programme of vitrification for the storage of high-level waste prior to eventual burial is under way at British Nuclear Fuels.

NRPB, as the principal adviser on radiological protection to government and the nuclear industry in the UK, points out that there are technical advantages in continued storage of high-level waste but it is also important that research on HLW disposal continues and that there is no de facto decision to store HLW indefinitely after vitrification. Reluctance to host such long-staying guests is quite understandable, even though the risks associated with high-level waste disposal are very low. This has been demonstrated in another European Commission project, PAGIS (Performance Assessment of Geological Isolation Systems), during the period 1982–7, when disposal in granite, salt and clay land formations was reviewed together with disposal in seabed sediments.

Other research and development projects to find a suitable disposition include 'Synroc', a project based upon the properties of certain natural minerals (i.e. zircon and feldspar) to survive extreme geological conditions for millions of years. The principle is to lock up high-level waste into synthetic titanate minerals which would simulate the radiation characteristics of natural rock. 'Synroc' specimens have been made and the process is under investigation in Australia, the UK, the USA, the FRG, Italy and Japan.

The US Department of Energy proposes to develop Yucca Mountain on the Nevada Test Site as a high-level waste burial site. Computed-modelled geological stability studies are under way on the probability of containment failure from a list of 57 independent and interdependent factors. Apart from materials and general reliability studies, these concern predictions and effects of the Earth's orbital changes, mass and momentum fluxes, the likelihood of climate changes within the period of burial (10,000 years), man-induced climatic changes and the imminence of a new Ice Age, all or a combination of which might lead to migration of radionuclides into the hydrological cycle.

Table 2.8 Occupational exposure: average individual doses by occupation, 1987

occupation	numbers employed	annual collective dose (man-sieverts)	average individual dose (mSv)
Mining (non-coal)	2,000	28.0	14.0
Nuclear industry	50,000	92.0	2.0
Air Crew	20,000	40	2.0
Mining (coal)	81,500	96.0	1.2
Defence	16,900	17.0	1.0
General industry	21,000	13.0	0.6
Health	64,000	10.8	0.2
Academic	13,000	1.3	0.1
Total (rounded)	265,000	300.0	1.1

Source: NRPB

EC nuclear (Euratom) directives

New Basic Standards for the Health Protection of the General Public and Workers against the Dangers of Ionizing Radiation (80/836/Euratom) of 15 July 1980 and amended 5 October 1984 (84/467/Euratom)

Laying Down Basic Measures for the Protection of Persons Undergoing Medical Examination or Treatment (84/466/Euratom) of 3 September 1984

International conventions relating to nuclear energy

Convention	Place of adoption Depository state/organization	Date
Convention Concerning the Protection of Workers Against Ionizing Radiation	Geneva (ILO)	1960
Convention on Third Party Liability in the Field of Nuclear Energy	Paris (OECD)	1960
Convention Supplementary to the Paris Convention on Third Party Liability in the Field of Nuclear Energy	Brussels (Belgium)	1963
Convention on Civil Liability for Nuclear Damage	Vienna (IAEA)	1963
Treaty Banning Nuclear Tests in the Atmosphere, in Outer Space and under Water	Moscow (UK/USA/USSR)	1963
Treaty on the Prohibition of the Emplacement of Nuclear Weapons and other Weapons of Mass Destruction on the Sea Bed, the Ocean Floor and in the Subsoil thereof	UK/USA/USSR	1971
Convention on the Physical Protection of Nuclear Material	Vienna (IAEA)	1979
South Pacific Nuclear Free Zone Treaty	Raratonga (SPBEC)*	1985
Convention on Early Notification of a Nuclear Accident	Vienna (IAEA)	1986
Convention on Assistance in the Case of a Nuclear Accident or Radiological Emergency	Vienna (IAEA)	1986
Joint Protocol Relating to the Vienna and Paris conventions to avoid conflicts in their application	Vienna (IAEA)	1988

* South Pacific Bureau For Economic Co-operation

3 ATMOSPHERE AND CLIMATE

The ozone layer, acid rain and global warming

World climate

Climate, or the average weather conditions of places and regions throughout the seasons, is governed by latitude, altitude, location relative to continents and oceans, local topographical conditions such as vegetation cover and prevailing atmospheric phenomena affecting temperature and humidity. The relationships that determine climate are both subtle and complex, involving the orbital influences of the Earth, ocean circulation, chemical balances and energy fluxes between the land, atmosphere and oceans, solar radiation and the more recent influences of human activities.

The scientific study of climate concerns energy fluxes and the biospheric and anthropogenic influences that may result in climate change, particularly in the temperate regions of the world, which would most severely be affected by even relatively minor alterations in average temperature. Variations in the temperature of the Earth are determined by the balance of solar energy absorbed by the Earth's surface (short-wavelength ultra-violet radiation) and the re-radiation of long-wavelength infra-red radiation. Outbound infra-red energy is trapped by water droplets, water vapour and carbon dioxide, creating the 'greenhouse effect', and maintaining the Earth's average temperature at 16.7°C.

Albedo, another determining factor of the Earth's temperature, is the fraction of unabsorbed ultra-violet light reflected from the surface back into space by deserts, seas, snow-covered land masses and intervening cloud formations. Forests and cultivated areas retain more ultra-violet energy than they reflect.

With regard to the scientific study of these phenomena, the main international initiative to obtain data for climate prediction is the World Ocean Circulation Experiment (WOCE), first proposed in 1980 by the World Meteorological Organization and ICSU as a key element in a World Climate Research Programme (WCRP). The first five-year field phase began in 1990, with satellite missions, including the joint France–USA TOPEX–POSEIDON and the European Space Agency's first environmental satellite ERS-1 and research cruises in the Antarctic Southern Ocean.

To determine the possible global warming produced by increases in CO_2 concentrations in the atmosphere, ocean biology, chemistry, vertical and horizontal circulation and the global carbon cycle will be studied. A focus will be measurement of sea-level changes (ocean variability) and air–sea energy flows. At the intergovernmental level, the joint WMO/UNEP Intergovernmental Panel on Climate Change (IPCC) is under political and economic pressures by the US and UK governments in particular concerning fuel and transport policies.

The IPCC was set up in 1988, coinciding with the UN General Assembly Resolution 43/53 on the Protection of Global Climate for Present and Future Generations of Mankind. This was followed by a series of meetings in 1989, in Ottawa (February), The Hague (March), Paris (July), in November at the Noordwyk ministerial meeting and most recently in 1990 (May) at Windsor.

Noordwyk agreed upon a programme towards the WMO Second World Climate Conference (SWCC), which is to be held in the first week of November 1990, co-sponsored by Unesco, UNEP and ICSU/SCOR. Immediately following Noordwyk, Mrs Thatcher pledged £100 million bilaterally for rainforest regeneration and £5.5 million annually for five years on the UK Centre for Climate Change Prediction which she officially opened at the May IPCC meeting.

The polar regions

The polar regions exert significant influences upon global patterns of weather and climate and both the Antarctic and Arctic are sensitive to the increasing atmospheric concentrations of carbon dioxide and other 'greenhouse gases', including chlorofluorocarbons associated with ozone depletion. These are among the least contaminated areas of the world, and therefore provide an opportunity for establishing benchmarks against which to measure the levels and effects of a wide range of terrestrial, aquatic and atmospheric contaminants and radionuclide pathways.

The Antarctic ice cap

The 1820 Bellinghausen expedition from Imperial Russia first confirmed the existence of an ice-covered southern continent. In 1911 the German geographer, Wilhelm Meinardus, calculated the average elevation of the ice as 2,100 metres. During 1957 the International Antarctic Glaciological Project (IAGP of ICSU) recorded the mean elevation of perpetual ice to be 2,200 metres and 4,500 metres at the extreme.

Antarctica is an uninhabited continent set aside for science, protected for the time being by the 1959 Antarctic Treaty, under international study for information on the Earth's evolution and its influence on the global climate. Signatories to the Treaty are Argentina, Australia, Belgium, Brazil, Chile, China, the Federal Republic of Germany, France, India, Japan, New Zealand, Norway, South Africa, the UK, Uruguay, the USA and the USSR, all of which maintain national research bases in Antarctica.

The Treaty resulted largely from the 1956 International Geophysical Year (ICSU), which concentrated on geophysical research in Antarctica and studies of the upper atmosphere. Its purpose was to protect the Antarctic from territorial claims and disputes and to establish a framework for international co-operation via scientific research. The Scientific Committee for Antarctic Research (SCAR of ICSU), although non-government, is the principal source of scientific information for governments party to the Treaty.

Since 1959, several amendments to the Treaty have been made in order to conserve and protect all Antarctic Marine Living Resources (1980) and to extend the regional definition of Antarctica by biological rather than geographical boundaries. Currently, the Treaty nations are discussing terms and conditions of future exploitation of Antarctic minerals. Data on the structural and chemical properties of the ice obtained from the analysis of ice cores provide an historic record of global atmospheric conditions and climate from the levels of trace gases and radioactivity from natural and anthrogenic sources.

The Arctic and sub-Arctic

Important to UK interests in the Arctic is the 1920 Svalbard Treaty, which confers rights of access upon its signatories to stipulated commercial and industrial activities such as hunting, fishing, mining and shipping. The Treaty provides the opportunities for long-term research and the basis of the work of the NERC Polar Sciences Committee. Signatories to the Svalbard Treaty are Australia, Canada, Denmark, France, India, Italy, Japan, The Netherlands, New Zealand, Norway, South Africa, Sweden and the USA. The Svalbard archipelago is under Norwegian sovereignty.

While vastly different in age, physical structure, oceanography, biota and human habitation, the cold and intensely seasonal environment of the Arctic provides a valuable area for comparison with the Antarctic. The Arctic has a major influence on global systems of climate and ocean circulation, especially in the North Atlantic. The region is economically important to the fishery, forestry and mineral industries of Arctic rim countries (Canada, Greenland, Iceland, Norway, the USA and the USSR) and to the defence of north-west Europe. The protection of Arctic wildlife is vital to the socio-economic wellbeing of the indigenous peoples, and the conservation and replenishment of many mammal and fish stocks has wide economic and ecological significance.

Climatic perturbation in the Arctic is characterized by Arctic haze. It is also suggested that stratospheric ozone may be an Arctic phenomenon.

Atmospheric pollution

The emission of trace gases into the atmosphere is both a natural and a man-made phenomenon, having short- and long-term effects on climate and human health. Trace gases have a range of effects which are inseparable, since they give rise to a multitude of complex chemical processes and cause–effect relationships involving the oceans, radiative activity, the hydrological cycle, the carbon cycle, agricultural practices, albedo, cloud formation and energy flows — in short, the entire balance between the four main physical zones of the Earth's system. Here we outline some of these relationships in terms of the anthropogenic contribution of trace gases.

Emissions, trace gases and particulates

A single 1,000-megawatt coal-fired plant, uncontrolled, emits 275 kg of carbon dioxide, 14 kg of particulates and 5 kg of sulphur dioxide per second, and a volume of nitrogen oxide equivalent to about 150,000 vehicle exhausts. The practice in the 1970s to build taller smoke stacks in order to reduce ground-level concentrations of these emissions had the effect of dispersing them over a wider area, turning a local problem into a regional or international one (trans-boundary pollution).

The pollution of one country's atmosphere by the industrial activities of another lent a strong impetus to international environmental co-operation. International control, impinging upon national sovereignty, has already proved to be a bone of contention. This is mollified somewhat by the growing weight of meteorological evidence concerning the fate of emissions of industrial gases, which not only affect adjoining countries but also have the potential for climatic and ecological disturbances on a global scale. The present intergovernmental philosophy in relation to these problems is to seek data and information which can assist in reconciling environmental with political and economic considerations.

Typically, the range of harmful chemicals, gases and particulates emitted into the atmosphere from industry and transport are as shown in Table 3.1.

Climate- and atmosphere-modifying gases

Oxygen, nitrogen and the inert noble gases make up some 99.9% of the atmospheric gases (Table 3.2). The volumes of trace gases indicated are from natural and anthrogenic sources which will be identified in more detail below. From the scientific evidence thus far adduced, it has been demonstrated that naturally occurring trace gases play an important role in climate determination, and that any additions to them may have untoward consequences outside the normal ranges of climatic variation, as well their recognized contributions to respiratory disease.

The hydroxyl radical is the scarcest of the gases identified in Table 3.2, but provides an important element in the atmosphere's self-cleansing mechanism. It is also subject to depletion, from anthropogenic methane and carbon monoxide, gases which also assist in the build-up of ozone. The observed effects on the ozone layer, the predicted climatic changes from ozone depletion, acid rain, photochemical smog, etc., are attributed to the build-up of trace gases.

Table 3.1 Chemicals, gases and particulates in the atmosphere

Chemical	Source	Health effect
Arsenic (As)	Combustion (oil and coal); glass manufacture	Lung and skin cancer
Benzene (C_6H_6)	Oil refining; vehicle exhausts	Leukaemia
Cadmium (Cd)	Combustion (oil, coal and waste); smelting	Lung, kidney and bone damage
Carbon dioxide (CO_2)*	Combustion (oil, coal, natural gas)	No direct effects
Carbon monoxide (CO)	Combustion (oil and coal); vehicle exhausts	Heart disease
Chlorine (C_{12})	Chemical industry	Nasal damage
Chlorofluorocarbons (CFCs)*	Chemical industry; aerosols, etc.	Respiratory, cardiovascular and central nervous systems
Fluoride (F)	Metal manufacture	Fluorosis
Formaldehyde (HCHO)	Chemical manufacture; vehicle exhausts	Eye and lung damage
Hydrocarbons (HC)*	Vehicle exhausts	Carcinogens
Hydrogen chloride (HCl)	Waste combustion	Eye and lung damage
Hydrogen sulphide (H_2S)	Oil refineries and sewage	Nausea and fatalities at concentrated levels
Hydroxyl radical (OH)*	Combustion (coal and oil); vehicle exhausts	
Lead (Pb)	Smelting; vehicle exhausts	Physiological and mental disorder; high blood pressure
Manganese (Mn)	Power stations; steel making	Parkinson's disease
Mercury (Hg)	Combustion (oil and coal); smelting	Brain damage; physiological disorders
Methane (CH_4)*	Sewage, wastes, rotting vegetation; cattle	Lung irritant
Nickel (Ni)	Combustion (oil and coal); smelting	Lung cancer
Nitric acid (HNO_3)*	Photochemically from nitrogen dioxide	Lung damage
Nitrogen oxides (NO_x)*	Combustion (oil and coal); vehicle exhausts	Respiratory disorders
Ozone (O_3)*	Photochemically from nitrogen oxides	Eye and lung irritant
Peroxyacetyl (PAN)	Photochemically from NO_x and HC	Eye and lung irritant
Silicon tetrafluoride (SiF_4)	Chemical industry	Lung damage
Sulphur dioxide (SO_2)*	Combustion (oil and coal); smelting	Eye and lung damage
Sulphuric acid (H_2SO_4)*	Photochemically from SO_2	

* Climate- and atmosphere-modifying gases

Table 3.2 Distribution of atmospheric and trace gases

Atmospheric gases	Parts per billion	Trace gases	Parts per billion
Nitrogen (N_2)		Sulphur dioxide (SO_2)	50 (max.)
Oxygen (O_2)	9.99^8	Nitrogen oxides (NO_x)	50 (max.)
Noble gases		Nitrous oxide (NO)	310
		Methane (CH_4)	1,700
		Carbon dioxide (CO_2)	350,000
		Carbon monoxide (C)	40–200
		Clorine, fluorine, carbon hydrogen compounds (CFCs)	3 chlorine atoms
		Hydroxyl radical (OH)	0.00001

Mathematical models of the atmosphere provide the data for predicting climatic behaviour, and much work is being carried out to determine the effects of airbone particles, including dust, particularly their effect on temperature variations. The variations in atmospheric temperature, i.e. cooling and heating patterns within the various layers of atmosphere, predicated upon the presence of natural and anthrogenic sources of particles reflecting solar radiation, is described as the Albedo Effect. Thus the combined effects of gases and their non-soluble particles are taken into account in assessing the Earth's thermal balance (Table 3.3).

Table 3.3 Principal sources of man-made trace gases

Source		Trace gas emissions (million tonnes)	
		Low est.	High est.
Fossil fuel and biomass combustion	Carbon monoxide and NO_x gases	700.0 10–20	1,300.0 20–30
Fossil fuel combustion and deforestation	Carbon dioxide	5,500.0	8,000.0
Fossil fuel combustion and ore smelting	Sulphur dioxide	50–70	100–130
Rice paddies, cattle, landfills and fossil fuel production	Methane	150–250	250–400
Nitrogenous fertilizers, deforestation, biomass burning	Nitrous oxide	19.0	6.0
Aerosol sprays, foams, refrigerants	CFCs	1.0	—
Worldwide		6,495.0	7,270.0

Trace gases play an important role in the energy cycle and in climate determination. While it may be difficult to appreciate the effects of additional levels in such proportionately small quantities relative to the total atmosphere, anthrogenic sources make a significant contribution at least to short-term effects. Scientific propositions concerning long-term climatic changes based upon mathematical models are more contentious, but that effects will occur are authoritatively agreed. Total industrial emissions of carbon dioxide are estimated to have increased from 1.5 million tonnes in 1950 to the current level of 5.5–8.0 billion tonnes. Glacial core samples indicate that the levels of carbon dioxide in the pre-industrial atmosphere were in the order of some 260 ppm, compared to some 350 ppm today.

Levels of methane and nitrous oxide in the atmosphere are increasing at twice the rate of carbon dioxide. By the end of the century, together with CFCs, these gases could be the principal greenhouse gases (NERC), at the orders of magnitude shown in Table 3.4.

Table 3.4

Gas	Concentration (ppb), AD 2000
Carbon dioxide	3,600
Methane	1,700
CFCs	2.4–? chlorine atoms*

Source: ICSU
* Based upon industrial production of 750 kilotonnes/year

Ozone depletion (stratospheric)

The stratospheric ozone layer which surrounds the Earth acts as a filter to ultra-violet radiation from the sun. Stratospheric ozone (O_3) results from the re-formation of oxygen by short-wave radiation. Losses of O_3 from the ozone layer were first noticed in 1975 above Antarctica during the southern spring. The phenomenon has become increasingly pronounced and similar losses have been observed in the higher latitudes of the Northern Hemisphere.

Ozone depletion is a consequence of insoluble inert trace gases (mostly chlorofluorocarbons — $CFCl_3$ and CF_2Cl_2) from terrestrial sources reaching the troposphere, where they react with direct ultra-violet radiation from the sun. These liberate chlorine, which catalyses the conversion of ozone into molecular oxygen. Low temperatures accelerate chlorine catalyst cycles, which confirms the geographic distribution of the observations.

Rate of ozone depletion

The inertness of CFCs is the very characteristic which allows them to reach the stratosphere unchanged. In the 1989 edition of *Social Trends* it is stated that, despite reductions in manufacturing, the chemical industry currently produces CFCs six times more quickly than the atmosphere can break them down. Uses of CFCs in refrigerators, aerosol propellants (banned unilaterally by Canada, Norway, Sweden and the USA in 1978), air-conditioning systems, foaming agents, etc. are now well recognized.

An interesting anecdote illustrating how CFCs react with ozone concerns a Russian comparison of fuels used in the American and Soviet space shuttles. The rocket motors on the space shuttle and Titan IV launch vehicles use solid fuels made from aluminium chips and ammonium perchlorate. These burn to produce chlorine gas and hydrogen chloride, which destroys ozone at the rate of 100,000 molecules per molecule of hydrogen chloride. The Russians calculated that Columbia alone, per flight (first launch, January 1989), would deplete some 10 million kilotonnes of stratospheric ozone (0.33% of the total). The volume of ozone in the stratosphere is estimated to be of the order of 3.0 billion kilotonnes. The Russian space shuttle, Energia, burns oxygen and hydrocarbon fuels, which it is claimed, destroys ozone at a rate 7,000 times less than this.

Subsequent research by NASA in the course of a presidential enquiry, based upon a programme of nine space shuttle and six Titan IV launches a year, provided the information in Table 3.5.

Table 3.5 Chlorine inputs to the stratosphere

Source	Annual volume (kilotonnes)	Parts per billion stratospheric chlorine
Space shuttle launches (15)	0.725	0.075
Industrial sources	300	3.0

Source: NASA

NASA calculated that the total amount of chlorine released into the atmosphere by the solid rocket motors is 0.725 kilotonnes per year, which compares to the 300 kilotonnes per year from industrial sources. The latter represents nearly 50.0% of the chemical industry's annual production of halogenated chlorine (WMO/UNEP, 1990), contributing some 3.00 ppb to the ozone column. NASA calculate that a steady-state distribution of stratospheric chlorine over a number of model years, based upon the current launch schedule, will add about 0.25% to the total level of inorganic chlorine, with ozone perturbations occurring in the northern mid-latitudes (0.10–0.15% depletion), Antarctica (0.10% depletion) and the Arctic (0.50% depletion).

Cumulative reductions on the production of industrial sources of halogenated chlorine, as envisaged in the Montreal Protocol, while leading to lower background levels, are not expected to result in concentrations much less than 2 ppb before the end of the next century.

Local initiatives

Some local initiatives to control the use of CFCs are worth noting in order to illustrate the wider possibilities for local unilateral action pending legislation. These include the city of Irvine in Southern California, which has enacted muncipal regulations that require industries using CFCs to prevent their escape into the atmosphere (from 1990). It is expected that more US cities may enact similar restrictions and that the Irvine initiative will be regarded as a model. In a similar vein, the city of Los Angeles restricts the use of CFCs in plastic food packaging. The Irvine-based Centre for Innovative Diplomacy (CID) has suggested that an international mayoral conference be held to arrive at a 'stratospheric protection accord'.

Low-level ozone and photochemical smog

The presence of ozone has been observed since the late nineteenth century, when natural ground-level occurrence was first measured (Table 3.6). Evidently, ozone has increased to typical ground-level concentrations two to four times greater than earlier in the century, and ten times higher in conditions associated with photochemical smog. Smog in tropical urban conurbations is exacerbated by stronger solar radiation.

Table 3.6 Rise in ground-level ozone (parts per billion)

	1900	Present average	Present (max.) (cities)
Western Europe			
California	10	20–40	100
Australia			
Tropics	—	50	

Ozone at low altitudes and at ground level as an oxidizing agent corrodes building surfaces, metal, certain vegetation and the leaves of trees. It is also associated with lung disease. It tends to build up its levels of concentration during the day in urban areas where sulphur dioxide and other pollutant gases are present and decays at night.

Vehicle exhaust emissions

Combustion engines' exhausts produce carbon monoxide (CO), carbon dioxide (CO_2), nitrogen oxide (NO), nitrogen dioxide (NO_2), sulphur dioxide (SO_2), lead particulates and a variety of hydrocarbons. These pollutants can be reduced by altering combustion cycles, modifying fuels and treating exhaust gases.

Nitrogen oxides and hydrocarbon emissions from vehicles

Nitrogen oxides and hydrocarbons are subject to photochemical reactions in the presence of sunlight, producing ozone and other products. In the 1960s, from observations particularly in Los Angeles, it was evident that exhaust emissions from vehicles were the most significant contributor to photochemical smog. This led to early legislation in the USA to reduce hydrocarbon and carbon monoxide emissions from cars and to decrease the amount of lead in petrol, which has now been followed by most industralized countries (Table 3.7)

The installation of three-way (nitrogen oxides, hydrocarbons and carbon monoxide) catalytic converters to the exhausts of larger cars (above 2 litres) burning unleaded petrol would meet the 1989 EC emission standards, although the system is costly and gives relatively poor fuel economy. For smaller cars, 'lean-burn' engines are expected to be available during 1992, offering an alternative to catalytic converters.

Table 3.7 Vehicle emission standards in North America, Europe and Japan

Austria	US model legislation
Canada	Californian model legislation
EC	Large cars (2+ litres) 1989; medium cars (1.4–2 litres) 1993; small cars (less than 1.4 litres) 1991
	From October 1989 all new cars to be capable of running on unleaded petrol; from 1991, all vehicles
Japan	US model legislation
Sweden	US model legislation
Switzerland	US model legislation
UK	EC regulations
USA	Current legislation requires catalytic converters on all vehicles

Tax incentives for installing catalytic converters are available in Austria, Denmark, West Germany, The Netherlands, Norway, Sweden and Switzerland. In West Germany they are based upon a remission of vehicle excise duties for periods up to three years.

Global warming (the 'greenhouse effect')

The 'greenhouse effect' is a natural phenomenon first observed in 1896, independently by the Swedish chemist Arrhenius and the American geologist Thomas C. Chamberlin. Arrhenius suggested that by doubling the natural CO_2 level, average temperatures would rise by some 5–6°C, a proposition confirmed by recent global climate models but with crucial gaps, particularly concerning the role of the oceans and the stability of the ocean–atmosphere relationship in global temperature patterns.

'Greenhouse gases', principally carbon dioxide, help to maintain the temperature of the Earth's surface at a level which enables life to thrive. Climate and temperature are determined by ocean current circulation, atmospheric turbulence, cloud formations, terrestrial vegetation cover, etc., mitigating the effects of natural and man-made carbon and sulphur oxide emissions by absorption and photosynthesis.

The discussion on global warming centres around the effects of additional carbon gas emissions into the atmosphere, the principal sources of which are carbon dioxide from scrub and forest burning (20–40%), power station emissions and carbon monoxide from vehicle exhausts. To these may be added the emission of methane, ozone-destructive gases (CFCs, etc.) and carbon releases from the depletion of peatlands. It is suggested that the total contribution of fossil fuel combustion (wood, oil and coal) to global warming is around 50%.

Since the Industrial Revolution, atmospheric content of carbon dioxide has increased by about 20%. Thus the products of combustion have contributed an amount equivalent to some 60,000 ppb to natural levels of CO_2.

Natural emissions of CO_2 from photosynthesis help to maintain the average temperature of the Earth, within a variation of 1–2°C, since the end of the last Ice Age, 10,000 years ago. The greenhouse debate is based upon the proposition that the additional relatively minor changes in the composition of the atmosphere from man-made CO_2 and other trace gases will lead to increased average surface temperatures of between 3° and 5.5°C, beginning within the next 50 years or so (ICSU and others). This would match the 5°C warming since the peak of the last Ice Age, but occurring some ten to a hundred times faster, in a timescale of 180–1,800 years hence. Although carbon dioxide enhances heat entrapment and thus affects average temperatures, it is difficult to explain short-term random climatic fluctuations, dry spells, droughts, hurricanes, etc. in these terms, nor the exact extent of ocean absorption of carbon dioxide.

An increase in the average temperature of between 0.3° and 1.1°C over the last hundred years has been postulated. This range of estimates suggests, on the one hand (MIT, and, most recently, NASA and the University of Alabama), that no untoward global warming has taken place. On the other (for example, the US Goddard Space Center, the UK Meterological Office and the University of East Anglia, among others), it presages the thin end of a wedge that will lead to long-term dire consequences, raising sea levels by ocean expansion, melting glaciers, extensively flooding low-lying areas and modifying local climates. The dry spell in Texas in 1988, which turned parched fields to sand and devastated the US grain crop, does not escape consideration. The lower level of temperature is based upon ocean-surface measurements, also taking into account the range of natural and man-made emissions. The higher level derives from land readings which, it is claimed, discounts the interference from urban heat radiation.

In short, the effects of global warming would first alter planning that assumes climatic stability. Its physical manifestations would be coastal flooding, altered distribution of agriculture, abnormal variations in patterns of plant growth, desertification of fragile croplands, population movements and the political tensions resulting therefrom.

Carbon dioxide reaches the very heart of economic activity, with its implications for energy and transport. Sulphur and nitrous oxides are more readily controlled, at a nominal cost of $2–3 billion, but the costs of reducing athropometric CO_2 are of orders of magnitude greater, and need a structured approach to balance the relative inputs from industry and other sources (Table 3.8).

Table 3.8 Estimated capital cost of CO_2 control on US power plants ($ billion)

Replacing power deration with nuclear	193.0
Removal by scrubbing	155.0
Liquid pipelines to ocean	125.0
Compression and liquefaction	111.0
Total cost	584.0

Data presented at the OECD/IEA Seminar on Energy Technologies for Reducing Emissions of Greenhouse Gases, April 1989

It would appear that the cost of effectively controlling CO_2 emissions in the USA from the power-generating industry, based upon a mixture of fossil fuel replacement and clean-up technology, would be the equivalent of 12% of US GDP. By comparison, it would cost EC member countries, at a rough estimate based upon 50% of US energy consumption, nearly $300 billion. This sum, by itself, is 700% more than the total world level of economic aid to developing countries. Given the more modest financial requirements of forest and agricultural regeneration in the Third World, for example, it would be not only of greater practical value but also of greater benefit to mankind, humanistically, economically and climatically, to create the incentives for greater fuel efficiency in Western societies and strengthen the mechanisms for Third World co-operation.

Before leaving the subject of carbon dioxide, unbalanced natural levels are demonstrably hazardous to health. A bizarre example of carbon dioxide poisoning occurred in the Cameroons in 1986, when 1,700 villagers and 3,000 cattle were killed by natural emissions from Lake Nyos.

Nitrogen oxides and sulphur dioxide

Nitrogen oxides (NO_x) are emitted from power plants and the exhausts of combustion engines. Nitrogen dioxide is the most dangerous form of NO_x, as an irritant which causes pulmonary edema. It reacts in the atmosphere to produce low-level ozone and combines with sulphur dioxide to increase levels of acid deposition.

The effects of nitrous oxides, in the form of nitric acid in rainfall, on coniferous forests and on fish populations in river and lake systems are more severe than those of sulphuric acid. Output from power plants, the main source, is increasing, although the technology for reducing emissions costs approximately the same as for sulphur dioxide.

Anthropogenic nitrogen oxide emissions from power-generating plant and vehicle exhausts are estimated to be some 30–50 million tonnes annually, to which the USA contributes about 46% of the total and EC countries some 8%. Phased reduction targets for NO_x emissions are shown in Table 3.9.

Sulphur dioxide and suspended particulates in smoke and dust are the principal air contaminants, and hence more attention has been given to

Table 3.9 EC phased reduction targets for nitrogen oxides emissions among the largest volume producers (million tonnes)

Country	1980	1993	1998
UK	1.0	0.9	0.7
West Germany	0.9	0.7	0.5
Italy	0.6	0.6	0.4
France	0.4	0.3	0.2
Spain	0.4	0.4	0.3
Total	3.3	2.9	2.1

Source: EC

reducing output levels. Economic factors also operate in the determination of which pollutant to reduce. Recovered sulphur is a more valuable commodity than oxides of nitrogen, and the costs of reducing NO_x emissions are claimed by industry lobbyists in the USA to be higher. Anthropogenic emissions of sulphur dioxide worldwide is estimated to be between 100 million and 130 million tonnes, to which EC countries in 1980 contributed some 14%.

WHO guidelines set the criteria for sulphur dioxide levels at 40–60 micrograms per cubic metre, a level which is exceeded in most Third World cities. Similarly, the criteria for suspended particulates, of 60–90 micrograms per cubic metre, are met only by some twelve cities. Both sources of air pollution have been declining in Europe and North American cities at an average rate of about 5% per year, while in Third World cities levels are increasing at an annual rate of 10%.

EC targets are to reduce sulphur dioxide emissions to 40% of 1980 levels by the year 2003 (Table 3.10). Compliance by the UK to emission targets will still mean that it will emit more sulphur dioxide than any other EC member country. Average SO_2 emissions from all EC countries is currently 1.2 million tonnes.

Table 3.10 EC phased reduction targets for sulphur dioxide emissions among largest volume producers (million tonnes)

Country	1980	1993	1998	2003
UK	3.9	3.1	2.3	1.5
West Germany	2.2	1.3	0.9	0.7
France	1.9	1.2	0.8	0.6
Italy	2.4	1.8	1.5	0.9
Spain	2.3	2.3	1.7	1.4
Total	12.7	9.7	7.2	5.1

Source: EC

The technology to be applied to reducing SO_2 emissions is flue-gas desulphurization (FGD). Privatization of the electricity and coal industries presents the UK with problems in meeting the required EC standard within the allotted time span. Following privatization, the question will arise of who will bear the cost of meeting EC requirements. Reduced demand for electricity would make a contribution to a decrease in emission, but more significantly, the installation of control equipment in new electricity generating plant, within a framework of tax benefits, would bring more permanent reductions.

Factors affecting variations in air pollution, apart from the siting of pollutant sources, are meteorological and topographical conditions which determine atmospheric dispersion. Some 66% of urban dwellers (1.2 billion people) throughout the world are exposed to high levels of airborne sulphurous contaminants which also include carbon dioxide and lead (Table 3.11).

Table 3.11 SO_2 averages worldwide

Lowest	Highest
Bangkok	Beijing
Bucharest	Brussels
Cali (Colombia)	Calcutta
Chicago	London
Craiova (Romania)	Milan
Melbourne	Moscow
Tel Aviv	New York
Toronto	Paris
Vancouver	Rio de Janeiro
	Sao Paulo
	Seoul
	Shanghai
	Shenyang
	Teheran
	Xian

Source: MARC

Sulphur pariculate emissions, which are a major contributor to acid deposition, can assist in the formation of cloud droplets, making them denser and brighter, thus increasing their cooling effects. This may have inhibited greenhouse warming and offset the effects of CO_2 in the Northern Hemisphere, where industrial activity is at its most intense.

Emissions of volatile organic compounds (VOCs)

Volatile organic compounds (VOCs) occur naturally in conifer forests and woodlands (30% in OECD countries) but are derived industrially from the evaporation of solvents used in paints and industrial processes, from vehicle exhausts and hydrocarbon evaporation in refining and gasoline distribution. In Europe, they contribute some 10 million tonnes per year of emissions into the atmosphere. Product reformulation to reduce solvent content would remove a significant amount of evaporation. However, costs of vapour recovery from refinery operations and gasoline distribution are considered to be too high in terms of the value of the hydrocarbons that could be recovered.

Natural disasters and climate

The year 1990 marks the beginning of the International Decade for Natural Disaster Reduction. Many natural disasters are the result of weather events such as tornadoes, hurricanes, typhoons, drought and flood. The distribution and severity of these events may well be modified by climatic change. Natural phenomena such as volcanic eruptions also make a significant contribution to levels of atmospheric sulphur dioxide and carbon dioxide, to which industrial particulate pollution adds a multiplier effect to the coolant properties of volcanic dust.

The three coldest decades recorded in England (from 1781, 1811 and 1881) were coincident with the eruptions of Mount Asama (1783) in Japan, Mount Skaptar (1783) in Iceland, Mount Tambora (1815) in Indonesia and Krakatoa (1883) in Java. The Tambora eruption emitted an estimated 150 cubic kilometres of ash into the atmosphere, resulting in an exceptionally cold summer in the northern USA and average July temperatures in England of 13.4°C. Similar eruptions today would create more serious effects on planetary albedo and climatic perturbation.

Acid deposition (acid rain, snow, fog, dew and particulates)

Acid deposition is the general term used for sulphur dioxide and nitrogen oxides in precipitation and dry aerosol particles and gases. This is a regional rather than a global phenomenon, affecting northern Europe (East and West Germany, Norway, Scotland, Sweden), north-west USA and south-east Canada (the Northern Temperate Zone). It characterizes the industrial nature of these regions, which have relied to a large degree upon coal for manufacturing and power generation. The level of acid in rain and snow in these parts of Europe and North America has increased from a nearly neutral solution two hundred years ago to a dilute solution today of sulphuric and nitric acids.

Acid deposition destroys conifer forests and woodlands, and acidifies river and lake systems. In the UK, the average acidity of rain in Yorkshire and the East Midlands is below a pH of 4.3. Acidity in rain is characterized by the presence of hydrogen ions (H^+). Levels are expressed as a pH measure, defined as the negative logarithm of hydrogen concentrations. The pH scale ranges from 0 to 14, with a value of 7 representing a solution which is neutral. Values below 7 indicate greater levels of acidity and those above 7, greater alkalinity. Since the pH scale is logarithmic, solutions of 6, 5 and 4 contain, respectively, 1, 10 and 100 microequivalents of acidity (H^+) per litre.

Under normal conditions, the pH of rain and snow, containing carbonic acid formed from water vapour and atmospheric carbon dioxide, and sulphur dioxide, hydrogen sulphide and nitrogen oxides from volcanoes and other natural sources would be about 5.6. Sulphur and nitrogen oxide emissions from the combustion of fossil fuels and the smelting of sulphide ores, together with additional levels of carbon oxides from vehicle exhausts, are converted to strong acids in the atmosphere, resulting in significantly lower pH levels, down to as little as pH 2.4 (the acidic equivalent of vinegar), a level observed during a storm at Pitlochry, Scotland, as early as 1974.

In general, the pH of precipitation is lower nearest the sources and increases with distance. However, the normal flow of air in Europe, from south-west to north-east, causes pollutants from UK emissions being removed in precipitation over Scandinavia. In southern Norway, acid precipitation has affected thousands of freshwater lakes and streams over an area of 33,000 square kilometres, reducing fish populations and the rate of bacterial organic decomposition.

International conventions relating to atmospheric pollution

Convention	Place of adoption Depository state/organization	Date
Convention on Long-Range Transboundary Air Pollution	Geneva (UN)	1979
Protocol to the 1979 Convention on Long-term Financing of the Co-operative Programme for Monitoring and Evaluation of the Long-range Transmission of Air Pollutants in Europe (EMEP)	Geneva (UN)	1984
Protocol to the 1979 Convention on the Reduction of Sulphur Emissions or their Transboundary Fluxes by at least 30%	Helsinki (UN)	1985
Convention for the Protection of the Ozone Layer	Vienna (UN)	1985
Protocol on Substances that Deplete the Ozone Layer	Montreal (UN)	1987
Protocol to the 1979 Convention Concerning the Control and Emission of Nitrogen or their Transboundary Fluxes	Sofia (UN)	1988

4 CHEMICALS

Production, management and control

The subject of chemicals is vast, as they are the very substance of life and the elements of the Universe. Thus, if ever there were to be a final analysis, it might be said that the Earth's environmental problems were brought about by chemical imbalances created by man's attempt to improve upon nature's work.

Having adopted such a hasty position, it would not take a great deal of additional reflection or observation to appreciate that every individual can attribute good health and living standards to the availability of chemicals or poor health and poverty to their absence. Both sets of circumstances are modified relatively by social and cultural conditions, but the role of chemicals as an aid to meeting economic and social objectives is clear.

The cycles of organic carbon, nitrogen and phosphorus determine what life shall be. Carbon flux and climate are interdependent factors; carbon-based fossil fuels produce energy for heat and the feedstock for chemical production; carbon, carbon compounds, synthetic chemicals, metals, minerals and their anhydrides that escape or succumb to physical or biological degradation play vital roles in industry, agriculture and medicine. That they can have serious negative side-effects is understood. Better management of their use and disposal is a common objective of industry, the scientific community and the regulating agencies.

The challenge of chemicals management is equally relevant in industrialized and developing countries. In the global perspective, chemicals and chemical developments are required to sustain standards of living in industrialized countries and, in the Third World, the need for fertilizers, pesticides, industrial chemicals and medicines to assist economic progress and to improve standards of living are pressing.

The most devastating accidents in industrial history have resulted from the loss of containment of chemicals, either in their transport or in their processing. Bhopal, the worst industrial accident in history, Flixborough, Seveso and Mexico City are well-known examples of the potential severity of loss of containment. Other less dramatic, higher-frequency events that have greater potential for ill-health and mortality among larger populations are accidental releases of toxic substances into air, soil and water, as well as the carcinogenic effects of persistent chemicals on living organisms. A new vector of threat to health is emerging in relation to the disposal of chemicals as waste. Moreoover, industrial and social activities are influencing global biogeochemical cycles of carbon, phosphorus, nitrogen and sulphur in cause-and-effect relations which are now subject to long-term research programmes stretching beyond the turn of the century.

The intentional, incidental or accidental release of chemicals, taking into account their reactive and catalytic nature and health and ecotoxicological aspects, are primary focii of environmental concern. A somewhat extreme view is that man's chemical output should not be greater than chemical levels that occur naturally. How this might be achieved without major sacrifices in human health and welfare is difficult to imagine. Most chemicals in use today are synthesized from organic carbon but do not exist in nature. Naturally occurring chemicals are not always benign (chlorine, for example, an halogen element, occurs widely as sodium chloride in oceans and rock-salt deposits). However, chemical releases are either the harmful byproducts of industrial processes or the residues of essential supports to standards of living and health. It is to the management of these aspects that modern chemical processing is concerned.

Reference has been made in the Introduction to Rachel Carson's *Silent Spring*. Since Dr Carson's book there has been signal progress in scientific knowledge of chemical pathways. Wide breaches have appeared in the defences of chemical producers and governments seeking often to discount the chemical downside, but there is some way yet to go in the reconciliation of social and commercial criteria. Lead times between identifying and evaluating new substances and their introduction as new products are fairly lengthy. Maintaining productivity and standards of living, redirecting investment and, where necessary, effecting structural changes are all factors that restrain instant change.

Reference to chemicals and chemical reactions permeate the environmental agenda, relating to their use, allegations of misuse, containment, disposal and control. While the carcinogenic or mutagenic potential of many persistent chemical substances at 'background' levels in populations is often of a speculative nature, occupational exposure has established morbidity patterns in the working environment. Accidental releases in manufacturing and processing have given rise to mass poisoning of humans and wildlife and to lifetimes of chronic ill-health.

All chemical substances in industrial and pharmaceutical use have been tested and verified for toxicity and carcinogenicity under national requirements (US Food and Drugs Administration, EC Directives, the UK COSHH Regulations, etc.). They are subject to Environmental Health Criteria (EHC) evaluations conducted by WHO/UNEP, in which environment effects are rigorously scrutinized. However, the continued use of substances which have had demonstrated ill-effects upon human health and the environment and the insouciant disposal or dumping of such substances can only engender dismay. The toxicity of PCBs (a chlorinated hydrocarbon) was recognized as early as the 1960s. In 1973 the OECD Environment Committee proposed that PCBs should not be used for industrial or commercial purposes except in a limited number of fire-sensitive applications such as closed-system electrical equipment. This was followed by an EC Directive in 1976, and a sequence of other events has effectively brought these substances into the 1990s.

Man-made chemicals

More than 7 million chemicals are known to man and some 80,000 are in common use. The principal raw materials for man-made chemicals are olefins (ethylene, propylene and butadiene), derived from natural gas, and aromatics (benzene, toluene and xylenes), from oil fractions. These carbon-based substances account for over 90% of world production of organic chemicals and for a large proportion of fertilizers (Table 4.1).

Table 4.1 World growth in base chemicals production (million tonnes)

	1950	1986
Organic		
Olefins and aromatics (petrochemicals)	2.0	96.0*
Other		10.0
Inorganic		
Ammonia	—	46.0
	2.0	152.0*

Source: * Shell

UNEP estimates that the total world production of organic chemicals is 250 million tonnes annually, from the 152 million tonnes of base chemicals produced by the petrochemical industry for the chemical, pharmaceutical, agrochemical and industrial markets. It is suggested that this volume will probably double in seven or eight years. Some 800–1,000 new chemical compounds are introduced each year. The task of listing, classifying and disseminating information on existing and new chemicals, generally and importantly to users and potential users in the Third World, as well as the organization of education and training in uses and effects and initiating programmes to prevent pollution, is the responsibility of WHO, FAO, ILO and UNEP, with the support of the scientific community, NGOs, etc.

Understanding the environmental effects of chemicals is greatly assisted by the ability to detect their presence at concentrations as low as parts per billion and by improved methods of toxicity testing. Chemical screening and classification is based upon three criteria:

Biodegradability (persistence and life)
Bioaccumulation (persistence and build-up in tissues mainly through the food chain)
Toxicity (affecting human populations and other species)

Physical laws demonstrate that matter cannot be destroyed but only reformed or degraded. Knowledge of environmental pathways is clearly of paramount importance, and imposes a high level of responsibility on chemical producers, users and control agencies. The ultimately desired degradation of chemical matter is re-formation to carbon and water, which, of course, is not in the nature of inorganic substances and certain persistent organic chemicals.

Threshold levels for contaminant clean-up

Recommended levels of chemical contaminant are made by WHO and the EC as well as national health and safety agencies. Examples of soil and water thresholds are provided in Table 4.2. The reasonableness of these standards, set out under EC schedules of chemical substances, is questioned in some government and industry quarters. Nevertheless, in European studies (EC-EFTA) of groundwater these low concentrations are consonant with levels that may be expected in high-quality potable water.

Table 4.2 Designated threshold levels for soil clean-up (UK) and EC standards for potable water

Substance	Threshold soil (mg/kg)	MAC* water (mg/litre)
Cadmium	3–15	0.001–0.005
Copper	130	0.02–0.05
Zinc	300	0.5–5
Polyaromatic hydrocarbons	50–1,000	0.001–0.0002
Organochlorine pesticides	—	0.001–0.005 (0.1–0.5 ppb)
Nitrates	—	25–50
Phosphates	—	0.4–0.7

* MAC: Maximum Admissible Concentration (EC)

Contamination of soil is often less apparent than water because the effects of pollutants on soil organisms, soil function, uptake by plants, passage to groundwater, etc. can be delayed, protracted or indirect. The excessive application of chemical fertilizers (ammonia, nitrates and phosphates), which is widespread throughout Europe and the Third World, decreases the take-up of natural nutrients, diminishes the ability of the soil to hold water and accelerates erosion. In addition, chemical runoff leads to the eutrophication of lake and river systems, with consequential loss of fish and wildlife populations. It can be argued, therefore, that a lowering of soil clean-up standards and of water quality will not encourage less dependence on synthetic chemicals.

Insecticides and pesticides

Chlorinated hydrocarbons (organochlorine compounds) were the first generation of pesticides, introduced following the Second World War to make a considerable contribution to European agricultural regeneration. They comprise DDT, Dieldrin, Heptachlor epoxide, and others, designed to kill insects and which, as broad-spectrum poisons, having an extreme range of biological activity, stability and affinity for living organisms, also inflicted heavy mortality upon vertebrate wildlife. In 1972, following a period of considerable reluctance by industry and governments, the use of organochlorine pesticides was banned in the USA and by many European countries. Extensive use of these substances continues in many Third World countries, repeating the well-documented experience of Europe and the USA of sanitizing the soil, contaminating groundwater, depleting the wildlife population and encouraging resistant pest strains.

Pesticides are the largest and most diverse group of chemical substances which now, for the most part, comprise organophosphorous and carbamate (urea) compounds. The majority of these compounds demonstrate greater solubility in water and shorter periods of efficacy (persistence), and tend, as used, not to produce chronic effects in ecosystems nor to deposition in living tissue. Health and environment hazards from these substances are most likely to be presented in effluents from their source of production and in agricultural runoff or from residues that remain on crops.

Chlorophenols (e.g. pentachlorophenol and chloraphenoxy herbicides) have broad pesticidal efficiency and are used as algicides, bactericides, fungicides, herbicides and molluscicides. Although the direct toxicity of these substances to animals is low, their modification and eradication of plants have a direct impact on animal populations. In terms of human exposure, adverse effects have been noted in occupational and non-occupational exposure through aquatic systems and drinking water.

The managed use of pesticides, particularly as insecticides in the control of the mosquito and locust for human health and crop protection, are highly important issues. Endemic malaria in the Third World accounts annually for some 2.0 million deaths and 400 million clinical attacks. Crop pests consume one third of the world's agricultural produce, with spectacular devastation caused by the tropical locust. The toxic side-effects and decreasing efficiency of pesticides is a matter of man outwitting the propensity of insects to deal evolutionarily with attempts to poison them.

It is interesting that historically, and to the present day, most (synthetic) pesticide programmes have been declared failures in meeting long-term pest-control objectives and exact a high ecological cost. The reasons for these failures have been readily available for at least two decades, even in the popular scientific press, and are reflected in the Brundtland Report.

Integrated pest management (IPM), a system promoted by FAO, UNDP and UNEP, consisting of biological, cultural as well as non-persistent chemical controls, is a natural systematic alternative to exclusive reliance on chemical pesticides. IPM involves breeding resistent plant varieties and integrating cropping patterns, which avoid pest-inviting monocultures, and obtaining detailed information about pests and their natural enemies (natural plant toxins and other defences). The IPM concept has been applied often enough in the last 30 years to establish its credibility. It is more labour intensive than the technological approach but also costs less.

The FAO/WHO International Code of Conduct on the Distribution and Use of Pesticides seeks voluntary standards among manufacturers and users but national legislation for the controlled use of pesticides is still generally weak.

World sales of pesticides have grown from $3.0 billion in 1972, $12.0 billion in 1980 with present world sales estimated to be in the order of $50.0 billion, in the distribution shown in Table 4.3. The sum of $50.0 billion represents approximately 5% of total world sales of chemical products of $1,000 billion, or 40.0% of the world agrochemical market, presently estimated to be $125.0 billion (Shell). On these figures, Third World expenditure on these items is some $40.0 billion annually, which is the equivalent of the net transfer of capital from the Third World to the developed world (World Bank).

Table 4.3 Proportion of world sales of pesticides by region (%)

	USA and Canada	OECD Europe	Japan	Rest of world	Total
Insecticides	23.0	12.0	11.0	54.0	100.0
Herbicides	52.0	23.0	7.0	18.0	100.0
Fungicides	9.0	47.0	17.0	27.0	100.0
	32.0	25.0	11.0	32.0	100.0

Source: OECD

International chemical controls

Standards and codes of practice for the manufacture of chemicals are established by the American Society for the Testing of Materials (ASTM) and the American Petroleum Institute (API). These are adhered to by chemical manufacturers, who tend to be multinational, and they provide a reference or benchmark for the work of national standards institutions. Regulations for the use of chemicals, the setting of threshold and exposure limits and disposal are matters for national legislation.

In Europe, these are also subject to EC Directives from 1967, concerning the testing, classification, packaging and labelling of chemicals that are dangerous to people or the environment. As well as these, other EC Directives concern industrial accidents and emergency response (the 'Seveso Directive') and the control of listed substances, including PCBs (polychlorinated biphenyls), PCTs (polychlorinated terphenyls) and asbestos. Chemical societies, trade associations and the medical profession have a role to play in maintaining standards and monitoring effects.

European chemical industry input to codes of practice and standards is organized by GIFAP (agrochemicals) in dealings with FAO, WHO, UNEP and OECD. CEFIC represents European chemical manufacturers, principally at the EC.

In Europe and the OECD countries, within the framework of generally high standards, there are nevertheless some variations in the attitudes and practices of different countries regarding environmental control, with, for example, the West German chemical industry subject to tougher environmental laws, and a stronger green lobby, than France, Italy or the UK.

The EC, in a somewhat uphill struggle, seeks harmonization of standards, which means that some countries would have to relax their laws and others introduce more stringent requirements.

There are, as yet, no international standards for the marketing and distribution of chemicals between countries outside the OECD as there is, for example, in the control of radioactive materials or the transport of oil and chemicals. The chemical industry does not have an internationally representative association which can support a dialogue between international agencies and Third World countries, which would assist in programme development and information exchange. In particular, such an association could support a number of important programmes identifying and classifying chemicals, by FAO (especially fertilizers and pesticides), WHO/ILO/UNEP (International Programme on Chemical Safety) and UNEP (International Register of Potentially Toxic Chemicals), which provide repositories of chemical data and a network for information exchange on the uses and effects of chemical substances.

Chemicals and health in the Third World

In Third World countries manufacturing standards and control is frequently dependent upon the voluntary actions on the chemical industry in the absence of Western-style legislation. Human and environmental exposure to chemicals is widely monitored by the WHO/UNEP GEMS Programme and subject to guidelines issued by the WHO-IPCS programme, the latter establishing criteria and promoting exposure-limit recommendations.

The promotion of chemical safety in the Third World addresses a range of daunting problems, which include misuse of pesticides and other agrochemicals, alfatoxins in agricultural produce, water pollution, air pollution from biomass burning, excess fluorides, silica, asbestos dust, containment of hazardous chemicals, etc. Most of the legislation and controls relating to chemical use and disposal in Europe and the USA are not applied in Third World countries for a variety of political, practical and industrial reasons. The Third World is a market for many of the chemicals banned in industrialized countries, particularly chlorinated hydrocarbons. National legislation is either lacking or difficult to implement. Except for the transport of hazardous materials, there are no enforceable international constraints, and the hand-to-mouth subsistence needs of Third

World peoples tends to overshadow the perceived conflicts with environmental considerations.

Apart from the generally high morbidity and mortality levels from poverty, malnutrition, gastro-intestinal diseases and malaria in the Third World, in the social environment, especially in Asia and in the USSR, endemic diseases present the greatest problem in the field of chemical safety. An overabundance of naturally occurring fluoride in drinking water is a common cause of fluorosis. Insufficient iodide salts in the diet leads to endemic goitre. Osteoarthritic disease, which has a chemical basis, is a seriously disabling environmental health problem in these countries, where several million people are affected.

The search for the chemical bases of endemic diseases and the development of methods of environmental epidemiology provides an important focus for the work of WHO and the International Programme for Chemical Safety (IPCS) and of the ICSU scientific community.

International trade in chemicals

Until fairly recently, the international trade in toxic and dangerous chemicals was conducted on the principle that it was up to the importing countries to improve their own regulations and monitoring programmes without relying on exporting countries to advise and inform. The rationale was that such assistance would interfere in free trade and also lead to the revelation of proprietary information.

Since 1987, work has been in progress on a system of 'prior informed consent' under the UNEP Provisional Notification Scheme for Banned and Severely Restricted Chemicals (IRPTC, 1984), which would cover a wide range of chemicals used in industry and agriculture that affect food safety, water and air pollution and the safety of the working environment. Without a legal framework, however, control of the chemical trade will continue to rely upon voluntary measures.

Transport of chemicals

Liquid commodities make up the bulk of chemicals carried by tankers in international trade — some 45 million tonnes annually of organic and inorganic chemicals, fuel additives and other products. The volume is expected to rise to approximately 55 million tonnes by 1992. The transport of bulk chemicals by tanker, road, rail and air is controlled by conventions, regulations and codes of practice issued by the International Maritime Organization, International Civil Aviation Organization, the Inland Transport Commission, the International Regulations for the Carriage of Dangerous Goods by Rail (RID) and the European Agreement for the International Carriage of Dangerous Goods by Road (ADR).

As with the oil tanker trade, cargo handling and transportation of chemicals is conducted to a large extent by companies independent of the chemical and oil industries, and are subject to different legislative regimes.

Legal and environmental pressures on the chemical industry

The environmental and health guidelines followed by major chemical manufacturers concern plant, process and product reliability, protection of employees and the public from accidental toxic releases, the safeguarding of water sources and soils from effluent and waste contamination, waste disposal and safe transportation. The chemical industry makes but a small contribution to atmospheric sulphur dioxide and nitrogen oxide emissions.

Chemical manufacturers in Europe and the USA are having to meet tougher environmental standards and the prospect in failure of almost exponential awards in litigation. Since the questions of quality, safety and toxicity of chemicals are already subject to existing controls, these new standards relate to waste disposal and the control of effluents (see Chapter 5); the transport of chemicals is subject to a different set of regulations.

Thus we can revert to the balance of benefit and harm of chemicals and the need for international standards to promote harmonization of safety and quality controls on a global scale. Harmonization and co-operation is hindered somewhat by national economic considerations and by industry's protectiveness of its proprietary secrets, arguing huge investment costs in research and development and sophisticated testing and control methods. In this respect, mistakes are expensive to the industry, where civil awards can be extremely high and embarrassing to its public image. Therefore external controls are considered to be superfluous and inconvenient. Future progress in all aspects of chemical control, nevertheless, will depend upon industrial co-operation with international agencies for the effective running and development of data-exchange systems and appropriate chemical strategies.

International and regional programmes

FAO/UNDP/ENEP Integrated Pest Management (IPM)
FAO/WHO/UNEP Panel of Experts on Environmental Management of Pest Control
UNEP International Register of Potentially Toxic Chemicals (IRPTC)
WHO/ILO/UNEP International Programme for Chemical Safety (IPCS)
European Inventory of Existing Commercial Chemical Substances (EINECS)

Regional intergovernmental co-operation

Nordic Council of Ministers (Denmark, Finland, Iceland, Norway and Sweden)
Council of Europe
Commission of the European Communities

International conventions relating to chemicals

Chemical conventions relate to the transport of hazardous substances, marine pollution and dumping but not to the manufacture or commercial distribution of chemicals

5 WASTE AND CONSERVATION

The polluter pays

In a narrowly defined sense, waste and pollution are inseparable issues. By the same token, chemicals, wastes and pollution provide the crux of the environmental agenda. This chapter covers the handling of wastes in the manufacture, use and disposal of products and materials. While the question of waste bears directly upon wider issues concerning energy, agriculture and natural resources, as well as the general question of chemicals in the environment, its principal focus is upon the management of the 'waste stream' (i.e. wastes generated in the production/use cycle), the minimization of the volume of wastes being generated and the protection of local urban and rural environments from pollution.

The generation and use of energy in industrial processes, transport, agriculture, construction, the production of goods and provision of services involves a transformation of material from one form to another and creates volumes of solid, liquid or gaseous residual matter which can be either re-used or disposed of as waste in the absolute sense of having no further economic value. Household and domestic waste output from the consumption of energy and goods more or less completes the picture and provides a management link between the consumer, waste-disposal authorities and industry.

Although waste management is largely a matter of local good housekeeping, it has two major international aspects. The first is its possible effects on the costs of goods and thus upon the conduct of international trade. Second is the more contentious matter of the transport of hazardous wastes for disposal or processing in other countries.

The national implications of a clean local environment emphasizes the very serious threats to public health and amenities from soil, water and atmospheric pollution through the mismanagement of domestic and industrial detritus, which includes many toxic and hazardous substances, and from the importation of hazardous substances from other areas for local disposal.

'Waste' can be defined as any unavoidable material resulting from an industrial operation for which there is no economic demand and which must be disposed of. The definition can be extended to domestic and consumer outputs which are perceived to have no further use or value. In this context, the discharge of liquid effluents to watercourses and gaseous emissions to the atmosphere are excluded. These aspects, relating to atmospheric, water and marine pollution and resource depletion, are discussed in other chapters.

Waste disposal has become a major hi-tech industry in EC countries and in the USA, the future growth of which will be based not so much upon rising volumes of waste but upon its more efficient disposal and recycling.

In 1975 the EC issued a Framework Directive for Waste in which member states could control the disposal of wastes nationally instead of locally and to take the necessary measures to ensure that waste is disposed of without endangering human health or harming the environment. The Framework Directive encourages recycling generally and the application of the Polluter Pays Principle.

A year later, the OECD recommended that its member states should develop waste-management policies to meet the objectives of environmental protection and the rational use of energy. The Recommendation and the subsequent establishment of an OECD Environment Committee work programme were made because of the substantial increases in the quantities of waste to be disposed of, the ever-widening range of hazardous chemicals and other pollutants contained in waste and the possibilities for resource conservation.

The Recommendation recognized the necessity to avoid transferring pollutants from one medium to another (e.g. from land to water or to the atmosphere) and, in common with many intergovernmental proposals, that any actions taken by one country should not have the effect of distorting international trade. The Polluter Pays Principle is thus a unifying feature of international environmental co-operation, and its application is most relevant in the waste/conservation debate.

A coherent waste-management policy is one that covers a product's lifecycle, from design, material selection, manufacture, packaging, use and the possibilities for reclamation and recycling. The logistics of disposal and reclamation must be added to this list, involving the manufacture and intermediary industries, local authorities and consumers.

Waste is the antithesis of conservation; conservation is an essential premise of environmental management. Planned obsolescence has been the post-war driving force of Western economic development and profit. A 'disposable economy' drawing upon diminishing resources is inflationary. Waste is effortless, expensive to the consumer and profitable to the producer.

In these conditions, sustainable economic growth, which relies upon the reduction of wasteful production and consumption and which sets parameters for universal responsibility, becomes something of a sensitive issue. National and international official reports on the subject characterize the general waste management infrastructure comprising waste producers, waste-disposal contractors and waste-disposal authorities as being 'thoroughly professional to [the] downright neglectful' (UK Hazardous

Waste Inspectorate, 1985). In more muted tones, at the same time, the OECD reported that the disposal of hazardous wastes has become a difficult and controversial problem. It remains so, despite the advances made in waste stream management.

Despite advances in waste management, there remain two essential problems relating to previous disposal practices and the transition to the adoption of more enlightened methods of site selection and management. The first and most immediately pressing is the improvement of industrial and domestic waste collection and disposal and the sanitization of old sites which pose future health threats. The second is the question of waste minimization, having the twin benefits of conserving energy and natural resources and reducing the volume of final wastes needing to be disposed of. Managing the disposition and disposal of industrial and consumer wastes presents a variety of problems associated with volume (a growing proportion of which is highly toxic and poses severe public health and environmental threats) and a diminishing number of secure or environmentally acceptable sites.

Broadly speaking, there are four classifications of waste: municipal, industrial, hazardous (toxic and otherwise dangerous) and a general classification to include agricultural, mining and quarrying detritus, dredging spoils, sludges, etc. A high proportion of paper, oils, plastics and glass, as well as fuel, that make up some of the volume of industrial and muncipal wastes can be recycled, re-formed and reprocessed, and would be more appropriately classified as residues. As residues, they have a value and can offer some positive cost benefits to companies that are able to make the necessary investments.

Problems of managing toxic and hazardous wastes

Off- and on-site disposal of toxic and hazardous wastes from industrial and chemical processes has caused critical groundwater and land contamination and has created several thousand abandoned sites (OECD, 1985) throughout Europe and the USA which require remedial action.

A number of programmes are under way in OECD countries, but it would appear, based upon experience in the Netherlands, that an average cost per site, to locate, restore or sanitize, would be in the region of £500,000. In 1978, the site of a housing estate at the Love Canal in the New York State, which had been previously used as a chemical waste dump and subsequently filled in, began to emit toxic gases. The cost of cleaning up that site, which apparently is now free from contamination, has been estimated at $260.0 million, to be paid for by Occidental, the company which took over the 'polluter' some time before the incident occurred. It is reported that the average cost of cleaning up hazardous waste sites in the USA is $70.0 million, and that the total cost of cleaning up landfill sites in the coming years could reach $250.0 billion.

Reference can also be made to 1,631 abandoned sites throughout

England and Wales, some 1,300 of which allegedly pose several degrees of threat to groundwater systems. Even from the limited amount of survey data available, it is clear that the management of waste-disposal sites, at least in Europe and the USA, is a matter of considerable urgency and forthcoming expenditures (Table 5.1).

Table 5.1 Pre-existing and abandoned landfill sites in Europe and North America with actual or potential groundwater or land contamination

Country	No. of sites	No. requiring immediate attention
Canada	—	1,000
Denmark	3,000	500
The Netherlands	4,000	350
UK	1,631	59
USA	'Several thousand'	2,000

Sources: OECD, 1985; Friends of the Earth, 1990; Environment Canada

That the chickens are coming home to roost is hardly on account of legislative frameworks being lacking, nor the relevant technologies. As with many other aspects of pollution control, the investment and organizational requirements are not insignificant, but the legal and financial incentives have hitherto been weak. The potential for public health accidents appears to be high, particularly since in many cases the precise nature and range of toxic substances hidden in these sites is unknown. Historically, health, safety and environmental legislation has tended to be reactive to a major disaster. When remedial or preventive costs have been high, the implementation of legislation has been slow and responses to the recommendations of intergovernmental agencies have not been prompt.

Community and voluntary organization involvement at the local level is already raising awareness of these serious problems. In 1985 a charitable organization (Clean Sites Inc.) involving community and industry was formed to identify and clean up hazardous sites. Also in the USA, site clean-up funds have been established in a federal 'Superfund', worth some $18.5 billion, administered by the EPA. Recently in the UK, Friends of the Earth have embarked upon a campaign to identify 'toxic tips'. Armed Green Police are patrolling at least one city in the USA to prevent fly-tipping and the illegal disposal of toxic and bulk materials.

The OECD estimated that the total amount of all waste generated by its member countries in 1980 was in the order of 8.0 billion tonnes. The three waste classifications being discussed, industrial, hazardous and municipal, are estimated to be something less than 2.0 billion tonnes, of which the greater proportion consists of industrial and hazardous wastes (Table 5.2).

In addition to the above, an estimated 6.0 billion tonnes of agricultural, mining, demolition and power-generating wastes, dredging spoils and sewage sludge is generated annually. Present waste levels are unlikely to be very much higher in view of the improvement of waste-disposal techniques and industrial conservation measures through the 1980s. Also, in several countries such as Norway, Sweden and the UK, quantities of municipal waste have either stabilized or are no longer significantly increasing.

Table 5.2 Volumes of waste in OECD countries (million tonnes)

	USA	Europe	Australasia/Japan	Total
Industrial	500	325	175	1,000
Hazardous	268	24	8	300
Municipal	180	120	50	350
Round est.	950	470	250	1,650*

Sources: OECD, 1980, 1983
* Excluding agriculture, mining, quarrying, sewage, etc.

Although the above data are not recent, they may be taken as a general guide. The USA accounts for nearly 60% of the developed world's waste output and 90% of hazardous wastes. The UKAEA estimates that the UK produces a total of 4.0 million cubic metres of toxic waste annually, some 44,000 cubic metres of which is made up of low-and intermediate-level radioactive material.

Disposal of industrial and municipal waste

It is estimated that up to 75% of industrial and hazardous wastes, chemicals, oils and metals are disposed of on-site. An increasing amount of waste, however, is being generated by air and water pollution abatement measures to meet the emergence of more stringent emission standards. The largest component of municipal waste is domestic rubbish (approximately 80.0%), mostly paper and plastic packaging material. Glass makes up a somewhat smaller proportion, and in some countries, such as West Germany, more glass than plastic is used for fluid packaging and it is also extensively recycled.

The principal disposal method in many countries is landfill, ideally organized to prevent seepage and migration of pollutants into subsurface soil, surface water and groundwater. It is becoming increasingly difficult to find additional sites for landfill, a method not suitable for highly toxic wastes, for which disposal demand is growing. In the UK, landfill disposal accounts for some 4.0 million tonnes annually. A further 250,000 tonnes is presently consigned to disposal at sea.

Other disposal options include incineration of toxic wastes or those that are resistant to natural breakdown, such as chlorinated compounds; underground disposal within impermeable rock formations (a method also under consideration for high-level nuclear wastes); co-disposal (mixing household with industrial wastes); or 'remediation' by bacterial action.

Composting of domestic wastes is the most ecologically sound of all methods of waste treatment but is relatively little used.

Every waste-disposal method has its drawbacks. Incineration creates emissions into the atmosphere. Landfill can lead to leaching of toxic chemicals into the soil and groundwater and to the emission of methane into the atmosphere. Composting can result in the deposition of heavy metals, and the co-disposal of industrial and municipal wastes is now being treated with caution and is subject to review in a new EC Directive.

Each classified waste type requires a specialized disposal method, and usually has an environmentally significant destination. A recent study by the Netherlands Ministry of Housing suggests, moreover, that although the disposition of wastes can be better managed to a considerable degree, the actual quantities of wastes produced by industrially advanced countries will not significantly decline.

Recycling and consumer behaviour

The EC intends that recycling should become a generally adopted national strategy among its member states in order to improve industrial efficiency and to reduce waste. There are several initiatives taken at the local levels in the UK (City of Westminster, Sheffield) in the selective collection of domestic refuse, but more nationally oriented programmes are under way in Europe (France, Sweden, the Netherlands, West Germany and Switzerland in particular), Japan and the USA in more comprehensive recycling programmes.

Effective recycling strategies depend upon close co-operation between the producer and the user, with local authorities acting as the intermediary collection agency. At the industry level, the recycling of production, fuel and chemical wastes is, in fact, becoming more widespread, but the volumes of dumped waste throughout the world remains enormous.

The consumer can make an important contribution to the implementation of conservation strategies. Rational consumer behaviour in the context of waste and recycling depends upon both education and financial incentives, in the same way as industry. After all, industrial and commercial enterprises are made up of consumers, and what is sauce for the goose is sauce for the gander.

Table 5.3 is a simple matrix in which producers and consumers relate in the management and disposition of waste materials and which provides some of the basis for the continued development of LWNT. The simplistic concepts of paper, glass and plastic recycling need to be supported by a complex infrastructure involving several industries, industrial processes, adjusted energy inputs, new perceptions of material values and investment strategies.

Waste paper recovery in the EC countries varies from 26% in Greece to 53% in the Netherlands, and a situation frequently occurs where supply exceeds processing capacity. Glass recycling is more firmly established in other EC countries than in the UK but will undoubtedly grow, given the present impetus. Many advances have been made in separation techniques to allow the recycling of plastics, but problems remain in re-using plastics as food and drink containers in view of the possibility that they were contaminated in their previous lives.

Table 5.3

Waste/material	Disposition
	Industry
Chemicals and toxic metals	Reclaim/recycle/degrade/dispose
Oily wastes	Collect/recycle/dispose
Construction materials	Reclaim/re-use/reduce bulk
	Industry/local authority
Domestic wastes	Conversion to biomass Utilizing wastes as fuel in combined heat and power schemes Reduce bulk
	Industry/local authority/consumer
Paper, glass, plastics	Collect/recycle

The use of recycled paper is one strategy to reduce deforestation. Technology for the production of good-quality recycled paper is available even to meet aesthetic criteria that British companies apply to their stationery output, but current costs are higher than for conventionally produced paper. It would not be economically feasible, for example, to produce this book on recycled paper.

Recycling of glass and paper as well as other domestic waste is a matter for local authority organization and management. Probably, among all conservation strategies, this is one area in which individual responsibility can best be demonstrated, given a local infrastructure to organize collection and redistribution.

Low- and non-waste technology (LNWT)

LNWT is a concept which was presented during the 1970s by the UN-ECE and thereafter promoted jointly with the UNEP Industry and Environment Office. Its continued development is intended to achieve environmentally sound economic growth and to contribute to the minimization of waste. The adoption of LNWT has been slow, although many of its principles have been taken up in national industrial and agricultural projects in Europe, Japan and the USA. One important principle of LNWT is that materials and products should be designed to maximize the potential for reclamation and recycling.

It is one thing for international agencies to promote environmentally sound industrial and consumer practices and yet another for these to be taken up enthusiastically by industry when there are no legal impositions or economic incentives. The potential distortion of international trading conditions is an ethos which presents many difficulties to the national adoption of many otherwise sound environmental policies. Intergovernmental agencies and the international scientific community more often than not find themselves in the uneviable position of making a sales pitch to reluctant and even hostile prospects.

Waste minimization is a principle to be applied to the whole product lifecycle, not merely at the end of it. Targets are thus to be applied to raw material extraction, production, product use and disposal, which require technology, planning and a redefinition of what constitutes good housekeeping practices.

Obviously, waste cannot be eliminated. Waste minimization can nevertheless be achieved ideally by preventive means and less ideally by so-called 'end-of-pipe' technologies.

Physical, chemical and biological processes are available to reduce bulk and toxicity. Chemical companies who make R&D and processing investments in on-site recovery techniques have found new sources of profitability, generally greater efficiency and are able to reduce the volume of their waste streams (Du Pont and ICI). Smaller companies are less able to meet legal, market and consumer pressures as flexibly as multinational corporations, and economies of scale can put them at a disadvantage in relation to the market and to legal controls.

Exporting hazardous wastes

In 1984 the OECD decided that member countries shall control the trans-frontier movements of hazardous waste. In the same year the EC published a Directive on trans-frontier shipment on toxic and dangerous waste. The OECD subsequently decided that monitoring and control of shipments to destinations outside the OECD area were also appropriate. The Basel Convention (see below) on the Trans-boundary Movements of Hazardous Wastes and their Control was signed in 1989.

The direction of hazardous wastes from Europe and the USA to Guinea-Bissau, the Congo, Benin, Nigeria, Peru, Argentina and Venezuela, countries mostly ill equipped to process and dispose of them, is coming under international scrutiny in a variety of programmes. However, the trans-shipment of waste is most frequently between one developed country and another, but it has been noted that in the near future more and more developing countries will be exporting their wastes (PCBs, for example) to Europe, Nigeria already ships hazardous wastes to the UK for disposal, which led to the *Karin B* fiasco, as well as being a repository for the hazardous wastes of developed countries.

The Basel Convention, as with any other attempts to arrive at international solutions, while establishing a framework for control, places far too much reliance on industrialized countries to exercise what are tanta-mount to voluntary constraints. The treaty states that 'illegal traffic in hazardous wastes is criminal'. By definition, this is not so for legal traffic.

In view of the relatively high risks attending marine transport and the nature of these cargos it was to be hoped that the convention would establish a period for phasing out this trade and therefore encourage the speedy development of disposal at source technology. It remains to be seen whether the UK and the USA ratify.

Legislation

In UK and US legislation, and in most EC countries, treatment, storage and disposal is the responsibility of the producer. Following the first EC Framework Directive, subsequent Directives cover toxic and dangerous wastes, transfrontier shipments, waste oils, the disposal of PCBs and PCTs, sewage sludge in agriculture and the recycling of beverage con-tainers as a major source of litter. A new Directive is presently being drafted with the intention of prohibiting co-disposal of wastes and pro-moting a 'Principle of Proximity' strategy to ensure that waste is disposed of at the nearest appropriate site, taking account of available technology and with the aim of reducing risks to public health and the environment.

The UK Environment Bill which will come before Parliament in Au-tumn 1990 is proposing integrated systems of pollution control to tackle waste at source. The US Environmental Protection Agency (EPA) is similarly changing its emphasis from traditional 'end-of-pipe' controls to preventive technology, on the sensible grounds that the former merely shifts pollutants from one medium to another. However, the EPA ap-proach appeals to industry to take voluntary initiatives to reduce source pollutants and embark upon recycling programmes.

Incineration at sea will be a closed option by 1992, by international agreement through the International Maritime Organization. The argu-ments against such incineration appear to be related to the difficulties of control and monitoring and to particulate fallout onto the ocean surface. Dumping at sea (discussed in Chapter 9) is subject to controls under the Oslo and London Dumping Conventions, and it can be anticipated that additional pressures will be put onto land-based solutions.

The high costs of reduction and sanitization of hazardous and toxic wastes and the difficulties in finding new landfill sites has attracted the in-terest of organized crime as well as the more *ad hoc* activities of fly-tippers. The high volumes transported lead to the risks of serious accidents.

International convention relating to waste	Depository state/organization	Date
Convention on the Trans-boundary Movements of Hazardous Wastes and their Control	Basel	1989

6 PUBLIC HEALTH, ACCIDENTS AND RISK
Perception, prevention and planning

This chapter discusses the environment in the context of health and safety impacts in the social and work setting, and taking these impacts into account in the determination of environmental risk. In general, noise, dust, smoke, fumes, noxious and toxic chemicals, waste, industrial effluents and urban air pollution have a significant influence on the incidence of ill-health, accidents and mortality in the working and social environments. Pollution abatement has critical implications for public health, the priorities for which are reductions in the background levels of chemicals entering the food chain through soil and water, emissions into the atmosphere of nitrous and sulphur oxides, managing domestic and industrial wastes, sewage disposal and social nuisances that have the potential for chronic ill-health and death.

The deleterious effects of urban smog on health, employment and productivity led to the first Clean Air Acts in 1956 (UK) and 1972 (USA), which brought about significant decreases in morbidity and mortality, particularly from lung and respiratory disorders. Current major concerns are the carcinogenic and mutagenic potential of many chemical substances, the persistence of photochemical smog and the implications for public health of climatic change. In the Third World, pollution and effluents have an even greater impact on mortality and morbidity in urban areas, but more fundamentally serious problems are presented by the quality and availability of water and sanitation.

As well as the direct and indirect effects of pollution upon the inhabitants of industrialized and Third World countries, industrial accidents and natural disasters take considerable toll of human life and health. Pollution reduction and accident prevention should be taken into account in planning and managing industrial activities in the methodologies of project evaluation and also in the development of policies which inevitably have a wide ecological significance.

Environmental impact assessment (EIA)

EIA is a method which can be adopted by organizations and governments to review the impact of their operations or actions on the environment, either at the planning stages of new projects or retrospectively. 'Impact' encompasses ecological, health, safety and socio-economic effects.

When followed, EIA procedures allow conservation groups and other members of the public to participate in the evaluation of public and industrial development projects, which since their introduction have included nuclear power, water and forestry, highways and hydrocarbon developments.

The first specific legislation enacted as a direct response to public pressure for environmental accountability was the US National Environmental Policy Act (NEPA) of 1969. Although the NEPA has not been replicated in other countries, several OECD member states have introduced some form of EIA requirements as a routine part of the land-use planning process. The 1985 EC Directive for harmonized EIA procedures concerning waste disposal and toxic substances, for implementation by 1988, is a clear indication that these procedures will generally become more common. In the UK, the application of EIA is a well-established practice within the oil and petrochemical industries but is little used outside.

Several international agreements advocate EIA, including the Vienna Convention and the UN–ECE Convention of Long-Range Trans-boundary Air Pollution and other agreements relating to activities which may affect the environment beyond national boundaries. However, there is no generally recognized rule of international law requiring it.

The conceptual difficulties of EIA are that the bases for quantification of goals and effects are inadequate and that criteria for both application and interpretation vary from country to country and from one enterprise to another. Because of its future relevance to international co-operation in matters concerning pollution control and nature conservation, much effort is being devoted by international agencies to establishing a harmonized conceptual and statistical framework.

Accident prevention and perception of risks

Accident prevention is a key issue in environmental management and pollution control. The association between accident prevention and pollution needs to be considered in the calculation and perception of risk, a subject which is highly controversial in the relationship between government and industry and in that between government, industry and the general public.

Table 6.1, as with attempts at statistical representation of social values, can give rise to all kinds of misconceptions. It does illustrate, however, that people are prepared to accept quite high risks in their everyday activities with less anxiety than the relatively very low statistical risks of events that might, as it were, come as a bolt from the blue. The question of 'How safe is safe enough?' is more readily answered in assessing the risks that people or societies are prepared to freely accept for their convenience, amenities or recreation. People do not generally seek a risk-free environment but naturally resent unnecessary risks being imposed upon them by the goods and services that are produced and supplied, or by government actions that do not take account of public susceptibilities.

Table 6.1 Voluntary and involuntary risks to the public

Voluntary annual risk of death (per 100,000)		Involuntary annual risk of death (per 100,000)	
Football	4	Falling aircraft	0.002
Drinking	7.5	Transport of oil	0.002
Rock climbing	14	Radioactive release	0.01
Car driving	17	Lightning strike	0.01
Car racing	120	Snake bite	0.02
Smoking	500	Run over by car	6
Motor cycling	2000	Leukaemia (natural)	8

Statistical risk calculation is based upon past occurrences of accidents and their impact upon the environment, including consequential injuries and death. New technology and redeployment of resources do not provide a reliable base for such calculations, and many environmental risks have not been quantified, even though the possibility of their occurrence is more than simple conjecture.

Past experience suggests that every human endeavour is or will be hazardous in one degree or another. Thus it might follow that future accidents are inevitable within any given population, be it to ships, aircraft, offshore oil structures, trains, nuclear reactors or people. The certainty is that an accident will occur, not to every unit but to at least one unit at some time. The uncertainty is to which unit or units or persons, when it will happen, in what manner and with what consequences.

Risks have varying levels of acceptability, explicitly related to the weighing of costs and benefits. Safety concepts and safety policies can be expressed as at between two poles – ALARA, which is maintaining the incidence of accidents 'as low as reasonably achievable' to ALATA, 'as low as technically achievable' (NRPB). Prudent action in the face of uncertainty, or without data to make plausible predictions, is often hard to take in the face of economic reality, particularly if an event has not yet happened.

Scientific and social arguments for the use of chemical substances and the higher risks of many industrial activities balance the incidence of death and injury with the greater social benefit. In the case of nuclear power stations, however, since the toxic effects of low-level radiation emissions are uncertain, and even though the risks of a serious nuclear accident from mechanical failure are low, to many, nuclear power risks are unacceptable at any order of magnitude, and future directions for nuclear power generation are uncharted beyond the turn of this century.

Nevertheless, more is known about the risks and consequences of nuclear accidents than in any other arena of industrial activity. Indeed, many of the models for determining risk and reliability were first developed by nuclear engineers. All things being equal, the probability of an accident involving an oil tanker is of orders of magnitude greater than one to a nuclear power station. Yet methods for dealing with nuclear incidents are considerably better organized. The frequency and severity of accidents, although unpredictable, are contained and controlled through the application of appropriate technology, management, training and cost benefit.

Consider, for example, the major industrial accidents that have occurred in the period 1970–89 and the relative severity of consequences depending upon whether they happened in the USA, Western Europe or elsewhere. Table 6.2 illustrates that the incidence and consequences of industrial accidents are not ameliorated by time or maturity. It also shows that not only are Western industrial societies prone to serious industrial accidents, but that the transfer of Western technology to Third World countries without mature management and containment techniques is actually disastrous.

Table 6.2 Deaths and injuries resulting from major accidents of environmental significance

	1970–75	1976–80	1981–5	1985–9
Europe and the USA				
No. of accidents	10	16	n.a.	3
Deaths and injuries	805	1,479	n.a.	310
Deaths, etc./accident	80	92	n.a.	103
Asia and Latin America				
No. of accidents	1	6	5	9
Deaths and injuries	92	408	>12,000	6,720
Deaths, etc./accident	92	85	4,000	747

Sources: OECD and UNEP

In summary, the point about environmental risk, or any risk involving the organization of people or the management of resources, is that the risk should be understood and quantified, even though quantification may be imprecise. To act on the basis of faith or blind hope, or trusting to luck, is not a sound enough basis for managing the future.

The cost of major accidents

Compensation and litigation expenses are escalating the costs of accidents to unprecedented levels. It is difficult, however, to draw many inferences from the comparative costs of recent major accidents since the total expenditures incurred directly and indirectly do not bear much relationship to accident severity but more to the prevailing economic conditions and societal expectations. For example, the USSR estimates that the cost to the Soviet economy of Chernobyl will be 8 billion roubles ($14 billion). The costs of the accident to OECD countries in Europe from agricultural repair could be a further $500 million. In the case of Bhopal, compensation of $3.0

billion was discussed, with settlement costs a fraction of this figure. The Piper Alpha disaster in the North Sea (1988) might have cost $2.0 billion, taking into account incidental losses and compensation, yet the *Exxon Valdez* cost nearly $2.0 billion, even without impending claims for compensation. Admittedly, much of this latter can be attributed to the 'public relations' nature of the clean-up exercise and to placate US environmentalists. It establishes a disturbing if not a salutary precedent. Shell was recently fined $1.6 million (£1.0 million) for spilling 20,000 tonnes of crude into the Mersey. The least one might say is that environmental and human cost accounting are both in need of realistic review, and that higher investments to protect life and the environment will be seen to be cost effective, particularly where company cash flow and profitability is undermined.

Bhopal, Three Mile Island and Chernobyl

The leak in 1984 of 30 tonnes of methyl isocyanate (MIC) from the Union Carbide plant in Madyha Pradesh, India, resulted in the world's worst industrial disaster in which 3,323 people died, 26,000 became chronically ill and a further 300,000–400,000 were affected with lung damage of varying severity.

The implications of Bhopal are many and varied for the exporting of technology, management expertise and training. According to the US Environmental Protection Agency (EPA), during the 1980s there were fifteen similar incidents of hazardous chemical releases in the USA exceeding the volumes and levels of toxicity of Bhopal in which, however, there were no fatalities. The laws of probability suggest that these releases were contained by a combination of contingency planning, management and technology rather than luck.

A similar comparison may be made between Three Mile Island and Chernobyl in terms of potential and actual severity. Nevertheless, both incidents severely reduced public confidence in nuclear energy programmes, and as a direct consequence of Three Mile Island, the then prime minister of Sweden, the late Olaf Palme, introduced measures to phase out Sweden's programme.

In view of the earlier comments on the inevitability of accidents and their increased severity in Third World countries, it is clear that industrial exports and assistance from industrialized nations to the Third World need to be either based upon low-risk technology or accompanied by appropriate scientific and management training programmes.

Distinctions, of course, may be drawn between the exporter–importer relationship and the activities of sovereign states. Nevertheless, a repository of scientific knowledge and expertise exists within intergovernmental and international industry associations, the influence of which is being strengthened by incidents and observations of the actual or potentially disastrous activities of industrial operations.

Contingency planning

The importance of pre-planning to manage the consequences of accidents cannot be over-emphasized. These principles apply as much to first aid as they do to containment and clean-up of oil spills or nuclear incidents. In the latter case, it is interesting to note that France, which relies on nuclear power generation for 70% of its electricity, is able to reach any national nuclear accident within 12 hours or a European accident within 24, using the railway network. It is claimed that fully equipped staff are able to treat 5,000 people a day.

Oil-spill contingency planning is a statutory requirement in many areas of offshore oil and gas exploration and production, and is discussed in Chapter 9. However, the ability to deal with tanker spills is still quite primitive.

Environmental law

There are some 140 international and regional environmental agreements (UNEP Register of International Treaties, 1989). A reference to the operation of intergovernmental conventions, treaties, etc. has already been made as well as to the frameworks within which national programmes are conducted. It should be remembered that, for the most part, the legislative programmes of Western countries often provide the basis for the development of international agreements, and that one of the problems to be overcome in international relations is the establishment of uniform and harmonized regulation to promote trade as well as providing the basis for other co-operative actions.

The establishment of a uniform legal framework also establishes the development of uniform standards, but the levels of stringency applied by mature and immature governments differ greatly according to public interest and the effects upon trade.

'Soft' laws are based upon recommendations for voluntary action, but frequently, as in the case of risk assessment, environmental impact assessments and environmental auditing, soft laws become the basis for introducing statutory obligations.

In Europe and North America, significant developments are taking place in broadening the concepts of legal responsibility and liability. For example, forthcoming EC Directives and UK environmental regulations are specifically concerned with determining responsibility for waste disposal, where the manufacturer can be held responsible for product life-cycle. Another fairly recent development has been in the dissolution of the doctrine of 'safe harbour', which has traditionally protected corporate directors from personal prosecution and litigation.

Environmental audit

Environmental audit is the term used for measuring how well a conservation, anti-pollution or clean-up programme is measuring up to the objectives set by internal company policy or the standards set by regulations. Its application has been growing since the early 1970s from its use by industries applying the principles of self-regulation to safety, health and environmental aspects of their operations. The importance of the audit for planning and prevention are clear, bearing in mind the extended corporate and personal liability for accidents causing injury and damage, and it is now becoming embodied in regulations to monitor compliance with effluent standards.

The environment and Eastern Europe

Most Eastern European countries are represented as UN member states at the UN Economic Commission for Europe (UN-ECOSOC) and participate routinely in matters relating to nature conservation and control of pollution. Nevertheless, the effluents from East Germany to West Germany and from within contiguous countries (not to mention the USSR) is a matter of both concern and alarm.

The problems of national levels of pollution in these countries, particularly in the USSR and East Germany, may well benefit from *perestroika*. The recent astonishing events in Eastern Europe towards the election of civilian governments raises hopes that these countries will evolve into genuine democracies. In the context of this book, while the possibilities for international co-operation on political and economic fronts will depend very much upon continuing détente between the USA and the USSR, the introduction of Western European technology will hopefully make some impact upon nearly half a century of environmental neglect.

Der Spiegel claims that Bitterfeld, north of Leipzig in East Germany, is the most polluted town in Europe. Chemicals, coal dust and diesel effluents are so awful that the grime itself has become a medium of written communication. Public health is characterized by high respiratory morbidity and infant mortality. According to another report in *The Times*, Copsa Mica in Romania claims this dubious distinction, where an area of 15 square kilometres is pitch black from the unfiltered effluence of the country's largest coal-refining plant. Ninety per cent of the fruit harvest is heavily polluted by lead and infant mortality approaches Third World levels.

Pollution in the USSR

The obligation of Soviet citizens to protect nature and to conserve its riches is embodied in the Constitution. The extent of the escape and hazardous and toxic materials resulting from inadequate or fraudulent management, ineffective or non-existent controls and obsolete plant suggests that these obligations are not being met.

Among the range of hazards that the Soviets face are unprotected gas pipelines, excessive use of pesticides and herbicides, negligent management of chemical plant, the domination of smokestack industries and wasted energy in the processing of raw materials. Pollution levels are:

Atmospheric pollution
60 million tonnes per annum
68 industrial cities have 'critical' levels of atmospheric pollution, higher than in most Third World countries.
Water pollution
The Aral Sea, the world's fourth biggest lake system, is largely depleted as a result of having had its rivers diverted to irrigate cotton fields. There are no fish left to support the local fishing community. The evidence of the pollution of Lake Baikal, the world's largest body of fresh water, from organic chemicals, heavy metals and petroleum products, is subject to disputes between politicians and the scientific community.

Many models for environmental cause and effect may be found in the USSR economy and social organization; central planning, weak local planning infrastructures, uncontrolled, subsidized industrial and agricultural production aimed at maximizing output; no consideration for environmental impact; lack of environmental expertise and knowledge within a government paying little or no attention to the scientific community; an overburdened defence expenditure; and rural poverty.

Perestroika, combined with the evidence of the consequences of past policies, have brought these crises into focus for the beginnings of a remedial programme and the establishment of a national environmental budget of some 30 billion roubles (£30 million).

Conventions relating to health

Convention	Place of adoption Depository state/organization	Date
Convention Concerning the Use of White Lead in Painting	Geneva (ILO)	1921
Convention Concerning Protection Against Hazards of Poisoning Arising from Benzene	Geneva (ILO)	1971
Convention Concerning Prevention and Control of Occupational Hazards Caused by Carcinogenic Substances and Agents	Geneva (ILO)	1974
Convention Concerning the Protection of Workers Against Occupational Hazards in the Working Environment Due to Air Pollution, Noise and Vibration	Geneva (ILO)	1977
Convention Concerning Occupational Safety and Health and the Working Environment	Geneva (ILO)	1981
Convention Concerning Occupational Health Services	Geneva (ILO)	1985
Convention Concerning Safety of Use of Asbestos	Geneva (ILO)	1986

7 ENERGY AND SUSTAINABLE ECONOMIC GROWTH
Survival in a finite world

The subject of energy, particularly conservation of energy, reinforces the theme of this book, which is that the principles of ecology and environmental management are long established in science. If, for a moment, we consider the first law of thermodynamics, concerning the conservation of energy, it would be clear that energy can be neither created nor destroyed. It is a constant; physical processes can change the distribution of energy among its various components but can never alter the sum of its parts.

The second law of thermodynamics is somewhat more complex. This states that in spontaneous processes, heat flowing between two objects moves from the hotter to the colder; that concentrations of energy tend to disperse. Thus disorder in the universe is ever increasing. No process is possible whose sole result is the transfer of heat from a cold to a hot body. Taking into account the accumulated energy expenditure of biological and technological processes, disorder in the ecological system results from the transfer of usable to degraded unusable energy, since while the total amount of energy remains constant, the fraction of usable energy is ever diminishing. The laws of thermodynamics place limits upon the efficiency of energy use and pose the threat that man may raise the temperature of the planet with degraded energy long before supplies of usable energy run out.

World energy demand in the future will continue to be determined by population growth and the requirements for higher living standards in the Third World; in industrialized countries by shifts in age distribution towards a more elderly population; and a tendency towards smaller households. Growth in energy demand will therefore continue, and it cannot be expected that energy conservation, industrial restructuring and improved technology will alter the demand curve very much. On the other hand, it is not expected that low energy prices, particularly of oil, will lead to additional energy demands, beyond those generated by other pressures.

The concepts of sustainable economic growth are based upon two principal objectives. These are to maintain economic growth in industrialized countries and to develop strategies leading to such growth in the Third World. Future global economic viability is held to be dependent upon meeting these objectives.

Strategies for sustainable economic growth mainly concern energy efficiency, conservation of non-renewable resources and the development of alternative energy supplies. To these can be added the transfer of technology from the developed countries to the Third World and economic assistance to promote environmental conservation.

Energy supply and demand patterns are not expected to change considerably, although trends in the redefinition of primary energy sources are likely to continue. Development, therefore, of alternative fuels and energy sources is essentially a long-term programme which will only become urgent nearer the predicted depletion dates for fossil fuels.

Energy and natural resources

Small is undoubtedly beautiful in its greater cleanliness and manageability. It does not reflect present or future strategies for energy organization at the global level nor does it meet the aspirations of the majority of the world's population seeking to improve its general living standards. Nevertheless, while it may be conceptually attractive to the lifestyles of well-educated and affluent minorities, it does fit the concepts of sustainable economic development in Third World countries if the historic problems of the industrialized countries concerning concentrations of population, pollution and waste are to be avoided.

Primary energy supply and demand

Electricity accounts for some 34% of primary energy demand, supplied from conventional thermal power generation supplemented to a relatively small degree by nuclear and hydro-power sources. The primary sources of energy which establish this pattern are oil, gas, coal, nuclear and hydro, to which in 1988 oil contributed some 38% to primary energy consumption (Table 7.1).

Table 7.1 Growth in world primary energy consumption, 1969–88

(1969=100)	1973	1978	1983	1988	Total consump. (million toe)	Percentage of total (1988)	Per cap. fuel consumption
North America	113	119	108	123	2,192	27.2	8.05
USSR	123	155	168	196	1,397	17.3	4.9
Western Europe	122	126	120	131	1,302	16.3	3.85
China	142	191	216	284	727	9.0	1.49
Japan	139	140	136	159	400	5.0	3.3
Australasia	121	149	162	202	107	1.3	5.35
South-east Asia	153	202	269	396	242	3.0	0.65
Latin America	128	161	197	233	425	5.3	1.14
Middle East	144	189	250	313	195	2.4	1.8
Africa	113	159	213	236	204	2.5	0.36
South Asia	111	134	185	261	243	3.0	0.23
Total world	121	127	141	164	8,058	100.0	1.61

World consumption of primary energy in the twenty-year period 1969–88 rose 64% from a total of approximately 5.0 billion tonnes oil equivalent (toe) to 8.0 billion toe. OECD countries increased their consumption by an average of 30%, South-east Asia by 396% and the rest of the world by 64%. Industrialized nations (including China and the USSR) account for some 76% of world energy consumption with the balance distributed somewhat unevenly among the Third World countries. In the period, Western European consumption has expanded least and in a number of countries, most notably Austria, Denmark, the Netherlands, Norway and Sweden, consumption declined in 1988 by approximately 1.5%. The overall increase in Western Europe in 1988 was 1.0% against a world average of 3.7%.

While energy consumption demonstrates a generally upward trend, this is most apparent in developing countries, although their annual gains are relatively small. The largest increases are in Asia, notably South Korea, Taiwan and India, with increases of around 10.0% a year.

Consumption patterns

Average per capita energy consumption in 1988 was approximately 1.6 toe. Assuming that OECD member countries can maintain a per capita average of 3 toe, worldwide energy requirements would be around 18 billion toe by the year 2000 and 25 billion toe in 2025, allowing an increase in developing countries to rise to similar levels (Table 7.2).

Table 7.2 Energy consumption by region (million toe, 1988)

Region	1988	Percentage change over 1987
North America	2,192.4	+4.5
EC member states	1,095.9	+1.0
EFTA countries	154.1	−1.0
Eastern Europe	621.9	+1.8
Latin America	425.5	+3.0
Asia	243.0	+8.0
South-east Asia	241.8	+11.2
Africa	204.2	+4.6
World total	8,058.4	+3.7

Source: BP Statistical Review of World Energy

EFTA countries, principally Norway, Sweden and Switzerland, are often ahead of the field in environmental protection, Norway, for example, exerts considerable influence in the development of maritime safety and pollution standards. Scandinavian stringency is sometimes viewed with dismay by industrialists in other European countries, but its approach appears to be bearing fruit in the fields of energy organization and effluent control.

Fuel options

The relative costs of different fuels traditionally have determined their usage for power generation. The first significant increases in the price of oil in the early 1970s led to the development of conservation strategies then largely on economic grounds, leading to reductions in oil usage in favour of gas, coal and nuclear power. It can be seen from Table 7.3 that the position of oil has weakened relative to other fuels since 1978, although it is still the dominant fuel, and is expected to retain this position, certainly up to the year 2000.

Table 7.3 Patterns in fuel usage

| (1978=100) | 1979 | 1984 | 1988 | Proportion of world consumption (%) | | |
				1978	1988	+/−
Oil	102	92	98	45.9	37.7	−21.7
Gas	106	117	134	18.0	20.2	+12.0
Coal	106	114	130	27.7	30.1	+8.7
Nuclear	103	190	289	2.2	5.4	+245.0
Hydro	104	123	130	6.0	6.5	+8.3

The most significant decrease in oil consumption in the near future would be brought about by smaller and more efficient automobile engines in the USA, where petrol is the dominant oil product, accounting for some 42% of consumption. This compares to 25% in Western Europe, 27% in Japan and 18% in the Third World. A 10% decrease in petrol consumption in the USA, of about 30 million tonnes, would be equivalent to Australia's total annual demand for oil.

Gas, coal and hydro have all seen fairly modest rises in their respective positions, while the most significant increase has been in the use of nuclear power, particularly in the USA, the USSR, West Germany and the UK, with increases of between 11% and 15% in its use during 1988.

Nuclear energy is a primary example of a cost-effective, renewable energy source, although in the short term this will be outweighed by low-cost predictions in the development of coal and gas. The rate of nuclear expansion in relation to other energy sources is predicted to rise to about 11% of primary energy supply by the year 2005. Because of high initial installation costs and the problems of decommissioning, as well as the possibility of accidents, it does not present a proposition for large-scale amelioration of Third World energy shortages, and its future contribution to energy supplies is as yet uncertain (Table 7.4). Nevertheless, 98 new nuclear power reactors are under construction throughout the world and are scheduled for commissioning within the next five years (Table 7.5). These could deliver on additional 16–20%, or between 50,000 and 70,000 megawatts to the grid worldwide.

Table 7.4 Total nuclear capacity (megawatta), 1989

Country	Capacity	No. of reactors	Average output (MW)	Percentage of world total
Western Europe	150,407	157	722	47.5
North America	109,808	128	858	34.6
USSR and E. Europe	46,143	81	570	14.6
Rest of world	10,480	67	156	3.3
Total world	316,858	433	732	100.0
Major users				*Percentage of national electricity*
USA	97,623	110	882	19.5
France	52,588	55	956	69.9
USSR	33,060	53	604	12.6
Japan	28,253	38	743	23.4
West Germany	22,716	24	934	34.0
UK	12,428	40	298	19.3
Canada	12,185	18	677	16.0
Sweden	9,693	12	807	46.9
Total major users	268,646	350	767	23.2
Other Europe				
Belgium	5,480	7	783	
Italy	1,120	2	560	
Netherlands	508	2	254	11.5
Spain	7,519	10	752	
Switzerland	2,952	5	590	
Total other Europe	17,579	26	676	
Eastern Europe	13,083	28	467	12.4
Latin America	2,215	4	554	11.0 (Argentina)
Asia	6,423	23	279	3.0 (India)
South Africa	1,842	2	921	7.3
Total rest of world	23,563	57	421	
Total world	316,858	433	732	17.1

Sources: UNSCEAR and IAEA

Oil

World proved recoverable reserves of oil increased from 50 billion tonnes in 1968 to 124 billion tonnes in 1988 of which 62% is to be found in the Middle Eastern countries. Annual consumption is approximately 3 billion tonnes. Proved reserves of oil are those which can be recovered with reasonable certainty under existing economic and operating conditions. These have increased from 65 billion tonnes in 1968 to 124 billion in 1988 (Table 7.6).

Table 7.5 Distribution of reactor types

Reactor type	USA	UK	France	USSR	Other	Total
AGR Advanced gas-cooled, graphite-moderated	–	13	–	–	–	13
BWR Boiling light-water cooled and moderated	36	–	–	1	49	86
FBR Fast breeder	–	1	2	3	1	7
GCR Gas-cooled, graphite moderated	–	25	4	–	2	31
HTGR High-temperature gas-cooled, graphite moderated	1	–	–	–	2	3
HWLWR Heavy-water moderated, boiling light-water cooled	–	–	–	–	Japan	1
LWGR Light-water cooled, graphite moderated	–	–	–	27	–	27
PHWR Pressurized heavy-water moderated and cooled	–	–	–	–	26	26
PWR Pressurized light-water moderated and cooled	71	–	49	25	89	234
SGHWR Steam generated heavy-water	–	1	–	–	–	1
	108	40	55	56	170	429

Source: UNSCEAR

Table 7.6 Distribution of oil reserves, 1988

Country/region	Billion tonnes	%
Middle East	77.3	62.3
Latin America	17.1	13.4
USSR	8.0	6.4
Africa	7.5	6.1
North America	5.5	4.8
China	3.1	2.6
Asia	2.5	2.3
Western Europe	2.4	1.9
Australasia	0.2	0.2
Total reserves	124.0	100.0

Source: BP

Coal

The world may well be on the verge of a second coal age which would reach its peak some time in the next century. World proved recoverable reserves of coal are 1,023 billion tonnes, representing 235 years' supply at present rates of consumption (Table 7.7).

Coal is the most abundant supply of fossil fuel, and is geographically widespread and relatively cheap. While most coal is consumed in the country of its origin there is a growing trend in international trade which is being led by China, Colombia, Indonesia and Venezuela, providing a lower sulphur commodity than that of European producers.

Table 7.7 Distribution of coal reserves

1988	Thousand million tonnes	Annual production (million tonnes)	1986 exports (million tonnes)
USA	262.2	868.0	77.0
USSR	243.2	785.0	
China	168.1	960.0	
Western Europe	94.5	433.0	11.0
Eastern Europe	74.4	761.4	
Australasia	74.5	178.0	92.0
Africa	44.5	20.0	
Japan	25.0	10.7	
South Africa	21.0	163.0	43.0
Asia	19.3	222.2	
Latin America	12.5	33.6	
Canada	6.5	70.2	
Total	1,023.0	4,701.0	225.0

Source: Shell

Power generation, which is the key area of growth in energy demand, provides the best prospects for coal and, of course, the greatest challenge to pollution control. Coal's contribution to acid rain and the 'greenhouse effect' have already been noted. While the legislation of OECD countries will undoubtedly lead to the development of economic scrubbing technology to reduce sulphur and nitrous oxides, carbon dioxide emissions are more problematic, and the prospects of environmental performance in China, the USSR, India and Latin America are less clear.

Natural gas
Oil and gas, at the level of currently proved recoverable reserves, share a similar expected life-span, of between 42 and 56 years (Table 7.8). The environmental advantage of natural gas is that it is sulphur-free and its carbon dioxide output from electricity generation is about half that of coal and somewhat less than fuel oil.

Energy conservation and alternative energy sources
Conserving natural resources is the central theme of environmental management, in the context of preserving them from destructive influences, decay or waste and extending the lifetime of their utility. Conservation and energy efficiency are complementary issues, both of which rely upon investment choices by industry and the consumer. Other European countries and the USA have introduced energy-saving technology, legislation and tax incentives more rapidly than the UK, despite the obvious economic and ecological benefits that result in both the short and long terms.

Table 7.8 Distribution of natural gas reserves

	Trillion cubic metres
USSR	42.5
Middle East	33.4
Africa	7.1
Latin America	6.7
Asia	6.2
Western Europe	5.7
USA	5.3
Canada	2.7
Eastern Europe	0.7
Australasia	0.6
Total world	111.9

While conservation measures by industry and the consumer can cut energy demand by valuable percentage points (perhaps up to 25% within the next decade), contributing to the reduction of atmospheric pollutants, more significant reductions in pollution levels will be made through the introduction of cleaner-burning technologies by energy producers. However, the question of carbon dioxide reductions need to be regarded with circumspection, and considered in the light of the other information presented in this book.

Micro-conservation

Micro-conservation, or aggregated energy savings by industrial and individual users, means that less energy needs to be generated. The energy consumption figures presented in this book for OECD countries illustrate the effects of more efficient technology and practices resulting from the various energy crises of the past twenty years as well as from changes in the balance of industrial structure between manufacturing and servicing.

The UK Department of Energy estimate that improved energy efficiency in offices, factories and warehouses has the potential of saving 20% of energy costs, amounting to some £8.0 billion a year savings nationally on heating, hot water and lighting. These estimates are supported by International Energy Agency studies which suggest that energy demand could be reduced by a further 25% by the end of the century, a significant proportion of which could result from consumer efficiency. In this regard, Friends of the Earth have suggested that 75% of the energy consumed by domestic appliances in the UK could be saved by more efficient design, similar to US and European products.

Investment in energy efficiency by users is motivated less by environmental considerations than by the return on capital and by payback periods, which are determined by fuel costs. Considering that pollution levels have been brought about by the historic volumes of fossil fuel consumption which are unlikely to fall within the next 25 years or so, while increased user efficiency can effect considerable savings, any significant reduction of pollution can only be achieved by technological advances in energy production. However, technology to control technology is itself a net energy consumer, and hence the emphasis on long-term structural changes towards energy efficiency rather than enthusiasm for a technological fix. Competition for natural resources is also a major management dilemma where national wealth and the income and livelihoods of existing and future populations is threatened by a diminishing asset base.

Contract energy management (CEM)

That the market has an important role to play in energy conservation is evident from the initiatives of the oil industry (Shell and BP in the UK) to offer contract services to major users in industry and local authorities in order to improve their energy efficiency. CEM operates on the principle that energy savings should be accounted as profit, to accrue both to the user and to pay for contracted services. The attractiveness of the concept and the approach for commerce and the consumer is that conservation can be compatible with maintaining lifestyles (i.e. consuming without waste).

In the area of consumer-related energy conservation, data from the Association for the Conservation of Energy (ACE) indicate declining home sales of insulating materials, which does not suggest that many householders are prepared to make the capital investments necessary for this kind of home improvement. Nor is consumer pressure apparent for more energy-efficient domestic appliances, including central heating. Market pressures to meet European standards are contributing greatly to energy-efficient efforts by UK industries, but apart from increasing awareness, considerable investment and re-adjustment needs to be made.

Macro-conservation

Fuel-specific energy conservation policies are difficult to impose in industrialized countries due to fluctuating fuel price differentials. The speed of the development of renewable energy supplies will continue to be determined by the price of oil relative to that of other non-renewable resources. Apart from the mainly traditional resources identified in this book, there are several options for alternative renewable supplies, which, despite their inherent long-term attractiveness in environmental terms, are not economic in the short term, largely on account of the long lead times needed for their technological development.

There is still a large potential for energy conservation in Europe. This is more so in the USA, where there is room to improve the efficiency with which traditional energy resources of oil, in particular, are used. However, it is probably true that the most cost-effective opportunities for conserving oil have already been exploited without inroads into living standards. In the last ten years consumption in volume has decreased by 11% in the USA and 15% in Europe. Although per capita oil consumption shows a declining trend in both regions, total energy consumption is increasing by between 3.5% and 4.5% per year, with gas, coal and nuclear energy playing important roles in integrated energy strategies.

Effective energy conservation combines energy savings by consumers with energy efficiency at the producer level, which requires a more positive approach by the power-generating industries to emission controls and strongly suggests the need for tax changes.

Alternative energy sources

Alternative energy sources are not expected to contribute more than 1–2 percentage points in the production of primary energy within the next 10–15 years. The value of alternative energy supplies, however, in the short term is to deliver electricity to rural areas of the Third World, where it may be difficult or too costly to supply from conventional sources.

Solar energy

Energy from the sun reaching the surface of the Earth is more than ten times the equivalent of estimated probable resources of fossil and uranium fuels and 15,000 times more than the world's annual energy consumption. Harnessing this source of energy is based upon solar thermal and photovoltaic systems.

In industrialized countries, solar energy for low-grade thermal generation in industry and domestic applications is an attractive supplement to fossil fuels on the grounds of environmental cleanliness, but, as in the Third World, it is only suitable for local applications. Solar energy in developing countries for domestic lighting, refrigeration, and small-scale water-pumping to replace diesel-fuelled engines is much more significant where populations cannot be served by conventional grid systems.

The Workshop on Alternative Energy Strategies estimates that solar energy could contribute between 50 million and 100 million tonnes annually of equivalent oil energy in industrialized countries by the year 2000. This represents between 0.125% and 0.25% of 1988 primary energy consumption in OECD countries, or between 0.3% and 0.6% of present oil use.

Biomass

The term 'biomass' encompasses natural vegetation, plants and crops. Biomass as energy is derived from both plant matter (fuelwood) and the derivatives from forest and crop residues, animal wastes and the organic content of municipal and domestic solid wastes.

Over half of the world's population relies upon wood as fuel for cooking and heating, of which there is an insufficient supply and few alternatives. This is a major cause of the deforestation of tropical areas, exacerbating the problem of soil erosion where animal wastes are used as fuel instead of as fertilizer.

Limits to growth and sustainable economic growth

The debate on limits to growth needs to be considered in the relationship between politics and economics and the population–resources–environment crisis. This debate essentially had its first airing at least 25 years ago, when the main elements of the present crisis were expounded in the principles of a global ecological need for change.

While not all economists and politicians are unanimous in their view of economic growth as an end in itself, the idea that GNP is a faulty index of economic health, natural resources, environmental stability or quality of life has gradually become conventional wisdom. The possibilities for economic growth in a finite world, the quality of growth in an expanding market (e.g. the EC single market) and the wider environmental implications of quality of life and disparities in standards of living are embodied in a declaration in the Treaty of Rome, but the reconciliation between anticipated growth in GNP and environmental quality is not guaranteed.

IEEP refers to the Cecchini report on the implications of the single European market. It suggests that economic growth in Europe following 1992 will be of an unreconstructed kind having an adverse environmental impact. Road freight, car ownership and tourism will increase; commercial and domestic building will expand; increased economic activity and consumption will lead to more roads, land-use pressure, air pollution, resource depletion and waste.

Even against this background, sustainable economic growth within Western societies is regarded as the necessary economic foundation for Third World development (Brundtland Report).

International energy conventions

Convention	Place of adoption Depository state/organization	Date
Convention on the Continental Shelf	Geneva (UN)	1958
Agreement on an International Energy Programme	Paris (Belgium)	1974

8 WATER, RIVERS AND SANITATION
Protecting the source of life

The inappropriate juxtaposition of water, chemicals and waste is a universal problem, and notwithstanding destruction of the world by other means, the protection of lakes, rivers, streams and groundwater from pollution is fundamental to food production, public health and the health of all living species. Dirty water is the world's major cause of disease and fresh water is the most fragile of the world's resources as well as being the source of life. Like other precious world resources, the volume of fresh water, while more than adequate for human use, is unevenly distributed and badly managed in both scarcity and abundance.

While untreated sewage is the world's most dangerous pollutant, human and other organic wastes are fully biodegradable, subject to caveats, in the open sea. Sewage contaminates fresh water and coastal systems, causing serious problems of public health and oxygen depletion. Industrial and agricultural chemicals and toxic wastes add considerably to sewage and contribute to the destruction of this finite resource. In developed countries water for human consumption is relatively safe but under serious threat, while in the Third World the mechanisms of distribution, protection and conservation are woefully inadequate.

Fresh water supplies
The Earth's supply capability of fresh water for human use is estimated to be some 9,000 cubic kilometres annually, sufficient in theory to sustain a total world population of some 20 billion people. Supply, however, is inelastic, unequally distributed and subject to increasing demands from industry, agriculture and growing populations.

Contaminated natural waters are the predominant cause of disease, principally from domestic wastes and sewage but less commonly from chemicals (UNEP, GEMS/Water). Toxic pollutants, however, can render water unfit for ever to support life and several major bodies of water are at or approaching this terminal state.

Crop irrigation consumes early three-quarters of the available fresh water in any given year, most of which is inefficiently used; industry and domestic uses account for the remaining quarter (Table 8.1).

Table 8.1 Uses of the world's fresh water (%)

Irrigation	73.0
Industry	21.0
Domestic	6.0
	100.0

Source: UNEP

Groundwater contamination

Groundwater makes up some 22% of the world's fresh water budget, with available surface water a mere 0.6%. The remainder is locked up in ice caps and glaciers.

Groundwater is contained in saturated voids between soil particles below the water table and are the reservoirs from which well waters are pumped. It is replenished by surface waters, and depths vary, from a few metres in humid and temperate regions, dependent upon geological conditions, to a few hundred metres in arid ones. The transit time of water and contaminants from the surface depends upon permeability and distance. For the most part, organic contaminants degrade by the time the water table has been reached.

The most serious threats that chemical contaminants from industry and agriculture pose is to groundwater, which is virtually impossible to purify once contamination has occurred, since the microbes that normally break down organic pollutants need oxygen, from which groundwater is cut off. In 1979 two cases of groundwater contamination, in New York State and in Lathrop, California, from Temik (a carbamic insecticide/nematicide) and DBCP (a chlorinated nematicide) affected thousands of drinking-water wells and led to the introduction of new legislation in the USA, Canada and Europe, and to the EC Directive on the Protection of Groundwater against Pollution (80/68/EEC).

Groundwater is an essential link in the hydrological cycle. It is subject not only to pollution but also to depletion from excessive withdrawals to supplement surface supplies from river and lake systems. In the most extreme practice, groundwater is 'mined' to meet the demands of irrigation projects in industrialized and Third World countries and cannot be renewed.

Eutropication of fresh water systems

Nitrogen-rich (eutropic) lakes are to be found in most countries where intensive agriculture is practised. In the UK, East Anglia and Staffordshire are particularly affected; and they are widespread throughout Europe and the USA. A quarter of China's major lakes are thus contaminated.

Inorganic nitrogen fertilizer accumulates in high concentrations in crops and results in a heavy flow of nitrates into the water supply. Nitrates in themselves are not especially dangerous, although in the presence of certain bacteria in the digestive tract of infants and animals they convert to highly toxic nitrites, affecting oxygen utilization ('blue baby syndrome').

Nitrogen enrichment of rivers, streams and lakes encourages the growth of algae, which in the process of decay causes de-oxygenation and the extermination of most aquatic life. Nitrate runoff, added to phosphates, sewage and other pollutants, has transformed many watercourses in Europe, the USA (Lake Erie), China, the USSR (Lake Baikal) and Third World countries into virtually dead water. Rising concentrations of nitrates from nitrogen fertilizers have been reported in deep groundwater aquifers in France, West Germany, the Netherlands and the UK.

Remedies to these problems are not short term and rely upon multi-faceted co-operative programmes between industry, agriculture, utility management and the consumer. The infrastructure and legal frameworks are, for the most part, already in place, but long-term commitments to time and investment need to be made.

Urban river systems in Europe

The pathogenic content and thus the quality of public water from European rivers is contained through chlorination, not a perfect method, considering the mutagenic risk from certain chlorine compounds. However, in view of the high level of dangerous pathogens which enter many water supplies, it is one that we shall doubtless continue to accept.

The series of North Sea conferences concerned with pollution levels and the relative inputs from adjacent countries identify the major polluting rivers as the Forth, Humber, Tees, Thames and Tyne in the UK and the Elbe, Ems, Meuse, Rhine, Scheldt and Weser in mainland Europe. Despite the levels of detritus in the North Sea contributed by UK rivers, all these major UK rivers have already illustrated the possibilities for river regeneration in which biological oxygen demand has been substantially reduced and fish have returned. These efforts have been under way since the 1960s. The job of industry and the water authorities has been made somewhat easier by the application of national pollution-control regulations rather than the need for international co-operation, as is the case of the rivers Rheine and Elbe, which are trans-boundary.

The Rhine provides an excellent example of the possibilities for combating trans-frontier pollution. It is also a salutary model for the timescale of international remedial actions. The Rhine, originating in Switzerland, runs 1,320 km through the major urban and industrial conurbations of France and West Germany, via the Netherlands into the North Sea. The river has been subject for many decades to large volumes of industrial effluents, and a programme of river water recycling and re-use is promoted through the Rhine Action Plan agreement, which has been in operation since 1980 following a series of regional agreements dating back to 1963.

The Elbe, flowing from Czechoslovakia through East Germany and emptying into the North Sea, is virtually a dead river. This is understandable in view of the characteristic ecological neglect of Eastern Europe since the end of the war and its passage through chemically overburdened farmlands and the heavily industrialized and equally neglected cities of Bitterfeld, Halte, Leipzig and Dresden. The structural problems of regeneration and the return to potability and ecological balance are similar to the general difficulties to be faced in cleaning up Eastern Europe.

Trans-frontier rivers in the Third World

The Amazon, Nile, Jordan, Ganges, Bramaputra and Malayasian and African rivers contribute most significantly to the problems of public health in the Third World, which include infantile diarrhoea as the world's greatest killer. Competition for fresh water for irrigation purposes and the continuous input of industrial, agricultural, human and animal wastes, as well as the effects of erosion and silting from deforestation, reduce the availability of clean water for human consumption by considerable margins.

High colliform counts from untreated sewage in Africa (Nigeria), Asia (China, India, Indonesia), Central (Mexico) and South America (Brazil) contribute to high infant morbidity and mortality rates. The lake and reservoir systems of Asian and Pacific countries tend to have nutrient levels ten to fifteen times higher than the world average, largely on account of faecal contamination.

Water management

Irrigation and domestic applications are more characteristically wasteful of water than industrial, even though considerable volumes are re-used many times through river systems. Management and conservation are of primary importance for the maintenance of health, food production and wider ecological considerations. The prevention of contaminants entering water, by recycling and re-use in closed and semi-closed industrial systems, are practical ways of avoiding the complex technology and huge costs of purification and restoration, although these costs need to be faced to clean up polluted bodies of water that already contain high levels of PCBs, DDT and heavy metal compounds. The reduction of nutrient inputs from agricultural runoff can be achieved efficiently by returning cattle manure to the land rather than by treating it as sewage.

International and regional agreements on managing fresh water systems have been operating in Europe since 1958 and since 1964 in Africa. International programmes with the purpose of improving water management and distribution, either as research or as a basis for international co-operation, were first introduced by Unesco in 1950.

EC water directives from 1975 to the present relate both to remedial measures and to the prevention of pollution by identifying pollutants and establishing Maximum Admissible Concentrations (MAC) for bathing, consumption, preservation of aquatic life and general water quality. For example, the total MAC for all pesticides in drinking water is 0.5 parts per billion, with a MAC of 0.1 ppb for any single pesticide. These levels are not high when one considers that one ppb is the time equivalent of one second in every 34 years. The UK argues that MAC thresholds should be calculated and set for each product according to its health risk. The probability, however, of the health effect of each substance is not fully known. Where water-monitoring surveys have been fairly extensively undertaken (in West Germany, for example) these targets of parts per billion appear to be eminently reasonable, since the results of the surveys have been in consonance with the current published standards.

In 1968 an early European initiative concerning water quality came from the Council of Europe, relating to the biodegradability of certain detergent products. This was subsequently taken up by OECD in 1971 as the first water recommendation of the OECD Environment Committee, followed by other recommendations to members concerning eutrophication and strategies for pollution control and water management.

Principal international and regional programmes concerning fresh water

Unesco Arid Zones Programme		1950–60
International Hydrological Decade		1964–74
International Hydrological Programme	IHP-1	1975–80
UN International Water Conference	(UNWC)	1977
	IHP-2	1981–83
	IHP-3	1984–90
WHO International Drinking Water and Sanitation Decade		1981–90
UNEP Programme for the Environmentally Sound Management of Inland Water (EMINWA)		1985 onwards

EMINWA includes:
  Zambezi Action Plan (ZACPLAN)
  Lake Chad Action Plan (proposed)
  Lake Victoria Action Plan		

Inland water-related conventions

Convention	Place of adoption Depository state/organization	Date
Convention Concerning Fishing in the Waters of the Danube and Environmental Co-operation in the Danube Basin	Bucharest (Romana) Regensberg	1958
Protocol Concerning the Constitution of an International Commission for the Protection of the Moselle Against Pollution	Paris (FRG)	1961
Agreement Concerning the International Commission for the Protection of the Rhine Against Pollution	Berne (Switzerland)	1963
Convention and Statute Relating to the Development of the Chad Basin	N'Djamina (Chad)	1964

European Agreement on the Restriction of the Use of Certain Detergents in Washing and Cleaning Products	Strasbourg (COE)	1968
Convention Concerning the Status of the Senegal River, and Convention Establishing the Senegal River Development Organization	Nouakchott (Senegal)	1972
Convention on the Protection of the Rhine Against Chemical Pollution	Bonn (Switzerland)	1976
Convention Concerning the Protection of the Rhine Against Pollution by Chlorides	Bonn (Switzerland)	1976
Convention Creating the Niger Basin Authority and Protocol Relating to the Development Fund of the Niger Basin	Faranah (Niger)	1980
Agreement of the Action Plan for the Environmentally Sound Management of the Common Zambezi River System	Harare (SADCC)*	1987

* Southern African Development Co-ordination Conference

9 THE OCEANS

Coastal and sea pollution

International research and oceans management

The most authoritative scientific assessments of the state of the marine environment have been made by GESAMP in two reviews dated 1982 and 1989. The significance of GESAMP's findings between the two periods are reflected in the change in name of UNEP's Regional Seas Programme to 'Oceans and Coastal Areas'.

In summary, the 1989 review observes chemical contamination and litter 'from the poles to the tropics and from beaches to abyssal depths'. However, in contrast to the open oceans, which contain detectable (although biologically insignificant) levels of contamination, coastal areas reflect the effects of rapidly growing concentrations of population, industrialization, mariculture, tourism, eutrophication and plankton blooms from sewage and nitrates, plastic litter, lost habitats from the destruction of beaches, coral reefs, wetlands and mangrove forests. In addition, rising levels of chlorinated hydrocarbons, particularly DDT and TBT, are to be found in tropical and subtropical sediments.

The 1982 report tended to concentrate on oil and trace element (cadmium, lead and mercury) contaminants and artificial radionuclides. It must be said that considerable progress has been made since that time, through international agreements and national regulations, in managing the disposal of oil and trace elements from seaborne sources. Similarly, contamination from artificial radionuclides emanating from nuclear installations has become more tightly regulated and monitored.

The recent shift in emphasis from the oceans to coastal areas in no manner diminishes the need for continued control and vigilance of these sources. However, coastal area destruction from land-based activities is now the major cause of immediate concern in the marine environment on a global basis.

It appears that no areas of the ocean nor its principal resources are irrevocably damaged at present. Nevertheless, the marine environment generally could soon deteriorate beyond repair in some areas in the absence of international co-operation regarding coastal development and national action to reduce waste inputs.

The oceans constitute nearly three quarters of the Earth's surface, and include enclosed and inland seas, such as the North and Irish Seas, the Mediterranean, the Baltic and the Aral Sea as well as five great oceans, the Atlantic, the Pacific, the Indian, the Arctic and the Southern Ocean.

Oceans and seas are fed by rivers through many estuaries and outlets which also act as channels for agricultural, industrial and chemical effluents. The great oceans have a high capacity for absorbing organic and inorganic materials from both man-made and natural sources. The extent of this capacity can only be speculated, but the effects of pollution on coastal zones and enclosed seas is very apparent. Estuaries, coastal and littoral zones provide natural habitats for mammal and fish species, wetlands for migrant birds, lower organisms of the food chain and principal recreational areas for the human population.

The most seriously polluted marine area is the Mediterranean, from tankers and land-based sources, but indeed, many coastlines, shores and marine habitats, such as coral reefs, are under continuous threat (as well as assault) from deliberate and accidental discharges of oils, chemicals, wastes and tourist developments.

Managing marine pollution

The International Maritime Organization (IMO), based in London, is responsible for the regulation of international shipping, safety of life at sea and the protection of the marine environment. Its function is to establish co-operation between maritime nations in the development of legislation to prevent and control pollution from ships, to promote technical standards for the design, construction and safe operation of ocean-going vessels engaged in international trade and to establish standards of training and working conditions for mariners. The most influential national delegations at IMO are the UK (Department of Transport), the USA (US Coast Guard), the USSR and Norway among the maritime nations. In common with other organizations and agencies in the UN system, the IMO works to a tight budget of some £12 million, which is diminished by the non-payment of contributions due from member governments.

The principal instrument of IMO's environment programme is the Convention for the Prevention of Pollution from Ships (MARPOL), 1973, and its subsequent amendments and annexes covering the handling and discharge of oil, oily wastes, oily water discharges and noxious liquid (chemical) substances. In the conduct of its environmental programme, IMO works in collaboration with UNEP and associated agencies in the development and implementation of international pollution agreements within the context of the Oceans and Coastal Areas Programme. Similarly, IMO provides an international forum for promoting regional environmental and pollution initiatives, such as the Oslo Commission, responsible for the Oslo Convention and party states to the London Dumping Convention (LDC).

Marine transport

Oil pollution from tankers and other vessels is a major threat to the marine environment, particularly in semi-enclosed seas, where its effects on birds, marine life and recreational amenities can be devastating. Particularly vulnerable areas are the Red Sea, the wider Caribbean, Indonesia and the

Philippines, Pakistan and the Indian west coast, West Africa and the Mediterranean.

Most pollution is the result of routine uncontrolled discharges. More severe effects are caused by major accidents, from the *Torrey Canyon* (Scilly Isles, UK) in 1967, the *Amoco Cadiz* (English Channel) in 1978 and, more recently, the *Exxon Valdez* (Prince William Sound, Alaska) in 1989.

There is general agreement that since 1979 there has been a significant reduction in beached tar, which is the principal physical manifestation of oil pollution. This is accounted for by reductions in marine transport of oil following the 1979 price increases, the entry into force of the MARPOL Convention and the systematic and regular cleaning of beaches.

Apart from oil, many other substances having a potential to cause serious damage to the marine environment are carried in ships' bulk cargoes, including radioactive, toxic, infectious, corrosive, organic peroxides and oxidizing materials, explosive and flammable liquids, solids and gases (Table 9.1).

Table 9.1 Estimated contribution to marine pollution from human activities

Source	All potential pollutants (%)
Land-based discharges	44.0
Atmospheric inputs	33.0
Marine transport	12.0
Dumping	10.0
Oil exploration/production	1.0

Source: GESAMP

Protection of the marine environment, as with other issues of global importance, relies upon international co-operation, but, at the end of the day, also upon the economic benefits which might be accrued from efficient practice. These benefits include the public relations value of a clean record or a well-managed response to accidents, and by presenting difficulties to ships of nations with poor pollution performance in their trading relationships and port reception.

Pollution clean-up is a very costly business, and accidents incur higher future insurance premiums as well as more direct financial penalties. The *Exxon Valdez* clean-up has cost the operating company, Exxon, up to $2.0 billion. Since US legislation requires complete site restoration, and in the face of a multi-billion dollar lawsuit by Alaska State, the final cost to Exxon is expected to be considerably in excess of this figure.

The *Exxon Valdez* incident killed about 33,000 birds and 1,000 otters, caused considerable damage to shorelines in Prince William Sound, polluted marine organisms and vegetation and disrupted the local fishing industry. The oil slick spread over 3,000 square miles and onto some 350 miles of beaches. Despite the immediate impact of the spill upon what had been described as a pristine and magnificent natural area, long-term injury to wildlife and marine life is expected to be minimal.

Along with other major oil tanker pollution incidents, the *Exxon Valdez* incident illustrated government and industry plans to be wholly insufficient to handle a serious oil spill. As noted earlier, marine transport is subject to quite rigorous control, but the *Exxon Valdez* highlighted how far research and development into oil spill containment, response and clean-up techniques declined following the last oil crisis and subsequent budget cutbacks by industry.

The political effects of this incident are likely to have a beneficial international impact. Long-overdue US domestic legislation on compensation and liability for incidents of this nature will undoubtedly emerge, together with US ratification of the 1984 Protocols to the 1969 International Convention on Civil Liability for Oil Pollution Damage and to the 1971 Establishment of an International Fund for Compensation for Oil Pollution Damage. These legislative measures would have the effect of stimulating adoption of international standards among countries which look to the USA for leadership on handling oil spills.

It may also have the effect of increasing expenditures by the oil and tanker industries on contingency and accident response planning. There are proposals to set up a Petroleum Industry Response Organization (PIRO) in the USA, with a five-year budget of £250 million. But control of pollution from ships proves to be more difficult than that from fixed marine installations such as oil and gas production platforms, where national legislation and regulation can be more readily applied (Table 9.2). In any event, while contingency planning and clean-up are important aspects of environmental management, accident prevention through technological containment and training to minimize the consequences of human error is likely to be a more effective long-term strategy.

Table 9.2 Major tanker spills

	Quantity (tonnes/1,000)	Routine discharges/year (tonnes/1,000)
Torrey Canyon (1967)	117.0	
Amoco Cadiz (1978)	221.0	
Exxon Valdez (1989)	36.0	
Khark 5 (1989)	60.0	
Aragon (1989)	25.0	
Estimated annual inputs	>500.0	600.0

The total quantity of oil discharged into the sea is estimated to be in the order of 3.2 million tonnes annually (NAS, 1985 based on 1980 data), some 40% of which originates from industrial effluents and other consumer-related sources. An estimated 20% of the oil comes from routine tanker operations and a further 0.01% from natural seepage. Similar amounts originate from coastal refineries, other shipping and offshore exploration and production.

Bacterial degradation of toxic waste, including oil, through the stimulation of bacterial growth by nitrogen and phosphate-based chemicals ('bioremediation': use of nutrients to hasten the growth of microbes that consume petroleum) is one of the test measures adopted in the Prince William Sound clean-up. However, from all reports and also from the experience of the *Amoco Cadiz* incident, following the immediate damage, oil that cannot be recovered from such spills is normally dealt with more efficiently by natural degradation and wave action.

In the case of the Iranian-owned *Khark 5*, which lost some 60,000 tonnes in the North Atlantic following storm damage and a series of explosions and fire in December 1989, the oil was naturally dispersed and degraded without reaching the Moroccan coastline, as the Spanish and Moroccan authorities had originally feared.

Offshore exploration and production
In view of its relationship with the marine environment, offshore production platforms and oil-drilling rigs are subject to IMO discharge and dumping controls, and drilling rigs to IMO design and construction codes. Oil spills and discharges from submarine pipelines tend to occur mostly in the immediate vicinity of platforms, due to pipeline failure and damage from marine transport. Quantities of oil spilt from pipelines is measured in barrels rather than tonnes, and bears no comparison with other sources of oil pollution

Pollution of the North Sea
In respect of the North Sea, a possible consequence of the high volumes of detritus which emanate from Europe is the decline in fish stocks. The effects of pollution, however, are not clear, nor indeed are those of weather and temperature changes which have been noted in this area from 1980, since which time there has been a declining trend in cod and haddock landings and spawning stocks. The effects upon the Scottish fishing industry are severe, subject as they are to EC fishing quotas which are set annually.

Coastal pollution from industrial waste, sewage and oil spills and contaminants from rivers, as well as from atmospheric sources, is a well-documented universal occurrence. In addition, soil erosion from traditional agricultural and forestry practices overburdens estuary and wetland habitats.

However, in 1987 the quality of popular coastal bathing water in England and Wales failed to meet EC colliform standards (EEC Bathing Water Directive) of 10,000 colliforms per 100 millilitres at 109 beaches out of

360 tested. The 1987 figure shows an improvement over similar measurements taken in 1986.

In 1988 a canine distemper virus (CDV) gave rise to an epidemic causing the deaths of 13,000 common seals in north-west European waters. The population of seals and fatalities caused by the virus is shown in Table 9.3.

Table 9.3 Common seal population and fatalities

	1985/7	1988	1989
UK waters	100,000	12,000	
The Wash	7,000	3,900	2,000
Orkneys	6,600	Less affected	
Waddensee	n.a.	60% mortality	
World population	200,000		

Source: SRMU

At present, there is still no confirmed link between pollution in the North Sea (PCBs and dioxins, however, are known to reduce resistance to disease of marine mammals) and CDV, although persistent organic compounds have been found in Waddensee and Baltic seal populations (SMRU). Recent SMRU studies of seal morbidity in UK waters suggests that grey seals are not particularly healthy in the wild and, set against natural mortality, the CDV plague seems unlikely to have a significant effect on future seal populations.

Quantities of waste into the North Sea

A principal contributor to the continued pollution of the North Sea is the UK's 250,000 tonnes of toxic waste dumped annually and sewage sludge.

Table 9.4 Volumes of waste into the North Sea (tonnes)

	1980	Current
Wastes discharged from vessels (sewage sludge, dredged soil and rubble)	153,000,000	64,000,000
Nitrates and phosphates from rivers	n.a.	1,433,000
Atmosphere (industrial nitrogen, lead, copper)	n.a.	626,600
Incineration at sea	n.a.	96,000
Oil (ships and platforms)	1,000,000	90,000
Heavy metals (cadmium, mercury, lead, etc.)	70,000	13,200
Chemical spillage from vessels	n.a.	2,800
Radioactive material (caesium, strontium, plutonium)	n.a.	5,500 Tbq/year
DDT and PCBs from the Rhine	10,500	n.a.
Total volumes (estimated and rounded)	156,000,000	66,300,000
Estimated total volume of sewage (mostly untreated) 70 m³ daily		

Table 9.4 illustrates that total volumes of waste into the North Sea from the North Sea Conference countries since 1980 have not only declined by nearly 40% but are being more accurately monitored.

In common with other polluted seas, the North Sea is afflicted with red algae (phytoplankton bloom) with an unusual alga causing great damage to seaweeds, invertebrates and fish along the coasts of Denmark, Norway and Sweden, noted in 1988.

Pollution of the Mediterranean

The Mediterranean is a shallow sea having an average depth of 1.5 kilometres, containing 3.7 billion cubic kilometres of water and representing about 1% of the world's oceans. Pollution of the Mediterranean from marine and land-based sources presents extremely serious ecological and public health problems. It is estimated that some 1.5 million tonnes of industrial and agricultural effluents from 170 refineries and chemical plants, 70 rivers and ship discharges enter the Mediterranean annually together with between 30 million and 50 million tonnes of largely untreated sewage.

The consequences of these effluents is pollution of coastal resorts, extensive poisoning of marine life and fish for human consumption, interference with breeding grounds of endangered species (for example, the Monk Seal, Loggerhead Turtle and Dalmatian Pelican, among others), destruction of wetland habitats and extinction of sea meadows.

One manifestation of this high level of detritus are red tides of algae formed along the nutrient-rich littorals from Gibralter to Alexandria and again westwards along the North African coastline. Similar red tides are also noted around the Bahamas, and these have become quite a common feature of the world's oceans.

The Mediterranean Action Plan resulting from the 1976 Barcelona Convention and co-ordinated by the UNEP Oceans and Coastal Areas Programme is a large political and practical initiative to control dumping and oil discharges from ships and to persuade the Italians and the French to treat and reduce the quantities of industrial, agricultural and human effluents and restore the sea for wildlife and human amenity.

Pollution of the Baltic

The 1974 Helsinki Convention was the first regional agreement to protect an enclosed sea from land-based pollutants. As with all seas and oceans, the Baltic is the repository of toxic wastes, fertilizer runoffs, oil spills and discharges and domestic wastes, from Denmark, both Germanies, Finland, Poland, Sweden and the USSR.

The Baltic is a haven for wildlife, recreation and war games. It is tideless, sluggish and its stagnation has counteracted the natural saline flushing mechanisms of the North Sea. The Baltic seal, along with the white-tailed eagle, are virtually extinct and fish are highly contaminated, although in the past ten years, PCB, DDT and mercury concentrations have apparently decreased. The control and reduction of effluents, as agreed in the Convention, given the 35 million population of the littoral borders and the presently unmanaged industrial and agricultural effluents from East Germany, Poland and the USSR, suggests at least one priority for *perestroika*.

Metals in the sea

Mercury enters the freshwater and marine environments naturally and via the effluents of industrial processes, particularly petrochemical plants. Methylmercury is its particularly hazardous form, to be found in Mediterranean fish stocks, in the high-fish diets of coastal villages and among the fish-eating populations of South America, the Pacific and Australasia. The worst recorded incident of mercury poisoning, during the late 1950s, caused 788 deaths as a result of dumping into Minamata Bay, Japan.

The release of metals is most evident in coastal waters and shallow seas, particularly the North Sea and the Mediterranean. Long-term effects of pollutants upon the oceans and their absorption capacity is less clear.

The Southern Ocean

Twelve of the Antarctic Treaty nations are collaborating in a programme entitled 'BIOMASS' (Biological Investigations of Marine Antarctic Systems and Stocks), in order to describe and explain the physical and biological processes of the Southern Ocean. The programme is being co-ordinated by SCAR (ICSU).

The ocean as a food resource

Conservation and pollution are, of course, key issues in the Antarctic programmes, but in general they are concerned with monitoring climate change and the longer-term global effects of human activity on the marine environment. However, the changes in the distribution and abundance of the world's fish stocks brought about by overfishing and the anomolies of atmosphere and ocean circulation present problems which appear to be more severe than any known pollution effect in open waters.

Competition is fierce for the world's fish stocks. Overfishing of commercially valuable species is well above the levels that allow stocks to replenish. Larger vessels and the use of monofilament driftnets on a large scale in the open oceans catch dolphins, whales, turtles and seals as well as the target tuna and salmon.

Quota systems and other management methods are politically difficult to establish. The dynamic balances between species are adversely affected by a variety of other factors, including rapidly expanding fish farming (mariculture), the disturbance of the seabed by heavy trawling gear and human intervention to conserve seal stocks.

The world's fisheries provide about 10% of the protein available to human populations, and rather more in many developing countries. It is quite possible that the maximum sustainable annual fish catch, which some believe to be some 100 million tonnes, has already been overtaken, given the variety of pressures on fish populations, and that decline may now be predicted (Table 9.5).

Table 9.5 Global fisheries yield (million tonnes)

Year	Tonnage
1979	71.3
1987	92.7
1988	94.0

Sources: FAO and GESAMP

Scientific study of the oceans

Reference has already been made to the work of the WMO, ICSU and NERC in the development and co-ordination of ocean studies for information on chemical, physical and biological processes of seas and oceans. Main areas of interest are the exchange of gases between the sea and atmosphere, plankton productivity and absorption of CO_2, chemistry at various depths and the movement of sediments.

Long-term programmes that are presently under way include the World Ocean Circulation Experiment (WOCE), the Joint Global Ocean Flux Study (JGOFS), the Study of the Tropical Ocean and the Global Atmosphere (TOGA) and the Biogeochemical Ocean Flux Study (BOFS), which are being conducted within the World Climate Research Programme (WCRP). The question of the uptake of anthropogenic CO_2 in the ocean by the Committee on Climate Change and the Ocean (CCCO) has resulted in a programme to measure the concentration of dissolved inorganic carbon during the period of WOCE.

The oceans absorb carbon dioxide from the atmosphere and bury it in sea-floor sediments, thus balancing the overall warming effect of carbon dioxide in the atmosphere. The annual net uptake by the ocean of carbon from the atmosphere is estimated to be in the order of some 3.0 billion tonnes and a further 1–2.0 billion tonnes by terrestrial biota. The annual input of carbon into the atmosphere from man's activities is estimated to be 6–8.0 billion tonnes. Thus, carbon input exceeds uptake by some 1–3.0 billion tonnes annually and could double within 50 years (Table 9.6).

Table 9.6 Global carbon reservoirs

	Billion tonnes	%
Oceans	35,000	95.0
Terrestrial biota and soil	1,750	
Atmosphere	740	
Total 'mobile' carbon	37,490	

While carbon fluxes are the focus of several biogeochemical studies of the relationship between carbon balances and climate, from the point of view of marine pollution, the detection and measurement of synthetic organic chemicals, trace metals and radionuclides in the oceans and marine organisms is straightforward technology. Prevention and control, however, give rise to basic dilemmas concerning appropriate levels of effort and cost benefit. While the capacity of the oceans to absorb contaminants (EC — environmental capacity) is still subject to considerable speculation, its ability to absorb a given contaminant at a particular site is quantifiable on the basis of the site's physical, chemical and biological characteristics. On these grounds alone, the framework for controlling pollutants and effluence is already established, but the problems of monitoring and application of legislation require new levels of co-operation.

Nevertheless, it is not only apparent but generally accepted that the routine discharges of oil and other pollutants into the oceans has been reduced significantly within the last decade as a result of international and regional agreements (GESAMP). The first national legislation in the UK, the Oil in Navigable Waters Act 1922, resulted largely from pressure brought to bear by the Royal Society for the Protection of Birds (RSPB) following accidental pollution and seabird mortality on the island of Annet in the Scilly Isles in 1907 and a series of other incidents involving the deliberate discharge of oily wastes from oil-fired vessels and tankers. A number of international conventions were drafted in Washington in 1926 and under the auspices of the League of Nations in 1936 which were abandoned for lack of signatories. The *Torrey Canyon* incident, also afflicting the Scilly Isles, led to the first international agreement to restrict the discharge of persistent oils close to land, which was the Convention for the Prevention of Pollution of the Sea by Oil, 1954.

Conventions concerning the protection of the marine environment and species

Convention	Place of adoption Depository state/organization	Date
Species protection and fishing		
International Convention on the Regulation of Whaling	Washington (USA)	1946
Establishment of an Inter-American Tropical Tuna Commission	Washington (USA)	1949
Agreement for the Establishment of a General Fisheries Council for the Mediterranean	Rome (FAO)	1949
Agreement Concerning Measures for the Protection of the Stocks of Deep-sea Prawns, etc.	Oslo (Norway)	1952
International Convention for the High Seas Fisheries of the North Pacific Ocean	Tokyo (INPFC)*	1952

Interim Convention on the Conservation of North Pacific Fur Seals	Washington (USA)	1957
Convention on Fishing and the Conservation of the Living Resources of the High Seas	Geneva (UN)	1958
North-East Atlantic Fisheries Convention	London (UK)	1959
Convention Concerning Fishing in The Black Sea	Varna (Bulgaria)	1960
Agreement Concerning Co-operation in Marine Fishing	Warsaw (Poland)	1962
International Convention for the Conservation of Atlantic Tunas	Rio de Janeiro (FAO)	1966
Convention on the Conservation of Living Resources of the South-east Atlantic	Rome (FAO)	1969
Convention for the Conservation of Antarctic Seals	London (UK)	1972
Convention on Fishing and Conservation of the Living Resources in the Baltic Sea and Belt	Gdansk (Poland)	1973
Convention on Future Multilateral Co-operation in the Northwest Alantic Fisheries	Ottawa (Canada)	1978
Convention on Future Multilateral Co-operation in the North-East Atlantic Fisheries	London (UK)	1980
Convention for the Conservation of Salmon in the North Atlantic Ocean	Reykjavik (EEC)	1982

* International North Pacific Fisheries Commission

International conventions on pollution, shipping and mining

International Convention for the Prevention of the Pollution of the Sea by Oil	London (IMO)	1954
Convention on the Continental Shelf	Geneva (UN)	1958
Convention on the High Seas (Pipelines and dumping)	Geneva (UN)	1958
Convention for the International Council for the Exploration of the Sea (ICES)	Copenhagen (Denmark)	1964
International Convention on Civil Liability for Oil Pollution Damage	Brussels (IMO)	1969
International Convention Relating to Intervention on the High Seas in Cases of Oil Pollution Casualties	Brussels (IMO)	1969
Amendments to the International Convention for the Prevention of Pollution of the Sea by Oil, 1954, Concerning the Protection of the Great Barrier Reef	London (IMO)	1971
Convention Relating to Civil Liability in the Field of Maritime Carriage of Nuclear Material	Brussels (IMO)	1971
International Convention on the Establishment of an International Fund for Compensation for Oil Pollution	Brussels (IMO)	1971

Convention on the Prevention of Marine Pollution by Dumping of Wastes and Other Matter	Washington (USA)	1972
International Convention for the Prevention of Pollution from Ships	London (IMO)	1973
Protocol Relating to Intervention on the High Seas in Cases of Marine Pollution by Substances other than Oil	London (IMO)	1973
Convention on Civil Liability for Oil Pollution Damage Resulting from Exploration and Exploitation of Seabed Mineral Resources	London (UK)	1977
Protocol to the International Convention for the Prevention of Pollution from Ships	London (IMO)	1978
United Nations Convention on the Law of the Sea	Montego Bay (UN)	1982

Regional pollution conventions (including UNEP Ocean and Coastal Areas Programme)

Agreement for Co-operation in Dealing with Pollution of the North Sea by Oil	Bonn (FRG)	1969
Agreement for Co-operation in Dealing with the Pollution of the North Sea by Oil and Other Harmful Substances	Bonn (FRG)	1983
Convention on the Protection of the Marine Environment of the Baltic Sea Area	Helsinki (Finland)	1974
Convention for Prevention of Marine Pollution by Dumping from Ships and Aircraft (North Atlantic and Arctic Oceans)	Oslo (Norway)	1972
Convention on the Prevention of Marine Pollution from Land-based Sources (North Atlantic and Arctic Oceans)	Paris (France)	1974
Convention for the Protection of the Mediterranean Sea Against Pollution	Barcelona (Spain)	1976
Protocol for the Prevention of Pollution of the Mediterranean Sea by Dumping from Ships and Aircraft	Barcelona (Spain)	1976
Protocol Concerning the Co-operation in Combating Pollution of the Mediterranean Sea by Oil and Other Harmful Substances in Cases of Emergency	Barcelona (Spain)	1976
Agreement for the Protection of the Waters of Mediterranean Shores	Monaco (Monaco)	1976
Protocol for the Protection of the Mediterranean Sea Against Pollution from Land-based Sources	Athens (Spain)	1980
Protocol Concerning Mediterranean Specially Protected Areas	Geneva (Spain)	1982
Kuwait Regional Convention for Co-operation on the Protection of the Marine Environment from Pollution	Kuwait (Kuwait)	1978
Protocol Concerning Regional Co-operation in Combating Pollution by Oil and Other Harmful Substances in Cases of Emergency	Kuwait (Kuwait)	1978

Convention for Co-operation in the Protection and Development of the Marine and Coastal Environment of the West and Central African Region	Abidjan (Ivory Coast)	1981
Protocol Concerning Co-operation in Combating Pollution in Cases of Emergency	Abidjan (Ivory Coast)	1981
Convention for the Protection of the Marine Environment and Coastal Area of the South-east Pacific	Lima (PCSP)*	1981
Agreement on Regional Co-operation in Combating Pollution of the South-east Pacific by Oil and Other Harmful Substances in Cases of Emergency	Lima (PCSP)	1981
Supplementary Protocol to the Agreement on Regional Co-operation in Combating Oil Pollution of the South-east Pacific by Oil and Other Harmful Substances in Case of Emergency	Quito (PCSP)	1983
Protocol for the Protection of the South-east Pacific Against Pollution from Land-based Sources	Quito (PCSP)	1983
Regional Convention for the Protection of the Red Sea and Gulf of Aden Environment	Jiddah (Saudi Arabia)	1982
Protocol Concerning Regional Co-operation in Combating Pollution by Oil and Other Harmful Substances in Cases of Emergency	Jiddah (Saudi Arabia)	1982
Convention for the Protection and Development of the Marine Environment of the Wider Caribbean Region	Cartagena (Colombia)	1983
Protocol Concerning Co-operation in Combating Oil Spills in the Wider Caribbean Region	Cartagena (Colombia)	1983
Convention on the Protection, Management and Development of the Marine and Coastal Environment of the Eastern African Region	Nairobi (Kenya)	1985
Protocol Concerning Co-operation in Combating Marine Pollution in Cases of Emergency in the Eastern African Region	Nairobi (Kenya)	1985
Convention on the Protection of the Natural Resources and Environment of the South Pacific Region	Noumea (SPEC)†	1986
Protocol for the Prevention of Pollution of the South Pacific Region by Dumping	Noumea (SPEC)	1986
Protocol Concerning Co-operation in Combating Pollution Emergencies in the South Pacific Region	Noumea (SPEC)	1986

* Permanent Commission for the South Pacific
† South Pacific Bureau for Economic Co-operation

10 AGRICULTURE

Problems of both over-efficiency and mismanagement

The world's permanent agricultural cropland (Table 10.1) is around 9.0 million square kilometres, use of which is characterized either by over-efficiency in the major OECD countries or by a combination of under-efficiency, mismanagement and structural problems in most of the Third World. In both circumstances, natural resources for agriculture, land, water and genetic material have been (and are still being) depleted or degraded. While soil erosion and desertification, water pollution and loss of biodiversity may not significantly affect world global food production, at least in the short term, at the local level these effects are quite devastating. In aggregate, they influence the lives of millions of people as well as being associated with the wider climatic aspects of biogeochemical cycles.

Table 10.1 Global distribution of agricultural cropland

Region	Percentage of landmass cultivated		GDP share of agriculture	Cultivated area (per person—ha)
Europe	88.0	Except Eire	> 6%	0.42
Asia	83.0	India and China	< 30%	0.18
USSR	64.0			0.86
North America	51.0		> 6%	0.75
Africa	22.0	Sub-Saharan	< 30%	0.29
Latin America	11.0	Brazil and Mexico	10–19%	0.21
Australia	10.0		> 6%	1.00

Source: World Bank

Agriculture in the EC and OECD countries

OECD countries are virtually self-sufficient in dietary food production, consumption is high, population growth is low and there is a structural surplus of cereals, dairy products, fruit and sugar. Internal demand for agricultural products is unlikely to increase very much, subject to regional variations, and growth in the agricultural sector is most likely to come from trade with the Eastern bloc and with the richer developing countries.

The agricultural scene is characterized by maximum utilization of productive land, and in certain countries (in the UK, for example) there is a surplus of farmland which can be put to alternative uses, or more crucially, be rehabilitated from the effects on soil and water of chemically induced productivity. Thus the principal concern, particularly in Europe and the USA, is conservation of the existing land base in order to remedy or prevent future soil erosion and land degradation, to maintain water quality, protect groundwater and, in the process, aim at the least possible use of chemical fertilizers and pesticides. It is interesting to note that in the USA most crop residues are recycled for the purpose of soil maintenance, retention of moisture and protection against erosion. Use of nitrogenous fertilizers at approximately 2 tonnes per square kilometre of agricultural land is considerably lower than in most of Europe, and compares to nearly 8 tonnes per square kilometre in the UK and nearer 12 tonnes in Belgium, Denmark and West Germany. Although US agriculture is not so intense as in Europe, increases in production throughout the OECD countries has been achieved on an acreage that has remained more or less constant.

The general stability of land and the efficiency of agriculture are factors which are able to support considerably more attention to conservation in present and future agricultural policy. The encouragement of organic farming techniques to reduce reliance on chemicals, improving the quality and health aspects of food production, protecting water supplies and creating an environment which is more congenial for human and wildlife populations are principles which are in the mainstream of international and regional policy, if for no other reason than to ensure future productivity of a land base which agriculturally is fully committed.

The implementation of these principles, which in a formal sense are embodied in the work of OECD, Council of Europe and the relevant UN agencies, can be brought about only by some modification to the capital-intensive structure of European farming. This devolves upon the relationship and dependence of the farming community on its suppliers and the agro-food industry. Thus the role of the consumer may well be the key to the consolidation and improvement of European agriculture if the growing demand for organically produced food is sustained.

EC agricultural policy (CAP) is presently concerned with the internal and international competitiveness of European farmers, restoring markets and assisting rural development. The problem of food distribution is clearly greater than that of food production *per se*, and the universal problem of land and water conservation is such that few ecological sacrifices may now need to be made in the short-term interest.

Agriculture in the Third World
Sustainable economic growth and agricultural practices that do not deplete the land but anticipate the food needs of the growing world population are complementary and mutually supporting obverse sides of the same coin. The world has more than adequate agricultural resources to feed its entire population at least the minimum required to meet dietary demands, yet it is common knowledge that two-thirds of the world goes hungry, and many daily starve to death. Agriculturalists and economists predict that

enough food can be produced to feed 10 billion people. There is no reason to doubt that this quantity can be produced in the absence of an intervening major ecological disaster, but whether these 10 billion people will be more adequately fed than the 5 billion at present will depend upon a political determination to participate in problem solving.

Assuming all things to be otherwise equal, there are two related objectives to be met. The first is to organize resources in such a way as to adequately feed the present population and, meeting this objective, to apply the same principles and skills to feed the next 5 billion. It need hardly be said that the present and continuing constraints are more severely economic and cultural than agricultural.

Rural–urban migration is both cause and consequence of Third World rural decline. Cash and food crop imbalances created by government intervention and mismanagement of its agricultural base; water shortages; drought and other natural disasters; local hostilities; national debts; international trade barriers; badly planned economic aid programmes; poverty, unemployment and despair; lack of education and training; high morbidity and mortality resulting from malnutrition and poor sanitation – all these problems (and others) call for a new dimension of co-operation between politics, economics and trade, to tackle local and regional factors which prevent people from producing enough food to feed themselves.

There is both challenge and opportunity for economic growth in the organization of food production and distribution, use of water, land and forests in such a way that can support present and future generations. The populations of India, China, Latin America and tropical Africa, numbering a total of some 2.7 billion people and representing 54% of the world's population, rely upon agriculture for their basic livelihood. Cultivated area (Table 10.1) per person is an index of population density on cultivated land, which is highest in Asia, Latin America and Africa and lowest in Australia. The levels of agricultural intensity, in terms of the proportion of areas under cultivation, is not necessarily related to the abundance of food (comparing, for example, US output with Russian output), but is a function of agricultural efficiency and land planning.

Examining abundance, the daily calorie supply per capita in India, Sub-Saharan Africa and eastern Latin America of fewer than 2,300 calories, the minimum required for health, is substantially less than in Western societies, who consume more than 3,300 calories per capita, operating efficient agricultural systems.

Concerning relative densities (Table 10.1), large areas of the tropics are not farmed or grazed; the extensive flat, grassy plains (the Llanos) of Latin America are largely unexploited tracts, as are the savannah lands south of the Sahara, incompatible with extensive human habitation because of the presence of onchocerciasis (river blindness). The southern Sudan, one of the potentially richest farming regions of the world, is subject to continuous flooding by the headwaters of the White Nile.

There are two basic aspects of improved agricultural output in Latin America and Africa, both of which concern the transition from traditional farming to modern methods and the utilization of marginal lands. These two apparently simple concepts require considerable investment in organizational skills and equipment and adjustments in political attitudes to the balances between agriculture, industrialization and urbanization.

Turning again to the data, people in developing nations do not starve on account of land shortage, but for a variety of economic, structural and political reasons – low productivity, losses in storage from spoiling and infestation, transportation, distribution and competing energy demands. Added to these problems are urbanization contributing to rural poverty, an ill-managed balance between cash and food crop production, lack of political will and, in Africa, non-co-operation among political leaders seeking 'an African solution to an African problem'.

The nature of African soil adds to the general litany of woes. Only 7% of its arable land consists of rich alluvial soil. The remaining soils are highly leached latosols (the reddish soil of tropical forests), desert soils and sandy undifferentiated soils, all of which require chemical fertilizers, a variety of minerals, stable farming practices, irrigation and floodplain management to be agriculturally productive.

Arid and marginal lands

The productivity of arid and marginal lands are reduced by erosion, salination and flooding by irrigation, poor agricultural practices, obsolete land-tenure systems, overburdening by fertilizer and pesticides, loss of forest and unsettled populations. According to UNEP, one-third of the world's land area, equivalent to 37 million square kilometres, is subject to the risk of desertification, due principally to the factors enumerated above, and affecting in varying degrees each of the world's continental land masses. These types of land, together with the populations that they support are represented in Table 10.2. Urban populations living within these lands is presently 850 million people, predicted to rise to 1.2 billion by the year 2000. Desertification tends to affect those countries which are

Table 10.2 Arid and marginal lands

Land type	Area (million km²)	Rural population (millions)	Population at risk (millions)			
			'Severe'	%	'Moderate'	%
Rangeland	37.0	66	25	38.0	23	35.0
Rainfed cropland	5.7	260	90	35.0	82	30.0
Irrigated cropland	1.31	175	20	11.0	40	23.0
Present	43.41	501	135	27.0	145	30.0
Year 2000	43.41(?)	600	?	?	?	?

Source: UNEP

within or contiguous to the great desert regions, which, of course, include the Sudan and Sahelian belt of Sub-Saharan Africa, as well as the fragile soils of countries with Mediterranean-type climates (which include California).

In a sense, discussions concerning the environmental aspects of agriculture and future agricultural potential are somewhat more complex than those relating to the effects of pollution and conservation, even though they are interrelated topics.

Land-management priorities in developed countries are consolidation and conservation; in developing countries, basic restructuring of domestic food production, access to international markets for other produce and management of marginal and arid lands.

Food production in China

Official Chinese data indicated that some 30.0 million people died as a result of the 1959–61 famine, brought about by prolonged drought in some regions, extensive flooding in others and Mao Tse-tung's 'Great Leap Forward'. Agricultural reform brought farmers increased inputs, wider markets and higher prices, which led in 1984 to grain surpluses to an extent that much had to be destroyed due to inadequate storage and transport systems. Today, China manages to feed more than a fifth of the world's population by farming only one-fifteenth of the world's arable land. This extraordinary feat has not been accomplished without ecological error, particularly during the first grain drives: indiscriminate deforestation, desertification within the reclaimed northern grasslands, and worsened seasonal flooding of alluvial lowlands resulting from the filling in of lakes.

Water pollution from untreated urban wastes and industry present large problems for nearly 50% of the farmland which relies on irrigation for its productivity. Moreover, excessive use of chemical fertilizers has seriously undermined soil fertility; recycling of crop residues is inhibited by shortages of energy in rural areas which use most of the straw for fuel. China, like Europe, is faced with the challenge of reducing chemical inputs to its arable land, introducing programmes of organic recycling and increasing the efficiency of water use. Chinese agricultural development is hindered by energy shortages and the need to develop an adequate transport system.

Genetic diversity

The 'Green Revolution' increased agricultural productivity during the 1960s by significant margins in developing countries, with Latin America and Asia benefiting from new strains of wheat and rice. The further application of these principles in African countries could decrease the high and persistent levels of malnutrition that exist, but clearly, many social, economic and political changes need to be made along the way.

Interestingly enough, the world contains some 20,000 species of edible plant; 3,000 of these have been cultivated as food at one time or another;

approximately 100 species are presently cultivated and 20 or so roots, grains and legumes provide the world's basic diet. The three most important food plants in the world are rice, wheat and corn, for which rather more than a half of the world's croplands are used to grow them.

Food production in Western countries relies upon a very small proportion of the world's genetic stock, in the interests of economies of scale, but monocultures are more vulnerable to pests and disease than mixed cropping. Similarly, the 'Green Revolution' has narrowed the genetic base of food crops and, overall, the maintenance of modern agricultural practice relies upon broad-based chemical fertilizers and pesticides.

Rural development programmes

Rural development is the main focus of aid programmes from developed countries to the Third World, which include irrigation projects, produce marketing, pest control, rural infrastructure, forestry, water supply and sanitation, aquaculture, education, training and management. In general, in view of the growing adoption of the principles of sustainable development, these programmes can be considered under the heading of 'natural resources and the environment'.

The multi-disciplinary input to rural development is becoming increasingly evident. In recent years the involvement of conservation NGOs, particularly in respect of tropical rainforests, has grown along with the greater awareness of the wider ecological implications of intervention.

Post-war history is replete with examples of futile but well-meaning funded or financed enterprises which, while being potentially or otherwise profitable, have been technologically, sociologically and environmentally inept at best and disastrous at worst. These range from early groundnut schemes, to dams, road, rural resettlement, forestry, land reclamation and mega-projects combining all, which have been unsustainable, unmaintainable and unmanageable. In general, the larger the scheme, the more damaging its effect upon peoples and their environments. The extent of Third World debt and the present plight of many peoples can be directly attributed to inappropriate intervention.

The sociology of development has in fact a sounder theoretical and practical anthropological and environmental basis than these projects might suggest. In direct contrast to grandiose misconceptions, the experience of government and non-government agencies in small-scale schemes, in nutrition, sanitation, rural and urban projects, developed in collaboration with local communities, have brought immeasurable benefits over the years. The late Fritz Schumacher's 'Small is Beautiful' concept was essentially the basis for an intermediate or appropriate technological response to improving the rural resource base in the Third World and consolidating upon the traditional skills of the people. Reference can also be made to the Overseas Development Administration's 'Partners in Development' programmes and the wider environmental policy basis for assessing future projects. This approach may be observed generally in the funding of partnership programmes involving government, conservation and development groups and the UN agencies.

The general futility of capital-intensive rural development schemes is well documented but unfortunately are very attractive to many Third World governments and banks. More unfortunate is the unwillingness of organizations like the World Bank to eschew such schemes which, although bureaucratically are easier to administer, often do not address the structural aspects of development.

The EC relationship with developing countries, most significantly from 1992, is through international agreements (the Lomé Convention and the UNCTAD–GATT rounds), regional trade and development agreements with African, Latin American and Asian countries to improve their access to the single European market, and the provision of assistance to countries with food deficits. EC is a partner, through the European Development Fund set up in the Lomé Convention, in multilateral assistance programmes to the Third World in ODA and World Bank projects as well as being associated regionally with the work of UN agencies.

Reconciling environmental and commercial criteria in agriculture will be of the same order of complexity as with industry generally. Success in this area will have the benefit not only in terms of human welfare but in making a contribution to the restoration of a fundamental natural resource.

Integrated Pest Management (IPM)

The subject of IPM is again raised (see Chapter 4) on account of the devastating role that pests play in tropical agriculture and the effects of indiscriminate use of chemical pesticides on benign organisms, human health, wildlife and water quality. Since there are many conventions concerning international co-operation in the control of locusts, it would be interesting to identify some of the possibilities for reducing them.

The control of migrant locusts and armyworm, which are windborne, by means other than saturation spraying requires accurate mapping of insect disposition and dispersal and weather data to calculate possible trajectories. Thus reductions in the use of pesticides seem to be dependent upon the ability to pinpoint swarming areas and probable destinations.

While opportunities for biological attacks on the locust have not been noted, biological intervention to pests endemic to particular localities are better documented. The breeding of rice crop strains that are unpalatable to the brown plant hopper and the spraying of secretions that are sexually attractive to insects (pheromones) in 'lure and kill' strategies are selective, and do not sacrifice predatory and parasitic insects that are beneficial nor have influence beyond the target organism. Control of the tsetse fly and the spread of trypanosomiasis causing widespread sleeping sickness in human populations and disease in cattle and horses can be accomplished by 'lure and kill' based upon host odours.

Research and development in biotechnology will lead to either the reduction or the elimination of direct application of chemicals in pest control. Cost and management are the two common factors particularly where the largest problems are among the poorest peoples.

International programmes relating to agricultural development

GLOBAL 2000 Programme to improve agricultural yields of maize and sorghum in Sub-Saharan Africa (Ghana, Nigeria, Sudan, Tanzania)
Consultative Group on International Agricultural Research (CGIAR)
UNEP/FAO/UNESCO World Soils Policy
International Board for Plant Genetic Resources (IBPGR)
UNEP/UNESCO Microbiological Resource Centres (MIRCENs)
World Data Centre on Micro-Organisms (Tokyo)
Microbial Strains Data Network

International conventions concerning agriculture and plant protection

Convention	Place of adoption Depository state/organization	Date
International Plant Protection Convention	Rome (FAO)	1951
Convention for the Establishment of the European and Mediterranean Plant Protection Organization	Paris (France)	1951
Plant Protection Agreement for the South-East Asia and Pacific Region	Rome (FAO)	1956
Agreement Concerning Co-operation in the Quarantine of Plants and their Protection Against Pests and Diseases	Sofia (CMEA)*	1959
International Convention on the Protection of New Varieties of Plants	Paris (France)	1961
Convention on the African Migratory Locust	Kano (Nigeria)	1962
Agreement for the Establishment of a Commission for Controlling the Desert Locust in the Eastern Region of its Distribution Area in South-West Asia	Rome (FAO)	1963
Agreement for the Establishment of a Commission for Controlling the Desert Locust in the Near East	Rome (FAO)	1965
Phyto-Sanitary Convention for Africa	Kinshasa (OAU)†	1967
Agreement for the Establishment of a Commission for Controlling the Desert Locust in North-West Africa	Rome (FAO)	1970
Convention Concerning the Status of the Senegal River, and Convention Establishing the Senegal River Development Organization	Nouakchott (Senegal)	1972
Convention Establishing a Permanent Drought Control Committee for the Sahel	Quagadougou (Burkina Faso)	1973
Treaty for Amazonian Co-operation	Brasilia (Brazil)	1978
Convention Creating the Niger Basin Authority and Protocol Relating to the Development Fund of the Niger Basin	Faranah (Niger)	1980

* Council for Mutual Economic Assistance (Eastern bloc)
† Organization of African Unity

11 FORESTS AND WOODLANDS

Turning the planet into a desert

The world's forest cover, the Taigas and the Selvas, deciduous and thorn forests, regulate climate though carbon dioxide synthesis, protect soils from erosion, river and lake systems from silting and maintain the local natural balance. They are also the repository of the world's botanical and biological wealth. Properly managed, forests and woodlands are a sustainable source of trade and livelihood for many peoples.

Wood consumption is proceeding at a faster rate than wood production. This is true in Europe as in the rest of the world. Within EC member states, the total wood deficit, as of 1986, amounted to some 90 million cubic metres, with the most pronounced imbalances occurring in the UK, the Netherlands and Italy. Nevertheless, taken as a whole, OECD countries have rich forest resources, and while the total area of forest is ecologically stable it is faced with pollution problems, aged growing stock and loss from wildfires. In Africa, Asia and Latin America forests are disappearing as a result of unmanaged commercial logging, unnecessarily subsidized logging, tree felling to clear land for cattle ranching and the plight of many landless peoples seeking food and habitation.

Ecology of forests

From the time of prehistoric man, the forests provided the archetypal ecological system where human society and the natural environment co-existed in a harmonious relationship. The transition from the subsistence to the economic and recreational use of forests has, of course, been a feature of Western society. There remain, nevertheless, conflicts between timber and non-timber uses, but this conflict is nowhere more marked than in the transition that is now taking place in Third World countries, where forest depletion is fuelling poverty for their indigenous peoples rather than providing a basis of economic growth or subsistence.

Man's earliest impact upon flora and fauna is to be found in the degradation of Mediterranean vegetation into desert, traceable from about 6000 BC. Four thousand years later saw the beginnings of Chinese deforestation, to be followed by the loss of forests in Europe from agricultural demands from about the fifteenth century and the similar sequestration of North American forests from the mid-nineteenth century. Total loss of world forests since the eighteenth century is estimated to be in the order of 6.0 million square kilometres. Reafforestation has provided Western countries with more forest cover than they had a hundred years ago, even though this has consisted of planting single species of conifer to replace the more botanically diverse deciduous varieties. The world's woodlands presently cover a total area of approximately 4.3 billion ha (Table 11.1).

Table 11.1 The world's woodlands (million hectares)

Europe and Turkey	USSR	Asia	USA and Canada	Latin America	Oceania	Africa	Total
159.0	928.0	468.8	734.0	988.0	298.0	743.0	4,320.0
3.6	21.5	10.8	17.0	23.0	7.0	17.0	100.0

Source: EC

The ecological value of forests and woodlands are in the habitats which they provide and their facility to absorb carbon and nitrogen elements and to replenish oxygen. In the former respect, tropical forests absorb some 50% of carbons emitted into the atmosphere, including those from industrial sources.

It has been suggested that forests feed rainfall as well as absorbing it. Deforestation can lead therefore to higher temperatures and increase the drought propensity of regions dependent upon forests for their climatic stability as well as to soil erosion and desertification.

Temperate forests

Temperate forests in North America, China and Japan characterize a primeval richness of species not to be found in Northern Europe. They were protected from the ravages of the Ice Ages by north–south running mountain ranges, allowing plants to retreat from the ice and then to return. In northern Europe mountains and sea formed a barrier extending from Spain to Poland, and the flora had been gradually thinned over millions of years during the northerly movement of the land mass. This left northern Europe on the same latitude as Hudson Bay and the Great Lakes, where a similar paucity of plant species is to be found.

The height of the Ice Age left the British Isles bereft of trees, and the only species that returned were near the land connection. Subsequent separation from the mainland put an end to natural propagation of new plant species and the history of silviculture in the UK is characterized by the introduction of species from Europe, Asia and North America. There are some 600 species and varieties of trees in northern Europe, and all except 33 broadleaf and conifer species have been introduced over the centuries from other parts of the world.

Conifer plantations established for commercial purposes (paper and building materials) are subject to acid rain despoliation and are less supportive of natural flora and fauna than broadleaf woodlands and forests. Efforts to re-introduce and protect broadleaf woodlands is part of the European conservation strategy.

Depradations of European forests

In general, the European forestry stock is increasing (UNEP), even though areas of exploitable closed forests are being turned to other uses. The effects of acid rain on Scandinavian and northern European conifer forests are the more serious examples of air pollution. Sulphur dioxide emissions from Europe's major industrial centres, vehicle exhausts, acid rain, high levels of ozone, soil erosion caused by human alteration and use of land surfaces, past forestry practice and extremes of weather characterize the poor health of many wooded areas, particularly the Swiss spruce and pine forests. Swiss forests have traditionally acted as avalanche barriers and protected local inhabitants from falling rock and earth slides. Many Swiss forests are classified as being severely damaged or disintegrating.

Table 11.2 State and privately owned forests and woodlands in OECD countries

Ownership sector	UK	EC	USA	Canada	Switzerland
State	1,271	39,262	75,175	332,325	248
Private	959	14,522	225,525	110,775	1,067
Community held	–	–	–	–	2,808
Percentage state and community	57.0	73.0	25.0	75.0	74.0
Hectares (000s)	2,230	53,784	300,700	443,100	4,130

Sources: EC; OECD; Council of Europe

The greater proportion of forests in the principal OECD countries, as shown in Table 11.2, are in state or community ownership, except in the USA, where 75.0% are private. National and state ownership accounts for 72.0% of the world's forests and 63.0% of the forests in OECD countries. Community ownership is peculiar to Switzerland.

In the UK, privatization proceeds, and by the year 2000 the Forestry Commission will have sold off some 100,000 hectares of forest to the private sector. Between 1981 and 1989, in the UK, some 70,000 hectares were transferred to the private sector. According to OECD, the greater the level of private ownership, the more complications can be expected in timber production and conflicts in land use and the implementation of national environmental policies.

Tropical forests

It appears that between 1980 and 1989 nearly one half of the world's tropical forests had been cleared. This observation is based upon estimates from several sources which vary from the optimistic to the pessimistic, but demonstrate consistency in the general order of magnitude of forest depletion in the Third World. Table 11.3 illustrates the world picture.

Table 11.3 Forest cover and deforestation in Asia, Africa and Latin America

Region/country	Forest area (000 km²) 1980	1989	Annual rate of deforestation %	Net loss %
Asia				
Indonesia	1188.0	860.0	1.4	28.0
Papua NG	382.0	360.0	1.0	5.3
Burma	319.6	245.0	3.3	23.0
India	593.0	165.0	2.4	72.0
Malaysia	210.2	157.0	3.1	25.0
Thailand	157.9	74.0	8.4	54.0
Laos	136.4	68.8	1.5	49.3
Cambodia	126.5	67.0	0.75	47.0
Vietnam	103.1	60.0	5.8	42.0
Philippines	98.1	50.0	5.4	49.0
Total Asia	3315.0	2106.8	4.6	36.5
Africa				
Zaire	1776.0	1000.0	0.4	44.0
Congo	213.6	90.0	0.8	58.0
Gabon	205.9	200.0	0.3	2.9
Cameroon	164.0	160.0	1.2	2.4
Nigeria	149.1	28.0	10.0	81.3
Madagascar	134.7	24.0	8.3	71.0
Ivory Coast	98.8	16.0	15.6	80.0
Total Africa	2742.1	1518.0	5.6	44.6
Latin America				
Brazil	5183.0	3171.0	2.3	38.8
Peru	707.2	515.0	0.7	27.0
Bolivia	667.9	70.0	2.1	89.5
Colombia	518.0	180.0	2.3	65.4
Mexico	485.1	166.0	4.2	65.0
Venezuela	339.9	350.0	0.4	–
Ecuador	147.7	76.0	4.0	48.7
Total Latin America	8048.8	4528.0	5.4	43.7
Total	14,105.9	8152.8	5.3	42.2

Sources: FAO and IUCN data provided by IUCN

Given that these data are estimates and subject to continuing work and revision, it does not appear that there are significant differences in the rates of depletion between the regions of the world covered. It is clear, nevertheless, that some countries are in serious difficulties as a result of forest policies. The Amazon basin represents approximately 37% of the total world cover of tropical forest and, because of its size and global ecological significance, has become the focus of international concern for the fate of the forest system.

Tropical forests and their vegetation protect much less robust soils than those which characterize temperate climes, but they provide both the wealth and the subsistence of half the world's population. Tropical closed forests (those with a continuous canopy) cover a total area of some 1.4 billion hectares and contain nearly half the world's species of plants and animals. Brazil, Indonesia and Zaire account for nearly half this forest area.

Deforestation of tropical rainforests for timber, land clearance for food production, cash crops, cattle grazing and industrial development proceeds at a steadily increasing rate in many Latin America, African and Asian countries. Table 11.3 suggests that about 5.0% of closed broadleaf forest were destroyed annually in the period 1980–89, at which rate it would have taken only a few more decades to deplete the entire stock. Rates of depletion appear to have dropped quite significantly in the most recent years to less than 1.0%, but many countries are above this level, and some (Ivory Coast, Nigeria and the Philippines) demonstrate extraordinarily high depletion rates. Thus, several countries in Latin America, Africa and Asia could lose their closed forests in their entirety before the close of the century.

Nigeria is a net importer of forest products. In general, the forest economies of most developing countries, based as they are on raw timber exports rather than on processed forest product exports, permanently destroy the forest fabric and most of the possibilities for regeneration. The greatest demands upon tropical rainforests throughout the world come from 250 million landless people, using up some 5 million hectares a year for new and impermanent sources of fertile land.

Apart from the topographical changes that forest destruction brings about (soil erosion, flooding, atmospheric and climatic disturbances from the loss of biota and carbon releases from forest burning), the reduction in the diversity of plant, animal, insect species and birdlife as well as the threat to indigenous forest dwellers provides a compelling argument for turning around the forest economies of developing countries and introducing policies which encourage stable agricultural practices. At the moment, there are no international constraints upon countries that wish to deplete their forests, although certain countries (Brazil, Indonesia and the Philippines) are exercising some control on the export of unprocessed logs. The International Tropical Timber Organization (ITTO), with a staff of no less than six people, responsible for implementing the UNCTAD International Timber Trade Agreement of 1985, provides a forum for producer and consumer countries to develop national policies for timber production and use.

The demand for tropical timber in Europe, the USA and Japan is high in a trade that is valued at some $6.0 billion a year. It is estimated that exports account for about 25% of forest losses, a large proportion of which is destined for the Japanese plywood industry.

Tropical rainforests contain a greater variety of plant, wildlife and insect species than other terrestrial ecosystems, many of which are unique. The value of these rainforests lies in their biological and botanical relationship to climate and atmosphere as well as in their economic importance to the livelihood of indigenous inhabitants. They are subject to traditional 'slash and burn' agricultural practices ('shifting agriculture'), the encroachment of new highways, conversion to cattle ranching and clearance for commercial and industrial uses. It is difficult to imagine how 260 square kilometres of forest in Amazonia could be burnt daily.

Amazonia and its rainforests cover an area of 1.564 million square kilometres (Amazonas State), nearly 20% of Brazil, representing nearly one-third of the world's 'Selva'. The region has abundant yet unexploited mineral deposits, particularly iron ore, as well as an enviable botanical biodiversity which, through management rather than destruction, could provide a valuable model for sustained economic growth. Fruits, nuts, rubber, aromatic oils, timber, medicinal herbs and plants are considered to be far more profitable than traditional industrialization or cattle ranching.

Many forest areas are already offered a degree of protection as Biosphere Reserves (Unesco's 'Man and the Biosphere' Programme) or in national programmes conserving biotopes of special significance. Some initiatives towards sustainable development of forests include Cultural Survival, a Boston (Mass.) based charity, Body Shop in the UK, which has an aromatic oils and brazil nuts project, and the Ecological Trading Company in the UK, set up to buy teak and mahogany from Ecuador and Peru. Processing and transportation present the greatest problems.

Forest fires

Wildfires are one of the greatest causes of forest damage, creating losses of some 16,525 square kilometres in the early 1980s throughout the OECD region. Each year a substantial area of the Mediterranean is ravaged by fire, in Italy and France, leading to losses of up to 1,000 square kilometres. Deforestation, changes in the dominant vegetation and the appearance of combustible undergrowth, declining agriculture, large unmanaged forest areas and increases in tourism all add to the forests' vulnerability to fire. The principal source of wildfires is man's careless and criminal activities.

In Third World forests, naturally occurring fires associated with excessively dry climatic episodes, possibly volcanic activity and traditional slash-and-burn agricultural practices are common. Fires are now even more frequent and widespread as a result of deliberate intervention.

One positive aspect of wildfires and ecologically managed forest burning is an improvement in natural nutrient soil cycles and new starts for vegetation. However, the result of fires in the regions discussed is calamitous to both natural and human populations.

European programmes

Under the European Community Aid for Forestry, the European Agricultural Guidance and Guarantee Fund (EAGGF) provides funds for afforestation and reafforestation projects, the improvement of deteriorated woodlands and related work to enhance and protect European forestry. Commitments to current projects (1986) amounts to the equivalent of £230 million.

A large number of forestry management programmes are under way throughout Europe, organized in the UK by the Countryside Commission and at a regional level by the Council of Europe. These are intended to balance wildlife, landscape and recreation considerations with farming and commercial requirements for timber production, and quota systems for conserving native broadleaf species in existing or planned conifer plantations.

The Third World

Tropical rainforests are providing a new focus for Western society's armies of conservation and aid agencies, and indeed, although largely characterized by individual 'deals' between agencies and host countries, the protection of the forests can provide the perfect opportunity for cooperation between health, population, forestry and rural development agencies and for the multidisciplinary approach to social science and Third World growth at the heart of the Brundtland Report.

Deforestation is not taking place therefore in the absence of concerted interventions, many of which are led or influenced by conservation agencies from Europe and the USA, either in conflict or in consonance with their countries' economic interests. Many of the countries subject to forest depletion have their own specialized professionally staffed institutions, albeit underfunded, addressing local problems. IUCN recognizes the greater importance of working in collaboration with local experts than the attempts to instigate unilateral political pressure, which have often proved to be both unproductive and unwelcome.

In 1985, the International Year of the Forest, FAO prepared a Tropical Forests Action Programme identifying 56 countries seriously affected by deforestation and estimating that an expenditure commitment of some $5.3 billion for development, management and conservation should be made in the period 1987–91.

Convention relating to tropical forests

Convention	Place of adoption Depository state/organization	Date
International Tropical Timber Agreement	Geneva (UN)	1983

12 WORLD POPULATION AND URBANIZATION

Exodus from the land

A decline in the birth rates of Western societies since the 'baby boom' years of the 1950s and 1960s and the continuation of high birth rates in the Third World characterize the global demographic scene. Modern population growth has not been subject to natural laws but to social and medical advances led by the phenomenon of the transition of human organization from an agricultural to an industrial focus and from rural to urban habitation.

Quite obviously, the determinant of population growth at the global level is the difference between birth and death rates. Migration is added as a factor to calculate population growth in individual countries. Birth and death rates in equilibrium result in zero growth, a situation which has been more or less achieved in North America and Europe, with an annual growth of 0.4%. High birth rates, high infant mortality and low life expectancy characterize Third World demographic patterns, although a general decline in infant mortality is occurring. The Third World's contribution to annual world population growth is some 87 million people a year.

The rate of world population growth declined from 1.99% in 1960–65 to 1.72% in 1975–80. Annual growth may fall to 1.5% by the end of the century. In 1988 the world population numbered 5 billion. It is anticipated to be some 6.25 billion by the year 2000 and between 7.5 billion and 9.0 billion by 2025 (Table 12.1). Demographic predictions do not suggest an inexorable growth in human population but a stabilization of around 8–12 billion people some time towards the end of the next century.

Historically, the demographic transition in Western societies from high birth rates and high mortality to low birth rates and greater life expectancy was associated with improved living standards brought about by industrialization, public health and medical advances, the spread of education, the higher status accorded to women and access to birth control.

Third World population growth

Rapid population growth in the Third World over the past 40 years has taken place against a general background of low or negative economic progress, a deteriorating rural environment, urban squalor and depletion of natural resources. Future population growth in the Third World will

Table 12.1 World and regional population

Country/region	Population (000s)	Growth rate (%)	Projection 2025
Developed countries			
European Community	324.4	>1.0	
North America (USA and Canada)	272.0	>1.0	
Japan	122.4	>1.0	
South Africa	34.0	2.3	
Australasia	20.0	1.4	
Scandinavia	17.5	>1.0	
Rest of Europe			
Austria	7.6	0	
Switzerland	6.5	0.3	
Israel	4.4	3.2	
Total developed countries	808.8	>1.0	
USSR and Eastern Europe	425.0	>1.0	
Total	1,223.8	>1.0	1,450.0
USSR, Eastern Europe, etc.			
Eastern Europe	139.4	>1.0	
USSR	285.6	>1.0	
Total	425.0	>1.0	
China and the Third World			
China	1,084.0	1.2	1,441.0
Asia	1,070.0	2.1	1,926.0
Africa	565.0	2.2->3.0	1,103.0
Latin America	371.5	2.5	528.0
South-east Asia	370.0	1.5–3.0	552.5
Middle East	109.5	2.2–<3.0	175.0
Turkey	53.8	5.4	88.0
Remainder	142.0	–	923.0
Total Third World	3,765.8	2.0	6,736.0
World Population	5,000.0	1.74	8,500.0

Sources: UN and World Bank

continue in these conditions, with or in the absence of industrialization, intensified by urban drift unrelated to employment or development, poverty, hunger and hopelessness. Deforestation, migration of rural populations onto marginal lands as well as into the cities, declining production of cash and food crops and persistent inequities in the distribution of food and availability of fresh water will widen the gap between developed and developing countries even more than at present. Finally, a massive contribution to global atmospheric pollution will come from China, India and

South-east Asia. These problems are well rehearsed in both the Brandt (1980) and Brundtland (1987) Reports, the first presented in a socio-economic context and the latter adding an ecological dimension to the argument for greater economic co-operation between the rich exploitative countries of the North and the impoverished, mismanaged nations of the South.

It is predicted, nevertheless, that reductions in the rate of population growth will occur in those countries in the process of socio-economic development, where it can be expected that positive influences on human welfare will be reinforced by a desire for smaller families, specifically in growing urban centres, where medical and other services are more readily available. The effects of economic development upon family size would be most apparent where there is also declining morbidity and mortality resulting from the control of air-, water- and foodborne diseases (see McKeown, 1976). Family planning programmes have already made a significant contribution to lower birth rates in those countries where socio-economic conditions are favourable. In these circumstances, the World Bank and others have estimated that these programmes can account for between 10% and 40% in birth-rate reduction.

How Sub-Saharan Africa will fare is a most vexing question. Most of the countries in this region have lagged sadly behind in every development index, and the search by African leaders for 'an African solution to an African problem' has been met with signal failure. Population growth in Nigeria, for example, the most populous country in this region (110.0 million), is 3.4%, in Ghana (14.0 million) it is 3.5%, rates which are among the highest in the world. In addition, both have squandered their resources with inept and corrupt government. Anecdote has it that both Asia and Latin America are more proficient even in corruption than these countries. If ever there was a backhanded compliment, that must be one of the best.

The health of the African continent, for its own sake as well as for the rest of mankind, depends upon establishing free market economies that can adjust to the vagaries of world-commodity price fluctuations and encourage food production. The other priorities concern disease eradication and continuing rural development programmes.

Urbanization

The efficiency of agriculture, transportation and communication in Europe and the USA, the cessation of significant rural–urban migration and the transition from manufacturing to service economies have established a situation in which urban growth has stabilized. Future predictions point to a redefinition of a city's social and economic function from being focal points of industrial production to becoming administrative and cultural centres.

Urbanization in the Third World

In the Third World, rural–urban migration is undertaken with the expectation of escape from a derelict agricultural subsistence to employment in emerging manufacturing and service industries. The urban reality, however, is high unemployment or underemployment, uncontrolled housing, inadequate disposal of domestic wastes and sewage, atmospheric pollution from industrial effluents and vehicle emissions which is exacerbated by long periods of low rainfall and low winds.

Table 12.2 Estimated population growth of selected Third World cities (millions)

	1985/6	2000	Increase (%)
Bombay	8.2	17.5	113.0
Calcutta	9.2	16.0	74.0
Jakarta	7.8	16.0	105.0
Mexico City	17.0	31.0	82.0
Peking	9.2	21.0	128.0
Rio de Janeiro	10.2	19.0	86.0
Sao Paulo	16.0	26.0	62.0
Seoul	9.6	15.0	56.0
Shanghai	11.2	22.5	100.0
Total urban population	98.4	184.0	87.0

In 1950, some 17.0% of the Third World population lived in cities. By the year 2020, well over 50.0% is expected to be urban, a total of some 3.5 billion people. The anticipated growth of Third World cities (Table 12.2) will result more from rural–urban migration than from natural increase, although this will make some contribution. Unfortunately, for the most part, the growth of these cities will not be a function of level of urban development so much as rural decline. The additional pressures on public services is difficult to imagine and the possibilities for intervention are limited. Arresting urban migration by agricultural regeneration would offer some hope. There has been some recent evidence from Nigeria, for example, where Lagos has actually lost population by people returning to the land.

Looking on the bright side, the growth of cities is likely to have a negative impact on population growth since urban fertility rates tend to be lower. Moreover, health care, education and other amenities can more easily be provided to urban dwellers. However, the structural pressures of urbanization are going to be enormous, defining new levels of economic and environmental co-operation.

Populations and roles of indigenous peoples

Man as an endangered species is nowhere more apparent than in the plight of minorities who have unwittingly found themselves untitled or dispossessed inhabitants of lands sequestrated by modern societies for colonization and commercial exploitation. Pastoral and primitive societies are the relict exemplars of man living in harmony with nature. These societies have been degraded and destroyed by their exposure to Western commerce, culture and settlement, an assault which began four centuries ago and continues today in the industrial search for oil and minerals and in the missionaries' quests for souls. Examples which immediately spring to mind are the conquest of the Inca and Maya civilizations by the Conquistadores, the subjugation of the North American Indians in the period of European colonial expansion, the plight of the Australian Aboriginal peoples divorced from their pastoral roots and the continuing assaults on the forest peoples of Asia and Latin America. Modern anthropological and sociological efforts to preserve the remaining artefacts of these peoples and persuade modern society to respect and protect the lifestyles of dwindling minorities from short-term and dubious economic or political aims are to be seen in the context of a general ecological debate.

Large-scale projects in Amazonia have been funded by the EC ($600.0 million in 1982 for iron ore extraction) and more recently by the World Bank, coming under considerable pressure from US environment groups to take more detailed account of investment impact on environmental and social degradation. Proposals for the protection of indigenous populations include the establishment of national parks, such as in the Xingu region of Amazonia. On the other hand, national park rights have been denied in the Peruvian Manu National Park. Similarly, rights were withdrawn from the Australian Pitjantjatjara and Yakunjatjara Aborigines as long ago as 1958. In Australia, as well as other parts of the world, national parks lose their protected status when confronted with mineral exploration and the demands of tourism.

There are estimated to be some 200.0 million tribal peoples throughout the world. Table 12.3, although patchy, illustrates the territorial distribution of named tribes and the range of threats that they face to their continued existence.

Table 12.3

Country	Tribe	Population	Habitat threat
ARCTIC			
Alaska	Inuit		
Siberia	Eveni		Industrialization and pollution
AUSTRALASIA			
Papua New Guinea			
AUSTRALIA			
Northern Territory	Oenpelli		
	Pitjantjatjara		
	Yakunjatjara		
	Yirrkala		Social disintegration
Queensland	Arukun		
	Mapoon and		
	Weipa		

Table 12.3 continued

Country	Tribe	Population	Habitat threat
South Western	Kokatha Fringeddwellers Warmun Yangngora		Social disintegration
Aboriginal population		200,000–300,000	
LATIN AMERICA Brazil	Apinaye Atroari		Demarcation and settlement
Vaupes region		15,000	Land security
	Barasana	300	
	Kaingang Kreen Akrore Nambiquara Panare		Demarcation and settlement
Carajas	Parakana	227	
	Pataxo Ha-Ha-Hai		Cattle ranching
	Satere-Maue		Oil exploration
	Txukarramae		Demarcation and settlement
	Uru-eu-wau-wau		
	Waimiri-Atroari		Hydro and mining
	Yanomani	21,000 (1985)	Mining, etc.
	Xavante Xikrin		
Total number of tribes:	300	120,000	
Chile	Mapuche	1,000,000	Government repression
Columbia	Barasana Cuiva Maku Sikuani		Cattle ranching
Ecuador	Shuar Waorani		Oil exploration and missionaries
Panama	Guaymi	80,000	Land ownership disputes
Paraguay	Ache Ayoreo		Missionary zeal
Peru	Amuesha		Road building and colonization
Venezuela	Piaroa		Cattle ranching
MALAYSIA (Sarawak)	Penan		Deforestation
AFRICA Botswana	Kalahari Bushmen		
Central Africa	Pygmy tribes	150,000–200,000	
Nigeria	Fulani		Land erosion
Zaire	Efe		Deforestation
ASIA Indonesia Tibet	Nomadic tribes		
USA	American Indians		Social destabilization
World population of tribal peoples		200 million	

Amazonian Indians

It is estimated that the population of Amazonian Indians numbered some 6.0 million people, reduced to its present level by genocide and the depradations of the diseases of Western societies. The Yanomani Indians, a forest tribe whose population has been reduced from 20,000 in 1985 to between 5,000–9,000 today, inhabit the Serra Parima in the Roraima (930 million hectares) area of the Amazonian rainforest. The Yanomani represent a Stone Age culture of nomadic hunters, fishermen and subsistence farmers. The tribe is classified as an endangered people now threatened with extinction by venereal disease, tuberculosis, river blindness and a malaria epidemic introduced by some 45,000 gold prospectors. In addition, mining methods using high-pressure jets against the riverbeds have caused the beds to silt up; oil and mercury have poisoned the people and killed the fish.

Indian reserves are, in theory, protected under the Brazilian Constitution from commercial activity without the approval of the Brazilian Congress and the tribes themselves. Nevertheless, the gold prospectors remain, and it would appear that the Yanomani are doomed if their demands for a Yanomani 'park' are not met.

Australian Aborigines

Some 600,000 Aborigines died in the years following European settlement. Today in Queensland, infant mortality is three times higher than the rate for whites and the Australian legal system is attacked for its 'cruel assertion of power' resulting in the destruction of Aboriginal culture and unparalleled rates of criminal conviction (Survival International). The cultural and legal plight of Aboriginal peoples in dealing with oil and mineral exploration and land development is worsened by the destruction of their sacred sites, high incidence of disease, malnutrition and alchoholism and by their curiosity value to the tourist industry.

Canadian Eskimos

The traditional hunting society of Inuit Indians of the North-west Territories and Baffin Island in the Canadian Arctic are subject not only to long-range European effluents such as PCBs entering the food chain via walrus and polar bear, the likelihood of petroleum and uranium exploration and all-year shipping through the North-west Passage but also to international criticism for their reliance on abundant Arctic wildlife, particularly seal meat and skins for subsistence. The life of the Inuit Indian is threatened both by the commerce of industrialized nations and by conservation strategies.

Recognizing that sustainable development for hunting peoples should be based upon a reinforcement of traditional lifestyles, the EC Directive on seal pups and products (83/129/EEC) prohibiting commercial imports specifically excludes products resulting from traditional hunting by the Inuit.

The inhabited Arctic already is faced with the problem of how to dispose of industrial wastes and further encroachment upon the Inuit Indians could easily lead to the disappearance of another minority society.

Programmes

United Nations Working Group on Indigenous Populations
Reference can be made to the work of Survival International and the Anti-Slavery Society

International convention

Treaty for Amazonian Co-operation, 1978

13 NATURE CONSERVATION

Maintaining biodiversity and protecting habitats

Biodiversity

Maintaining the number and variety of living species (biological diversity, or biodiversity) is the principal objective of nature conservation. Habitat protection and pollution control are the predominant interactive strategies. Loss of biodiversity from deforestation in particular has led to scientific and ethical arguments for preserving species and natural ecosystems. However, there is little hard evidence of the relationship between species diversity and ecosystem function. Although the concepts are probably correct, the arguments are postulated on extremely limited data.

The relationship of two key hypotheses will be subject to a major study programme organized by SCOPE during the 1990s. These state that there is considerable redundancy among species and species function; certain dominant and keystone species control both the structure and function of ecosystems. These relationships will be studied as well as that between ecosystem function and environmental conditions in the high-priority tropical rainforest and Mediterranean systems.

For the most part, the destruction of flora and fauna is a consequence rather than an intention of human activities. The factor determining conservation and preservation is whether flora and fauna matter, and whether they matter as much as short-term economic gain, or are even worth considering.

Even without data, in environmental and ecological contexts, it is quite clear that these short-term economic gains at the expense of nature cannot be sustained. This applies equally to a range of anti-economic and anti-social practices such as taking defensive positions on power station emissions, fishing with explosive devices, whaling, big-game poaching, inept subsidization of agriculture, silviculture and industry, waste dumping, litter, stealing birds' eggs, oil and chemical discharges into the oceans, sloppy accounting and so forth. Careless, persistent and inconsiderate behaviour poses a greater threat to biodiversity than accidental pollution.

Biological wealth suffers inasmuch as it is difficult to attribute economic value in the same way as to material or cultural wealth. Yet the biological wealth of forests and oceans is immeasurable. They have immense economic value in that their lifecycles and food chains provide the very foundations of our own existence.

Biodiversity is regarded as being crucial to the understanding of ecology for the reason that most of the species in the universe are either unrecorded or undiscovered and have potential importance to medicine, food and to the lifecycle. Estimates of the number of living species as organisms, excluding 250,000 plants and other vegetation, vary from between 5 million to 30 million. Identified and named species number some 1.4 million.

A clearer understanding of ecological relationships will therefore depend upon the expenditure of considerable scientific effort long into the future. The development of a biogenetic or taxonomic table from 250,000 species of wild plant species is itself an awesome task, made somewhat less so by their destruction. Darwinian observations and subsequent biological, zoological, medical and sociological discoveries demonstrate that living species play key roles in maintaining and regenerating natural vegetation, providing the habitats for their own survival, as well as serving mankind.

Industrialization, agricultural practices and urbanization are effectively reducing the number and variety of living species. In recent history and up to the present, the utilization of natural resources to meet human needs has been conducted in a manner which does not permit their regeneration. Moreover, the superiority of synthetic solutions promoted by science and medicine have relegated traditionally sustainable practices to a wholly inferior status. Ironically, researchers and scientists of every discipline have come to acknowledge that the chemicals derived from hydrocarbons can provide only a technical fix, and that the potential value of natural herbs and oils is immeasurable by comparison (Table 13.1). Needless to say, a sustainable future will depend on a more equitable balance between science and the natural world.

Other forest species are believed to have the potential for providing natural substances for the treatment of cancer, Aids and other diseases. It is entirely reasonable to speculate that nature can provide the antidote to most human conditions.

Table 13.1 Medicines derived from natural sources

Traditional and indigenous herbal remedies
Aspirin from white willowbark and fragrant meadowsweet compounds
Contraceptive pills from wild Mexican yams (diosgenin)
Heart stimulants (digoxin and digitoxin) from foxglove species
Malarial drugs (quinine) from Cinchona tree bark
Cancer-treating agents (vincristine and vindblastine) from the Madagascan rosy periwinkle

Conservation areas

In the OECD countries, national parks and nature reserves are estimated to cover an average of about 4.0% of the total land area. On a global scale, the designation of large tracts of parkland, forest, mountains, swamps and grasslands is growing quite rapidly for habitat protection and human recreation and for the study of the interface between man and the environment. National parks, country parks and nature reserves for conservation and recreation are managed by local authorities, local naturalists trusts, statutory agencies and the private sector (e.g. The National Trust in the UK) for public enjoyment and recreation.

Internationally, the numbers and land coverage of conservation areas of ecological and cultural significance have grown considerably for the preservation of biotopes such as forests, woodlands, parklands, deserts, grasslands, wetlands, coastal and island habitats. Biotopes are classified under international conventions and programmes as 'Biosphere Reserves', 'World Heritage Sites', 'Wetlands of International Importance as Wildfowl Habitats' (Unesco) and 'Biogenetic Reserves' (Council of Europe) and 'Special Protection Areas' (EC). The areas are distributed throughout Africa, the Americas, the Antarctic and Arctic polar regions, Asia, Australasia, Europe, the Middle East and the Mediterranean, representing the spectrum of global ecology.

Recreation and tourism

1990 is the EC European Year of Tourism, with the aim of increasing general awareness of the impact of tourism on the environment, to encourage tourist destinations away from concentrated areas and to promote low-season holidays. The annual number of world tourists increased from 50 million in 1950 to 400 million in 1988 and is predicted to grow to some 600 million by the year 2000.

Recent years have witnessed the growth of nature tours in the USA and 'green' tourism in Europe. Another term is 'eco-tourism', used to describe visits to the last bastions of underpopulated and uncluttered regions of anthropological, scenic and wildlife interest.

Tourist spending already brings significant income to East African safari areas, game reserves and national parks, to the Galapagos Islands and other sites throughout the world. On the other hand, tourists pollute, and their presence in numbers is frequently incompatible with the conservation of natural areas and preservation of the flora and fauna.

The Great Barrier Reef Marine Park is a prime example of zoning management, taking into account threats from international shipping movements and accommodating tourism and scientific research. The Reef is the most diverse ecosystem known. It has 15,000 fish species, 400 coral types, 4,000 molluscs, 242 bird species, whales, dolphins and dugong.

In the Third World, tourism related to conservation provides an opportunity to protect endangered species from hunting or poaching and preserve flora by giving them an economic value to the host country. Conflicts arise where nature conservation interferes with the livelihoods of pastoralist societies such as the Masai, who are denied access to grazing lands. The integration of indigenous peoples into the income-generating aspects of park management is being given considerable attention.

Environmental education

The UN Environment Programme (UNEP), in conjunction with Unesco, is responsible for the 'International Environmental Education Programme'. Environmental education is held to be the key to effective national and international programmes of nature conservation and pollution control. There is no shortage of initiative in this area. There is much popular and scientific material on ecology and wildlife produced by commercial publishing houses as well as from the output of wildlife and naturalists' societies and lobby organizations.

Environmental education is part of primary and secondary school curricula and there is wide public interest, reinforced by the media, in government, international and industrial initiatives taken in response to scientific discoveries. Moreover, environmental responsibility, extending from the individual to industrial corporations, is recognized to be a fundamental factor in reducing pollution, maintaining food production, protecting the atmosphere and ensuring sustainable economic growth.

Several multinational companies have established a board responsibility for dealing with environmental policy, particularly oil and petrochemicals. Commitment to programme development appears to be well established at all management levels. However, at the national level, most noticeably in West Germany, the UK and the USA, environmental awareness is most frequently observed among middle-management environmental professionals.

Principal conservation societies

The role of conservation societies in the UK is educational, increasing awareness and stimulating an active public interest in the preservation of local flora and fauna, through schools programmes and general promotional activities. Some societies are more politically directed towards challenging planning applications, in the case of CPRE, or towards speeding up the legislation process by gathering scientific and other evidence of pollution and environmentally destructive activities and initiating prosecutions under the Protection of Wildlife Act (Friends of the Earth, Greenpeace, RSPB, etc.) (Table 13.2).

Conservation societies have charitable status, relying primarily on membership subscriptions, legacies and bequests, donations from industry and government departments, and fund raising to cover their administrative and programme costs.

Conservation in the USSR

Reference has already been made to Eastern Europe and to its adherence to environmental conventions. Many land areas in these countries have been set aside for their ecological significance as Biosphere Reserves or World

Table 13.2 Membership of conservation societies and environmental lobby groups in the UK

Society/lobby group	Members	Country of origin
Friends of the Earth	190,000	USA
Greenpeace	327,000	Canada
The National Trust	1,800,000	UK
Royal Society for the Protection of Birds	680,000	UK
Worldwide Fund for Nature	220,000	UK
Other UK including members of local wildlife and naturalists' trusts, etc.	1,780,000	
Estimated membership	5,000,000	

Table 13.3 Conservation bodies in the USSR

Name of organization	Aims and objectives
Social-Ecological Union (Russian Republic)	Political pressure group
Ecological Union	Pollution controls and monitoring
Ecological Foundation	Toxic waste controls and alternative energy
Ecological Society of the Soviet Union	
All-Union Movement of Greens	

Heritage Sites. Some USSR conservation organizations are listed in Table 13.3, and it will be interesting to follow their future development.

Planning applications and pressure groups

Nature conservation at the national level is closely associated with agriculture and town and country planning policies. In addition to campaigns organized by established conservation societies, there are many examples, particularly in the UK and the USA, of the *ad hoc* formation of local groups to challenge industrial developments in their areas. More legal powers are being placed at the disposal of these groups by the designation of large tracts as Areas of Outstanding Natural Beauty (AONBs), upon which developments must not only be sympathetic to the local environment but also in the national interest. The political erosion of AONBs does require constant vigilance on the part of local inhabitants.

The National Trust is the largest private landowner and conservation society in the UK whose objectives are to hold and ensure its properties as inalienable from the encroachment of urbanization and development. In the UK it is generally easier for the public and conservation groups to intervene in development proposals and planning procedures. In the USA, where planning is the responsibility of several non-unified agencies, regulatory hearings are the only avenues open to the general public for expressing views on the management of the environment.

International conventions relating to nature conservation and species protection (see also Chapter 9)

Convention	Place of adoption Depository state/organization	Date
International		
International Convention for the Protection of Birds	Paris (France)	1950
Convention on Wetlands of International Importance Especially as Waterfowl Habitat (also, 1982 Protocol)	Ramsar (Unesco)	1971
Convention Concerning the Protection of the World Cultural and Natural Heritage (World Heritage sites)	Paris (Unesco)	1972
Convention on International Trade in Endangered Species of Wild Flora and Fauna (CITES Convention)	Washington (Switzerland)	1973
Convention on the Conservation of Migratory Species of Wild Animals	Bonn (FRG)	1979
Protocol to Amend the RAMSAR Convention	Paris (Unesco)	1982
Europe		
European Convention for the Protection of Animals During International Transport	Paris (COE)*	1968
Benelux Convention on the Hunting and Protection of Birds	Brussels (BEU)†	1970
Convention on the Protection of the Environment between Denmark, Finland, Norway and Sweden	Stockholm (Sweden)	1974
Convention on the Conservation of European Wildlife and Natural Habitats	Berne (COE)	1979
Benelux Convention on Nature Conservation and Landscape Protection	Brussels (BEU)	1982
Regional		
Convention on Nature Protection and Wildlife Preservation in the Western Hemisphere	Washington (OAS)‡	1940
Polar regions		
Convention for the Protection of Antarctic Seals	London (UK)	1972
Convention on the Conservation of Antarctic Living Resources	Canberra (Australia)	1980
Latin America and Asia		
Convention on the Conservation of Nature in the South Pacific	Apia (Samoa)	1976
Convention for the Conservation and Management of the Vicuna	Lima (Peru)	1979
ASEAN Agreement on the Conservation of Nature and Natural Resources	Kuala Lumpur (ASEAN)	1985
Africa		
Convention Relative to the Preservation of Fauna and Flora in their Natural State (Establishing nationals parks in Africa)	London (UK)	1933
African Convention on the Conservation of Nature and Natural Resources	Algiers (OAU)§	1968
Protocol Concerning Protected Areas and Wild Fauna and Flora in the Eastern African Region	Nairobi (Kenya)	1985

* Council of Europe
† Benelux Economic Union
‡ Organization of American States
§ Organization of African Unity

14 MONITORING AND COSTS

Surveillance systems and 'debt for nature'

Monitoring the environment

Policymakers need good data. Certain environmental propositions, related, for example, to global warming, biodiversity and other cause and effect phenomena, although plausible and probably highly desirable to tackle, are not always supported by the kind of data that can assist rational management decisions or national programmes or lead to international agreements. It is not prudent to rely on secondary or tertiary sources or alarmism. It we do not know what we are doing to the local or global ecology on the basis of present data, how can sensible changes be made? Nevertheless, there remains a large agenda of items where immediate action needs to be taken at both national and international levels.

Effective environmental management will rely upon the ability of control and monitoring agencies to interpret immense volumes of data. Landsat, Seasat and other satellites add to and assist the research and observations of a vast array of scientific institutions engaged in studying astrological, atmospheric, geological, biospheric, oceanic and terrestrial phenomena (see Appendix 2). Techniques in these areas include remote sensing, image processing and georeferencing, related to climatic change and ozone depletion. Micromonitoring the effects of individual substances on organisms, the modelling of ecological cause and effect, toxicological and taxonomic recording involve a huge computation requirement, not to mention manpower and training in hardware and software usage.

Having said this, the environmental issues to be tackled in the coming decade are more or less as outlined in this book. Computational requirements are required primarily for toxicology and taxonomy, for monitoring environmental 'behaviour' and for information sharing. Data development in all the areas listed here may well accelerate the policymaking process, meeting the needs of planners for more information and evidence of ecological perturbation.

Monitoring and evaluation are key strategic elements of the UN, EC, OECD and national administrations. We may yet see a resurgence of R&D expenditures, but the information aspects are already showing constructive developments in the relationship between industry and the environment at international and local levels.

IBM has donated £3.6 million ($6.5 million) of hardware and software to the UNEP Global Research Information Database (GRID), the database component of the Global Environment Monitoring System (GEMS), which is a repository of satellite data, aerial and ground surveys for the environmental work of UN organizations (WHO, WMO, FAO, etc.). GRID has monitoring centres in fifteen African countries and related training activities, with planned developments in South-east Asia and the Arctic region.

The technological core of much environmental monitoring is geographic information systems (GIS), which provides on-screen map displays of data generated from many sources, including remote-sensing satellites, on vegetation, soil types, wildlife populations, pollutants and pollution levels, atmospheric variables, natural resources and socio-economic factors. A major GIS undertaking is the Global Forest Mapping Project, under way at the World Conservation Monitoring Centre (WCMC) at Cambridge, examining actual versus potential forest cover. Other forest projects in the GRID programme include the Thailand deforestation survey.

WCMC is also in the process of setting up one of Europe's largest relational database systems, a five-year project which will maintain worldwide information on threatened species and other conservation data which will be available to governments, development agencies and industry. Hardware and software has been provided by IBM, DEC and Dell Computers. The system will operate over an Ethernet local area network and will be based upon an open hardware and software Unix system.

The UNEP Earthwatch programme includes the International Register of Potentially Toxic Chemicals (IRPTC), the Global Environment Monitoring System (GEMS) as well as the GRID database and INFOTERRA (Table 14.1).

Costs of environmental protection

The cost of pollution is greater than that of environmental cleanliness; conservation costs less than waste and destruction. These assertions are becoming easier to demonstrate even in the short term, with the availability of energy-efficient technology, growing consumer awareness, the tendency towards more stringent statutory controls and better data analysis.

The 'Polluter Pays Principle' (PPP), first aired by OECD in 1972 and now embodied in the Single European Act, is quite simple in application. Under this principle, industry should not be subsidized for its pollution-control costs. These costs should be met by the polluter who would generally pass them on to the consumer. PPP is intended to avoid distorting competitiveness in international trade.

PPP really means that the consumer pays. The operation of the market economy might suggest, however, that, given growth in the anti-pollution sector and developments in environmental accounting to take account of such things as health and amenity restoration, the consumer may end up

Table 14.1 Environmental data

GEMS: Climate, trans-boundary pollution, natural resources, oceans and the health consequences of pollution

    The monitoring of the world's glaciers is conducted through 750 glacier stations in 21 countries, run by WMO (Background Air Pollution Monitoring Network – BAPMoN), UNESCO and the Swiss Institute of Technology

    WMO/BAPMoN monitors air pollution in 95 countries

    The GEMS system co-ordinates data from FAO and WHO food and health-related monitoring activities also using an extensive network of country-based field stations

    Natural resource monitoring includes extensive work on tropical forests and desertification

INFOTERRA: Centralizes information from national focal points to produce a reference directory to the 6,000 or so environmental institutions and agencies as well as a glossary of related projects

ICSU World Data Centre (WDC)

Committee on Data for Science & Technology (CODATA)

National Oceanographic Database (UK)

NERC British Oceanographic Data Centre (BODC)

EC European Ocean Analysis Data Network (proposed)

ITE Environmental Information Centre (NERC)

Council of Europe, European Information Centre for Nature Conservation

EC, CORINE

See Appendix 2 for comprehensive database details

actually paying less for energy and for environmentally friendly goods and services.

Several European countries are presently managing to achieve a negative growth rate in total energy consumption and to bring down the quantity of effluents which they produce in a larger proportion. The point is made here because mature industrial societies are flexible enough to conserve and improve the environment without economic sacrifice, and that penalties and incentives offer many possibilities for flexible environmental policy.

The political and economic considerations of pollution control are thus less to do with costs to the producer than considerations of industrial competitiveness. Differences in production costs between goods produced under demanding pollution controls and those produced free of such controls can vary by as much as 5–20% or more. With these differentials operating, small companies, or even Third World producers, can find that meeting international standards of national statutory requirements puts them at a severe competitive disadvantage.

Considering the costs of environmental protection within the context of industrial competition leads to an argument for imposing uniform standards, according to activity, based upon a no-pollution general objective. An absence of uniform standards, i.e. varying emission standards between countries and regions, can create capital and investment movements towards less-regulated areas, or 'pollution havens', in similar fashion to locating industry where labour costs are less.

Standards based upon a no-pollution long-term general aim have several economic and practical advantages. The main one would be that industry would not be faced with the costs of making successive conversions to plant and equipment to meet progressively stringent unscheduled legislation. Long-term goals suggest progressive timetables, based upon a combination of regulations and taxation, which would vary according to the toxicity or hazard of substances and processes.

The political and economic aims of Western governments and industry are to avoid the environment becoming a net cost. The simple strategy of doing nothing until 'scientifically proven' does tend to operate, despite the fact that energy efficiency, which is the mainspring of sustainable economic growth, brings financial and environmental benefits. Nevertheless, scientific theory unsupported by hard evidence (e.g. global warming) can, if generally accepted in an alarmist fashion, deflect attention from the main issues facing industry, which should be the protection or clean-up of the locations where they operate.

Penalties on pollution

A range of financial penalties are imposed in a number of European countries but are generally considered to be too low to achieve significant reductions in pollution levels. For example:

West Germany:	effluent charges on waste water
The Netherlands:	,,
Sweden:	returnable deposits on car bodies
Norway:	,,
Switzerland:	extra handling fees for noisy aircraft
France:	effluent charges on waste water

The regulation and control of large industrial enterprises is relatively straightforward. New directions, mainly via taxation, are being explored to curb pollution output from smaller businesses and individuals. These may be based upon charges per unit of pollutant produced, and consideration of these issues is being given, for example, in West Germany (differential motor taxes on levels of exhaust emissions), the US Environmental Protection Agency and the European Commission Environment Directorate (carbon tax to reduce fossil fuel dependency).

Costs and benefits: income accounting

The adoption of accounting systems to quantify public health effects in national audit, particularly to balance the costs of environmental management and clean-up against the savings to national economies from lower morbidity, might encourage the wider application of tax incentives to industry. National audit systems to reflect the socio-economic and health costs and other consequences of pollution are highly desirable, but national data are hard to come by and criteria difficult to formulate. In the UK, HM Treasury directs that environmental costs should be considered in determining policy in social programmes, but the mechanisms for quantification are not well established.

Assigning values to the environment

It is argued that if economic values are not ascribed to natural resources, to 'intangibles' which determine the quality of life (in other words, to translate ethical values into monetary worth), then conservation will not be given its true weight in political and economic policy. The impending *Exxon Valdez* litigation will raise some very interesting problems in calculating a price for non-commercial flora and fauna. An initial estimate of Exxon's efforts on behalf of the seal population of Prince William Sound suggest that the cost per seal saved was some $40,000.

Cost-benefit principles are applied by governments and industry in the development of health, safety and pollution strategies, but on a very narrow base of calculation. Investment decisions take prevailing market sentiment and commercial requirements for profitability into account, in conscious acceptance of, let us say, ecological deterioration without attempts at cost quantification. The philosophy is that omelettes cannot be made without breaking eggs; the counter-argument is that we are killing the chickens.

The theoretically optimum environmental solution to industrial effluents is to eliminate them. But again, in theory there should be levels of pollution and effluence which can rely upon nature's capacity for absorption and self-cleansing. It might appear that this level has already been overtaken in some coastal areas. Without a re-rehearsal of the levels of gaseous emissions from industrial activities generally, this is probably true in many Third World countries, exacerbated by the inability to manage social and economic development.

Waste, effluent, accidents and disease are inevitable consequences of human behaviour as well as being natural ecological phenomena. Decisions regarding the control of socially derived undesirable events are determined by the incidence that society is prepared to accept. The growing concepts of international neighbourliness, however, brought about by the knock-on effects of pollution, adds considerable impetus to the need for developing internationally acceptable systems of environmental accounting, particularly since not only do different countries pollute at different levels but the degree to which they are subject to pollution from neighbouring countries also varies (i.e. acid rain, oil spills, chemical wastes in river systems, etc.).

Calculating pollution costs against the benefits to be derived from clean-up programmes is a complex business. The main factors which might be considered or taken into account are:

1. Extent of damage caused by a pollutant source:
   — Domestic damage from local or 'imported' pollutants
   — Damage to foreign neighbours from 'exported' pollutants
   — Penalty costs (direct and indirect)
2. Costs of control programmes:
   — Research and development
   — Equipment
   — Professional staff
   — Contingency planning
   — Risk analysis
   — Market effects and competitiveness
3. Benefits:
   — Improved public health
   — Waste control and recycling
   — Avoidance of clean-up costs and penalties
   — Market effects

Taxation strategies

Taxation strategies which discriminate in favour of energy-efficient, low-waste and low-pollution technologies and practices are considered to have the potential of raising revenue and encouraging sustainable growth. There appears to be some bias within the European Commission towards the development of environmental taxation strategies, including the imposition of high excise duties on products harmful to health or to the environment. Taxation as an instrument of national environmental policy may be restricted in the internal market except in the event of harmonization of indirect taxation within the EC.

The environment and Third World economic development

It has been pointed out that sharing Western industrial technology with Third World countries may increase Third World income but would not solve the problem of income distribution, or significantly affect unemployment, in view of the capital-intensive nature of Western technology. Nevertheless, industrial collaboration with these countries could provide the necessary capital for improving the agricultural base and food production, as well as alleviating the burden of Third World debt if some basic restructuring were allowed to occur (i.e. less government intervention).

The enormity of the economic restructuring that would be required to achieve sustainable economic growth is best understood in the traditional relationship between North and South, where the North has been happy to avail itself of plentiful (though presently declining) supplies of cheap raw materials and the South has not addressed itself to managing the natural assets upon which the livelihoods of its populations depend.

Aid transfers from the developed to Third World countries are running at about $35 billion a year. Debt transfers in the opposite direction amount to some $43 billion (World Bank). Developments in aid and debt policies are urgently required, but most importantly, Third World economic growth can only be brought about by realistic terms of trade, technological co-operation and less local government intervention in the operation of the market. Third World development issues differ in scope and nature according to economic potential, with each country on the continents of Africa, Asia and Latin America posing problems associated either with growing industrialization and wealth or declining agriculture and poverty. The application of conservation principles to industrial and agricultural planning in the Third World, as well as in addressing critical public health matters, has compelling economic arguments, but whether these can be applied in voluntary agreements remains to be seen.

Table 14.2 Estimated costs of sectoral losses versus restoration (from UNEP)

	Annual losses in productivity ($billion annually)	Estimated investment requirement ($billion annually)
Desertification	25–30	4–6
Topsoil protection	?	10
Reafforestation	?	4
Population programmes	?	16
Energy efficiency	?	18
Renewable energy	?	10
Debt remission	43	15
Suggested annual costs	(1990–2000)	79

Sources: UNEP; WorldWatch Institute

Without looking too deeply into how the costs in Table 14.2 have been calculated, let us assume that they are within a plausible order of magnitude. Except for desertification and debt remission, data on present capital losses are not available, nor have the returns on the indicated levels of investment been presented. Nevertheless, these figures do suggest that for relatively modest amounts of investment, both human and material resources could be made more productive.

Debt for equity/debt for nature

The history of 'debt for nature' is but three years old, based upon 'debt for equity', bringing creditor institutions and would-be investors together and relieving the creditor of the debt burden at a suitably discounted rate.

Debt for equity is a scheme in which an investor wishing to acquire assets in a debtor country may buy part of that country's debt, which is traded at a discount in the secondary markets. He then converts his newly purchased dollar assets into local currency which is then used to make a direct investment in fixed assets, equities or development projects. Several debt for equity arrangements were made from about 1985, notably with Mexico, Brazil, Chile and the Philippines.

These arrangements can be inflationary (where is the local currency to come from unless printed?). The question of sovereignty over the debt arises when the debtor country has no equity interest in the enterprise. They can be a cheap source of finance for projects which may have taken place in any case.

The release of Third World countries from their hard currency debts to finance local development projects has enabled several conservation schemes to be established as 'debt for nature'. These include a Worldwide Fund for Nature (WWF) initiative in respect of reafforestation programmes in Latin America and the Faith Foundation project to regenerate the black rhino population in Tanzania.

While debt liquidation is a much wider issue than nature conservation, nature-conservation programmes in relation to debt transfers bring economic value to nature's resources while making some contribution to Third World development. Debt for development has both potential and drawbacks, but basically, the opportunities for debt remission in this way are large enough only to make a marginal impact on a country's total debt, and the investor is subject to local politics.

The World Bank (IBRD), technology transfer and other assistance to the Third World

The aims and direction of aid and loans to the Third World are traditionally fraught, as fraught indeed as the grandiose plans for 'development' made by newly independent nations without regard for local ecological feasibility and doomed to failure. The World Bank (The International Bank for Reconstruction and Development) offers itself as a target for environmentalists, such as the US Environmental Defense Fund (EDF), urging the Bank to adopt principles of sustainable development in multilateral aid projects. Currently under attack by EDF is a $167.0 million project in the Rondonia province of north-west Brazil. The Bank had previously undermanaged a series of loans worth $434.0 million to the Polonoreste project from 1981 to 1985, a resettlement programme which led to land and rainforest depletion and the disruption of indigenous tribes.

The object of the Bank's loans to Brazil is to profitably finance sustainable development. However, the very size of the projects that are being funded, given the need for local management and control, defeat the environmental aims, although they may satisfy the lending institutions.

Environmental investment funds

A growing number of unit trusts are offering investment opportunities to those seeking ethical or social criteria in selecting their portfolios. In the USA (mutual funds) and the UK a number of trusts screen companies according 'green' criteria: sustaining use of natural resources and energy, waste consciousness, demonstrable management commitment to environmental principles, etc.

The Merlin Ecology Fund (UK), launched in 1988, excludes industries which it considers to be polluting, oil companies in particular. New Alternatives (USA), launched in 1982, invests in companies engaged in developing alternative energy and pollution-control equipment. Also in the USA the Social Investment Forum (SIF), a mutual fund club, has drawn up a set of guidelines, the so-called '*Valdez* Principles', for the purpose of evaluating companies' environmental performance for investment-screening purposes.

Appendix 1   CONSERVATION AND PROTECTED AREAS

There are currently some 940 reserves throughout the world which have been designated under international or regional conventions.

International and regionally designated sites

Designation	Number and area (km²)
1. Biosphere Reserves (Unesco)	269 (1,430,000)
2. Biogenetic Network and Reserves (COE)	158 (18,185)
3. Wetlands of International Importance (RAMSAR)	434 (286,777)
4. World Heritage Sites (Unesco)	79
	940 (1,734,962)

A number of the reserves are multi-designated.

In addition to these sites, national parks, nature reserves and other conservation areas are established under local statutes. The principal conventions and international agreements under which internationally important sites are designated are the RAMSAR (1971), Paris (1972), Washington (1973), Bonn (1979) and Berne (1979) Conventions. In Europe, the Council of Europe system of biogenetic reserves, established in a Resolution dated 1976 under the provisions of the Berne Convention, is a major part of the programme to conserve representative species of flora, fauna and biotopes of European significance.

Conservation objectives are generally adopted to protect, manage and enhance the natural environment and to resolve the conflicts between perceived natural and human interests. In particular, they ensure that wildlife does not disappear as a result of agriculture, industry or tourism. The European Network of Biogenetic Reserves was adopted in a COE resolution dated 1976. The number, area and classification of sites by country and the distribution of European national parks and nature reserves are shown in the following tables.

Council of Europe Biogenetic Reserves

Country	No. of sites	Ecosystem	Total area (ha) by country)
Belgium	8	Peatland	6,000
France	35	Alpine Coastal Dunes (inland) Heathland Littoral Marine Mountain massif Peatland Wetland Woodland	43,906
Greece	1	Ancient woodland	500
Ireland	4	Marine Peatland Woodland	1,398
Proposed	5		3,624
Italy	37	Alluvial Alpine and sub-Alpine Coastal dune Coastal marine Forest Lakes Limestone mountain Mediterranean Volcanic complexes	33,567
Netherlands	18	Alluvial Coastal Dry grassland Estuarine alluvial Heathland Peatland Riparian	18,000
Norway	1	Tundra	1,555,000
Proposed	10	Peatland	12,423
Sweden	10	Peatland	100,000
Switzerland	9	Alluvial valley Massif montagneux Wetland Wetland montagnarde	7,700
United Kingdom	30	Coastal Dry grassland Heathland Peatland Wet meadow	36,448
	158	Total hectares	1,818,566 (18,185 km²)

European national parks, nature reserves and other protected areas

Country	Area (km²)	Population (millions)	Protected areas etc. (No.)	(%)	National 'Red List' species* Fauna	Flora
Austria	83,849	7.4	334	20–25	n.a.	n.a.
Belgium	30,519	9.8	269	2.8	n.a.	n.a.
Denmark	43,079	5.1	678	25.0	343	1,325
France	551,000	55.3	87	2.5	260	n.a.
Finland	337,000	4.8	759	3.0	171	83
FRG	249,000	61.7	6,005	28.0	203	862
Greece	131,900	9.6	514	9.8	222	771
Iceland	103,125	0.24	31	7.2	32	131
Ireland	70,283	3.5	30	0.355	38	131
Italy	301,245	57.0	299	3.0	71	32
Lichtenstein	160	0.027	n.a.	7.0	n.a.	n.a.
Luxembourg	2,586	0.364	6	38.0	n.a.	n.a.
Netherlands	41,160	14.2	n.a.	4.0	969	1,394
Norway and Svalbard	323,900	4.1	677	3.86	75	126
	385,900	—	21	56.32	n.a.	n.a.
Portugal and islands	88,856	10.13	9	4.0	122	346
	3,205	0.514	5	33.9	n.a.	n.a.
Spain	504,000	37.7	75	4.0	398	64
Sweden	449,964	8.32	1,235	3.8	89	71
Switzerland	41,300	6.4	n.a.	n.a.	310	773
Turkey	788,000	51.4	125	2.32	401	2,990
UK	244,100	55.7	388	9.0	150	317
	4,774,131	403.3	11,547	—	—	—

Source: Council of Europe
* Mammals, birds, reptiles and amphibians; vascular plants

The Red Data list, first published jointly in 1977 by the Council of Europe and the IUCN, is the 'List of Rare, Threatened and Endemic Plants in Europe', then containing a total of 12,000 vascular plants from 1,200 taxa falling within the threatened categories laid down by the IUCN Threatened Plants Committee (revised by COE, 1982).

Conventions and charters promulgated by the Council of Europe

Convention/charter	Date
European Water Charter	1968
European Soil Charter	1972
Ecological Charter for Mountain Regions in Europe	1976
Convention on the Conservation of European Wildlife and Natural Habitats	1979
Charter on Invertebrates	1986

Nature conservation in the UK

Nature conservation in the UK is managed principally by local authorities in association with national conservation agencies, together with private landowners (including The National Trust) and county naturalists' and wildlife trusts. Rural conservation relates to the preservation of remaining natural habitats, ancient woodlands, traditional meadows and hedgerows. Naturalists' and wildlife trusts (see RSNC) campaign for wildlife conservation in rural and urban areas and national policies relating these interests to agriculture and forestry.

In the UK there are some 37 Areas of Outstanding Natural Beauty (AONB) and approximately 6,000 Sites of Special Scientific Interest (SSSI) designated by the Nature Conservancy Council and the Countryside Commission under the Access to the Countryside (1949) and the Wildlife and Countryside (1981) acts. Among these sites, and in addition to them, naturalists' and wildlife trusts in the UK own or manage some 2,000 nature reserves covering nearly 60,000 hectares.

UK site designations

1.	Areas of Outstanding Natural Beauty	37
2.	Areas of Special Protection	n.a.
3.	Biogenetic Reserves	30
4.	Biosphere Reserves	13
5.	Country Parks	250
6.	Environmentally Sensitive Areas	14
7.	Forest Parks	8
8.	Heritage Coast	10
9.	Limestone Pavement Orders	n.a.
10.	Marine Nature Reserves	7
11.	National Parks	8
12.	National Nature Reserves	235
13.	National Scenic Areas (Scotland)	18
14.	Sites of Special Scientific Interest	6,000
15.	Special Protection Areas	n.a.
16.	Wetlands of International Importance	40
17.	World Heritage Sites	9
	Number of designated sites	6,679

Source: NCC

Appendix 2   ENVIRONMENTAL INFORMATION SOURCES AND DATABASES

Worldwide information and data on the environment are available from United Nations libraries and databases as well as from European (EC) and US sources, several of which are commercial databases accessible on-line. All principal sources are described below.

United Nations data are available either directly from the agency indicated or via commercial databases by arrangement with the host organization. UN information as hard copy is usually provided gratis while on-line costs are determined on a connection or usage basis.

Data and information sources are organized by topic, name of database or bibliographic resource, accessibility of the information, whether on-line via terminal or computer, and by subject coverage. Contact addresses of agencies and hosts are provided in Appendix 4.

The listing of commercial databases covering the environment and related topics is comprehensive, and while the general range of information is not described exhaustively it will provide enough reference points to enable the reader or researcher to pursue any particular line of enquiry.

Headings under which the data are organized are as follows:

Topic/agency: Environmental topic listed alphabetically; 'AGENCY' indicates the intergovernmental originating source to whom direct enquiries can be made.
Database/bibliography: Name of the database, bibliography or library.
Access (on-line)/host: On-line host for direct access. 'External user' or 'External reference' indicates that direct contact should be made with the Agency.
Coverage: Summary of subjects covered in database or library.

Topic/agency	Database/ bibliography	Access (on-line)/host	Coverage
Accidents, safety			
ICAO, Montreal	ADREP and IBIS	External user	Aircraft, airports, birds, construction
IAEA, Vienna	INIS (International Nuclear Information Sys.)	Belindis, CISTI, ESA-IRS, FIZ, STN	Nuclear safety and protection (see INIS)
HSE/UKAEA	MHIDAS	ESA-IRS	Off-site impact of incidents and accidents involving hazardous materials
Agriculture			
CEC	AGINFO (EEC-CAP)	Telecom Gold	Common Agricultural Policy and European food trade
—	AGREP	DC/DIMDI	Agricultural research in EEC countries
—	Agribusiness USA	DIALOG	Commercial aspects of agriculture in the USA
—	Agricola	DIALOG/DIMDI	*Bibliography of Agriculture*
FAO, Rome	Agris (International Information System for the Agricultural Sciences and Technology)	DIALOG/ DIMDI/ESA-IRIS/IAEA/ TYMNET/ TELENET	Fisheries, food science, forestry and veterinary

Topic/agency	Database/ bibliography	Access (on-line)/host	Coverage
—	Agrochemical Handbook	DIALOG/DATA STAR	Pesticides in agriculture
—	AGPAT	STN	Chemical and biochemical patents and pest control
FAO, Rome	ASFIS and ASFA (Aquatic Sciences and Fisheries Abs.)	BRS/CISTI/ DIALOG/ DIMDI/ESA-IRS	Biological sciences, life resources, physical and chemical oceanography, marine technology and linology
—	CAB & CAB ADO	DIMDI/ESA-IRS	All agricultural sciences, legislation and marketing
FAO, Rome	CARIS (Current Agricultural Research Information System)	External reference	Current agricultural resources information system
—	EDAP	DATA STAR	European directory of agrochemical products
—	FIS ELF-ELFIS	DIMDI	Agriculture, food and forestry
CEC	RURALNET	ECHO	Rural development projects
Air pollution			
—	ACID	ESA-IRS	Acid rain abstracts; policy and planning
UN-ECE	EMEP (Co-operative Programme for Monitoring and Evaluation of the Long-term Transmission of Air Pollutants in Europe)		Sampling of NO_x, SO_2, etc. in 24 European countries
UNEP, Paris	UNEP Industry and Environment	External reference	Management of pollutants from industrial sources
Biosciences			
—	BBUS Biobusiness	DATA STAR	Biotechnology and genetic engineering
—	Biobusiness	ESA-IRS	Business applications of life sciences research
—	BIOL	DATA STAR/ DIMDI/STN	Zoology, botany, biophysics, environmental research
CEC	BIOREP	ECHO	EC biotechnology research projects
—	BIOSIS Previews	DIALOG/STN/ ESA-IRS	International biology and biomedicine
—	Biotechnology Abstracts	DIALOG	Biotechnology
—	Cancerlit	BLAISE-LINK/ DATA STAR/ DIALOG/ DIMDI/MIC-KIBIC	

Topic/agency	Database/ bibliography	Access (on-line)/host	Coverage
—	Cancerproj	BLAISE-LINE/ BLAISE-LINK	Includes IARC monographs and research projects
—	CELL	DATA STAR	Commercial aspects of biotechnology
—	CCRIS (Chemical Carcinogenesis Research Information)	BLAIZE-LINE/ BLAIZE-LINK	US National Cancer Research Institute
—	Chemical Abstracts	DIALOG	
—	CLINPROT (Clinical cancer protocols)	BLAIZE-LINE/ BLAIZE-LINK/ DIMDI	
—	Current Biotechnology Abs.	DIALOG	
WHO/IARC, Lyon	IARC database	External reference	On-going medical research
Chemicals			
—	AGPAT	STN	Worldwide chemical and biochemical patents
UN-ECE, Geneva	Annual Review of Chemical Industry	UN user only	
—	CAPF (Chemical Age Project File)	ESA-IRS/PFDS/ ORBIT	Chemical and related plant constructed since 1980
—	CAPREVIEWS	STN	Chemistry and chemical engineering
—	Chemical Abstracts (CAS/ CHEMABS/CA SEARCH)	DATA STAR/ DIALOG/ESA-IRS/QUESTEL	Chemistry and related field
—	Chemical Business Newsbase	DATA STAR/ DIALOG/PFDS	European chemical industry
—	Chemical Engineering Abs.	DATA STAR/ DIALOG/ESA-IRS	
—	Chemical Exposure	DIALOG	
—	Chemical Industry Notes	DATA STAR/ DIALOG	
—	Chemical Regulations & Guidelines	DIALOG	
—	Chemical Safety Newsbase	DIALOG	
—	Chem-Intell	DATA STAR/ DIALOG/PFDS	Chemical trade and production statistics
—	CHEMLINE (Chemical dictionary)	TOXLINE and MEDLINE	BLAIZE-LINE/BLAIZE-LINK/DIMDI/

Topic/agency	Database/ bibliography	Access (on-line)/host	Coverage
—	Chemname	DATA STAR/ DIALOG	Chemical nomenclature
—	Chemsearch	DIALOG	
—	CHI	DATA STAR/ STN	Chemical hazards in industry
ILO, Geneva	CIS	ESA-IRS	Occupational safety and health
—	CJACS (Chemical Journal of ACS)	STN	American Chemical Society
—	CJAOAC (Chemical Journals of AOAC)	STN	Association of Official Analytical Chemists
—	CORSC (Chemical Journals of RSC)	STN	Royal Society of Chemistry abstracts
—	CNEW (European Chemical news)	DATA STAR	European chemical news
—	DECHEMA and DEQUIP	STN	Chemical engineering and biotechnology equipment
EEC Joint Research Centre	ECDIN (jointly with IRPTC)	DC/JRC	Environmental chemicals data and information network; 65,000 chemical substances contained in environment resulting from human activities
—	EECM (East European Chemical Monitor)	DATA STAR	Eastern European chemical industry
UNEP, Geneva	IRPIC and MINISIS	National correspondents	MINISIS available to government institutions in developing countries
UNEP, Nairobi	INFOTERRA	National focal points	
UNEP/WHO, Geneva	IPDB (International Programme on Chemical Safety)	External reference	Monographs and publications on environmental health criteria (EHC)
—	PLAN	DATA STAR	Chemical plants worldwide
—	RTECS (Register of Toxic Effects of Chemical Substances)	BLAIZE-LINE/ BLAIZE-LINK/ DIALOG/ DIMDI/MIC-KIBIC	Toxic effects and toxic doses for man and animals; occupational health standards (US National Institute of Health)
—	TSCA Chemical Substances Inventory (and TOXLIST)	DIALOG/STN	Chemicals under the US Control of Toxic Substances Act and similar legislation (EPA)

Climate

Topic/agency	Database/ bibliography	Access (on-line)/host	Coverage
FAO, Rome	AEZ (Agro-ecological Zone)	UNEP-GEMS	Climate, soils, ecology and land use

Topic/agency	Database/ bibliography	Access (on-line)/host	Coverage
FAO, Rome	MANAGE	External reference	Agroclimatological data for Africa, Asia and Latin America
UNEP, Geneva	GEMS (Global Environment Monitoring System)	External reference	Climate, pollutants, health, oceans and natural resources
UNEP, Geneva	GRID (Global Resource Information Database)	External reference	GIS for inter-agency support and usage
WMO, Geneva	Infoclima	National Met. Offices	40,000 weather stations
—	Meteorological and Geoastrophysical Abs.	DIALOG	
—	MOLARS (Meteorological Office Library Accesion System)	ESA-IRS	Worldwide sources on meteorology (WCDP – World Climate Data Programme)
WMO, Geneva	WWW (World Weather Watch)	National Met. Offices	7,500 ship stations (WCDP)
Commercial enterprises			
UN-CTC, NY	Corporate database	NYCS	Trans-national corporations
ILO, Geneva	LID	ESA-IRS	Labour information
ITC, Geneva	TRADERS	UN user only	Company profiles
Conservation			
FAO, Rome	FOWCIS (Forests and Wildlands Conservation Information System) (see also **Forests**)	External reference/ WCMC	Wildlife, protected areas, conservation institutions, agrosilopastoral systems, watershed management, degradation of natural resources, acid zone forestry and fuelwood
Disasters			
UNDRO, Geneva	UNDRONET	External reference	International Disaster Management Information Network
Economic development			
UN-DIESA, NY	DIS	External reference	Development and resources
ESCAP, Bangkok	EBIS/Lib.	External reference	Regional data
UNCTAD	GATT	On-line	Tariff and Trade Data
World Bank	IBIS, IDMS & THESMAT	External reference	Environment, project operation reports
UNIDO, Vienna	INPRIS	On-line	Industrial investments and technical commission

Topic/agency	Database/ bibliography	Access (on-line)/host	Coverage
OECD, Paris	IRRD	ESA-IRS	
IAEA, Vienna	LION	External reference	Economics, science and engineering
Energy			
—	BIOMASS	STN	Biomass projects
—	CLRP	Belindis	Coal projects
—	COAL	Religious/ Inkadat	Coal
DOE-USA	DOE Energy (US)	DIALOG/STN	Energy sources and energy conservation
IAEA, Vienna	EEDB (Energy and economics)	On-line	Nuclear and non-nuclear energy and economics
—	Energie	STN	Energy research and technology
Unesco, Paris	Energy Information Programme	External reference	
—	Energyline	DIALOG/ESA-IRS/Inkadat	Energy, economics, policy, planning and research
—	NEI/NEIF/NEIL/ NEIX	DO	Energy in the Nordic countries
CEC	SESAME	ECHO	Information on EC-supported energy projects
Environment			
—	COMPENDEX	CEDOCAR/ DATA STAR/ ESA-IRS/STN	Engineering
—	DETEG	STN	Environmental engineering suppliers and equipment
CEC	ENREP	ECHO	Inventory of environmental research projects in EC
—	Enviroline	DIALOG/ DIMDI/ESA-IRS	Natural resources; pollution; transport; policy
—	Environ	GSI-ECO	Statistics and planning
—	Environmental Bib.	DIALOG	
UNEP, Nairobi	Library	COMPENDEX/ INSPEC/FSTA	Management, effects, industrial areas
Unesco, Paris	MABIS	MAB National Committees	Man and the Biosphere Information System
NASA	NASA	ESA-IRS	
—	PASCAL	ESA-IRS/ QUESTEL	Earth and biosciences, energy, pollution, transport
Forests			
FAO, Rome	Agric	(see **Agriculture**)	Forestry

Topic/agency	Database/ bibliography	Access (on-line)/host	Coverage
FAO, Rome	FORIS (Forests Resources Information System)	External reference	Tropical forests
Geology			
—	ADIGE	CILIA, Italy	Earth sciences (Italian)
—	Asian Geotechnology	ESA-IRS	Soil mechanics and hydrology of Asian origin
—	Geoarchive	DIALOG	
—	Geobanque	Questel	Drill sites and data
—	Geobase	DIALOG	
—	Geol	CNUCE	Earth science references and European GEOREF titles
—	Geoline	Inkadat	Geology, geophysics and economic geology
—	Georef	DIALOG	Earth sciences
—	QUAT	CNUCE	Geological events relating to the evolution of the Italian quaternary shorelines; sedimentology
Information systems			
UN, NY and Geneva	ADDIS	External reference	UN information and database systems
CEC, Luxembourg	DUNDIS	ECHO	Directory of UN information systems and databases
CEC, Luxembourg	ECHO	External user	Inventory of the EC Information Services Market
FAO, Rome	GIS	External reference	Geographic information systems
ESCAP, Bangkok	RIB		Remote sensing information systems
UN-RISD	Socioeconomic Development Indicators Data Bank	External reference	
UN-ECE	Statistical Division	External reference	
UNSIS	Statistical Information Sys.	External reference	
Legal			
—	CELEX	CERVED/ EDIOLINE/ EUROBASES/ ICEX/Profile Information/IBD	European Parliament, CEC and ESC legislation
—	ECC	CED	Ecology and environment legal documentation in Italy
UNEP, Infoterra	ELC (Environmental Law Centre)	WOMC/IUCN	Environmental legislation

Topic/agency	Database/ bibliography	Access (on-line)/host	Coverage
WHO, Copenhagen	Environment legislation	External user	Environmental legislation
—	ENLEX	CED	EEC ecological and environmental legal documentation
WHO, Geneva	Health legislation	DIALOG/ MEDLINE/ NEXIS	Health legislation
ICJ, The Hague	International Court of Justice	External user	International law
UNEP, Geneva	IRPTC	National correspondents	Legal protection
ILO, Geneva	LID/COOPLEG/ INFLEG	ESA-IRS	Legislation and labour information
IAEA, Vienna	LION	External reference	Environmental legislation
Marine environment			
—	Aquaculture	DIALOG	Aquatic science and fisheries
FAO, Rome	ASFIS	DIALOG	Aquatic science and fisheries
Unesco, Paris	Coral reef database	External reference	Coral reefs
Unesco/IOC, Paris	MEDI	UN user only	Marine science data collections
—	MARINELINE	FTZ Technik	Technology, law and environment protection
—	Oceanic Abstracts	DIALOG/ESA-IRS	Oceanography, meteorology, marine biology, pollution, geology, shipping
UNEP, Nairobi	Oceans and Coastal Areas	External reference (hard-copy documentation only)	
Natural resources and environmental management			
ECLAC, Santiago	BADEAUNU	External use	Regional natural resources, demographic and social data
ECLAC, Santiago	BIBLOS	External use	Regional development and trade
ECLAC, Port of Spain	CARISPLAN (Caribbean Information System)	CDC	Economic and social planning
UN, New York	DIS	External use	UN mission and project reports
ESCAP, Bangkok	EBIS	External reference	Agricultural development, energy and population
UNEP, Nairobi	GEMS	National networks	Renewable natural resources
UNEP, Nairobi	INFOTERRA	National Focal Points	International environmental information system
ECA, Addis Ababa	PADIS	External use	Pan-African Documentation and Information System
CEC	RURALNET	ECHO	Rural development projects

Topic/agency	Database/ bibliography	Access (on-line)/host	Coverage
Nuclear energy			
—	Nuclear Science Abs.	DIALOG	
IAEA, Vienna	INIS and EDIN	Belindis/ESA-IRS/STN	Peaceful applications of nuclear sciences; EDIN is a training file of INIS
IAEA, Vienna	LION (Library information on-line)	External reference	
Occupational safety and health			
ILO, Geneva	CIS	DIALOG/ESA-IRS	
ILO, Geneva	CIS BIT	Questel	
ILO, Geneva	CISDOC	ESA-IRS	
—	HSDB	BLAIZE-LINE/ BLAIZE-LINK	Hazardous substances; environmental fate and exposure; monitoring analysis, handling
HSE, London	HSE-Line	DATA STAR/ ESA-IRS	Health and safety at work
ILO, Geneva	LABORDOC	ESA-IRS/ Executive Telecom/ORBIT InfoLine	
NIOSH (USA)	Occupational Safety and Health	DIALOG	National Institute of Occupational Safety and Health
Pollution			
FAO, Rome	CARIS	On-line	
PAHO, Mexico	ECO-Line	External user	
UNEP, Nairobi	INFOTERRA	External user	
IAEA, Vienna	INIS	On-line	Radioactive pollution
Unesco/IOC, Paris	MEDI	External user	Pollution control monitoring
UNEP/UN-EC, Geneva	PACT (Pollution Abatement Control Technology)		
—	POLLUTION (Pollution Abstracts)	DATA STAR/ DIALOG/ESA-IRS	Air, noise, radioactivity, waste, water
WMO, Geneva	WWW	Local met. offices	
Population			
—	Popline	BLAIZE-LINE/ BLAIZE LINK	Population, family planning, fertility
—	Population Bibliog.	DIALOG	
Transport			
—	EXIS-1	EXIS	Transport of hazardous goods
—	TRANSDOC	ESA-IRS	Transport and the environment

Topic/agency	Database/ bibliography	Access (on-line)/host	Coverage
Waste management			
UNEP, Nairobi	INFOTERRA	National focal points	
UNEP, Geneva	IRPTC	National correspondents	
UNEP/UN-ECE, Geneva	PACT	UN user only	
FAO, Rome	Waste Paper Survey	External reference	Waste paper recovery, trade and utilization
Water resources			
—	AFEE (Association Française pour l'Etude des Eaux)	ESA-IRS	Fresh water, health and pollution
FAO, Rome	Asfis	DIALOG	Aquatic science and fisheries abstracts
WMO, Geneva	HOME	Nat. Referral Centres	Hydrological operations multipurpose sub-programme
UNEP, Paris	IEO database	UN user only	
UNEP, Nairobi	INFOTERRA	National focal points	
FAO, Rome	Irrigation Potential Database	External reference	Irrigation potential, Africa assessments
Unesco/IOC, Paris	MEDI	UN user only	
PAHO, Lima	REPIOSIBCA	External user	Water supply and waste management
—	Water Resources Abs.	DIALOG	
—	Waternet	DIALOG	

Sources: UNEP; IRS Dialtech

Appendix 3 GLOSSARY (INCLUDING ACRONYMS AND ORGANIZATIONS)

AAG Association of Arab Geologists (IBN of ICSU) — Geology
ABN African Biosciences Network (IBN of ICSU) — Bioscience
ABS American Bureau of Shipping (USA) — Marine transport
ACA Agricultural Chemicals Association (UK) — Agro. industry
ACAL Academia de Ciencias de America Latina (ICSU)
ACAST Advisory Committee on the Application of Science and Technology to Development (ICSU) — Development
ACC Administrative Committee on Co-ordination (UN) — Statistics
ACC American Chamber of Commerce (see also **ICC**) — Industry NGO
ACE Association for the Conservation of Energy (UK) — Energy
ACF Australian Conservation Foundation — Conservation
ACIA Australian Chemical Industry Association — Chemical industry
ACMRR Advisory Committee on Marine Resources Research (ICSU) — Marine science
ACOPS Advisory Committee on Oil Pollution of the Sea (UK) — Marine pollution
ACPS Advisory Committee on Pollution of the Sea (see **ACOPS**) — Marine pollution
ACS American Chemical Society — Chemical industry
ACTS Advisory Committee on Toxic Substances (UK HSC) — Chemical safety
ADIS Automated Data Interchange System (ICSU) — Data
ADR European Agreement for the International Carriage of Dangerous Goods by Road (EC) — Transport
AEC Australian Environment Council — Conservation
AEG Association of Exploration Geochemists (ICSU) — Geochemistry
AERE Atomic Energy Research Establishment (Harwell, UK) — Nuclear
AEZ Agro-Ecological Zone Data Bank (FAO) — Data
AGGG Advisory Group on Greenhouse Gases (ICSU) — Climate
AFRC Agriculture and Food Research Council (UK) — Agro.
AGCM Atmospheric General Circulation Model (NERC) — Atmosphere
AGRIS Agricultural Sciences and Technology (FAO) — Database
ALECSO Arab League Educational, Cultural and Scientific Organization (see also **PERGSA**) — Marine
ALPEX Alpine Experiment (ICSU) — Geology
ANBS Asian Network of Biological Sciences (ICSU) — Biology
AONB Area of Outstanding Natural Beauty (CC) — Conservation
AOPSC Anti-Pollution Standing Conference (UK) — Pollution
AOSB Arctic Ocean Sciences Board (ICSU) — Polar
APCA Air Pollution Control Association (USA) — Atmosphere
APHA American Public Health Association — PH
API American Petroleum Institute — Oil industry
APP Atmospheric Physics Programme (ICSU) — Atmosphere
ARC Agricultural Research Council (UK) — Agro.
ASA American Standards Association (see also **BSI** and **DIN**) — Standards
ASCOPE (ASEAN) Council on Petroleum — Regional
ASEAN Association of South-East Asian Nations — Regional
ASFIS Aquatic Sciences and Fisheries Information System (FAO) — Database
ASGA Association des Services Geologiques Africains (ICSU) — Geology
ASIDIC Association of Scientific Information Dissemination Centres (ICSU) — Data
ASSET Abstracts of Selected Solar Energy Technology (UNU) — Data/energy
ASTEO Association Scientifique et Technique pour l'Exploitation des Oceans — Marine
ATB Association of Tropical Biology (ICSU) — Biology
ATIS Appropriate Technology Information Services (ICSU) — Data
ATS Antarctic Treaty System — Polar
AUE Association Universitaire pour l'Environment (Belgium) — Conservation

BAA British Agrochemical Association — Agro.
BAEA British Atomic Energy Authority — Nuclear
BAPMoN Background Air Pollution Monitoring Network (WMO) — Atmosphere

BAS British Antarctic Survey (NERC)	Polar
BBSR Bermuda Biological Station for Research	Marine
BCIF Belgium Chemical Industries Federation	Chemical
BEE Bureau Européen de l'Environment (see **EEB**)	NGO
BES British Ecological Society	Ecology
BGC Berufsgenossenschaft der Chemischen Industrie (FRG)	Chemical industry
BGS British Geological Survey (NERC)	Geology
BIAC Business and Industry Advisory Council (CBI to OECD)	Industry
BIBRA British Industrial Biological Research Association	Biology
BIMCO Baltic and International Maritime Conference	Marine
BIOMASS Biological Investigation of Marine Antarctic Systems and Stocks (ICSU)	Polar
BIOTROP Regional Centre for Tropical Biology, Indonesia (ICSU)	Biology
BIRD Banque International pour la Reconstruction et Development (World Bank)	Development
BL British Library	Bibliography
BNF British Nuclear Fuels	Nuclear
BNSC British National Space Centre	Space
BOD Biological Oxygen Demand	Biology
BOFS Biogeochemical Ocean Flux Study (see also **JGOFS** of ICSU)	Climate
BOSCA British Oil Spill Control Association	Industry
BOSEX Baltic Open Sea Experiment (ICSU)	Oceanography
Bq Becquerel	Nuclear
BRS Bibliographic Retrieval Service (BL)	Data
BSBI Botanical Society of the British Isles	Botanical
BSI British Standards Institution	Standards
CAB Commonwealth Agricultural Bureaux	Agro.
CANSAP Canadian Network for Sampling Precipitation	Climate
CAP Common Agricultural Policy (EC)	Agro.
CAPER Committee on Air Pollution Effects Research (NERC)	Atmosphere
CARB California Air Resources Board	Atmosphere
CARICOM Caribbean Community and Common Market	Regional IG
CARIFTA Caribbean Free Trade Area	Regional IG
CARIS Computerized Agricultural Research Information System (FAO)	Database
CARPAS Regional Fishery Advisory Commission for the South-West Atlantic (FAO)	Fish.
CASAFA Inter-Union Commission on the Application of Science to Agriculture, Forestry and Aquaculture (ICSU)	Agro.
CAST China Association for Science and Technology (ICSU)	
CASTD Committee on Application of Science and Technology to Development (ICSU)	Development
CBGA Carpathian Balkan Geological Association (ICSU)	Geology
CBPA Chlorinated Benzene Producers Association (USA)	Chemical industry
CC Countryside Commission (UK)	Conservation
CCAMLR Commission for the Conservation of Antarctic Marine Living Resources (ATS)	Polar
CCC Central Classification Committee (ICSU)	Standards
CCCO Co-ordinating Committee on Climatic Changes on the Oceans (IOC/ICSU/SCOR)	Climate
CCE Commission des Communautés Européennes (CEC)	Regional IG
CCMC Comitée des Constructeurs d'Automobiles du Marché Commun	Transport NGO
CCMC Committee on the Challenges of Modern Society (NATO)	Regional IG
CCOL Co-ordinating Committee on the Ozone Layer (UNEP)	Climate
CCPA Canadian Chemical Producers Association	Chemical industry
CCRAC Co-ordinating Committee for Research in Atmospheric Chemistry (NERC)	Atmosphere
CCRX Co-ordinatie Commissie voor Meting van Radio-Ativiteit en Xenobiotische Stoffen (NL)	Nuclear
CDM Commission on Dynamic Meteorology (ICSU)	Meteorology
CEA Commission Economique pour l'Afrique (UN-ECA)	Regional IG
CEC Commission of the European Communities	Regional IG
CECAF Fishery Committee for the Eastern-Central Atlantic (FAO)	Fish.
CEE Communauté Economique Européenne (EC)	Regional IG
CEEN Centre d'Etude de l'Energie Nucléaire (CERN)	Nuclear

CEFIC Conseil Européen des Fédérations de l'Industrie Chimique	Chemical industry
CEPAL Commission Economique pour l'Amerique Latine (UN-ECOSOC)	Regional IG
CEPEX Controlled Ecosystem Pollution Experiment	Ecology
CEPLEO West European Coal Producers' Association	Energy
CEPM Comité d'Etudes Petrolières Marines	Marine
CEPPOL Commission d'Etudes Practiques de Lutte Anti-Pollution (Marine Nationale)	Marine
CERCLA Comprehensive Environmental Response Compensation and Liability Act (USA)	Legal
CERD European Research and Development Committee	Development
CERN European Centre for Nuclear Research	Nuclear
CESAP Commission Economique et Social pour l'Asie et le Pacifique (UN-ECOSOC)	Regional IG
CETEX Committee on Contamination by Extra-Terrestrial Exploration (COSPAR)	Space
CFP Common Fisheries Policy (EC)	Fish.
CGIAR Consultative Group on International Agricultural Research (also TAC)	Agro.
CGMW Commission for the Geological Map of the World (ICSU)	Cartography
CHEMRAWN Chemical Research Applied to World Needs (ICSU)	Chemical
CHEMTREC Chemical Transport Emergency Centre	Chemical
CHIP Chemical Hazard Information Profile (TOSCA)	Data/chemicals
CIA Chemical Industries Association	Chemical industry
CIAB Coal Industry Advisory Board	Energy
CICAR Co-operative Investigations in the Caribbean and Adjacent Regions (IOC)	Marine
CIDA Canadian International Development Agency	Development
CIDIE Committee for International Development Institutions for the Environment	Development
CIDST Committee for Scientific and Technical Information and Documentation	Data
CIEM International Commission for the Scientific Exploration of the Mediterranean	Marine
CIFE Council of Europe Industrial Federation	Regional IG
CIIT Chemical Industry Institute for Toxicology	Chemical
CIM Co-operative Investigations of the Mediterranean (IOC)	Marine
CIMMYT International Maize and Wheat Improvement Centre	Agro.
CINCWIO Co-operative Investigation of the Northern and Central Western Indian Ocean (IOC)	Marine
CIP International Potato Centre	Agro
CIRIA Construction Industry Research and Information Association (UK)	Industry
CIRN Centre d'Information et de Recherche sur les Nuisances	Pollution
CIS International Occupational Safety and Health Information Centre (ILO)	Data
CIS Chemical Information System (ILO)	Data
CISHEC Chemical Industry Safety and Health Council	Chemical industry
CITEPA Centre Interprofessional Technique d'Etudes de la Pollution Atmosphérique	Atmosphere
CITES Convention on International Trade in Endangered Species of Wild Flora and Fauna	Legal
CISTOD Confederation of International Scientific and Technological Organizations for Development (ICSU)	Development
CLC International Convention on Civil Liability for Oil Pollution Damage, 1969 (IMO) (also **CRISTAL, IFC, TOVALOP**)	Marine/legal
CMA Chemical Manufacturers Association	Chemical industry
CMAS Confédération Mondiale des Activités Sub-Aquatiques (ICSU)	Marine
CMEA Council for Mutual Economic Assistance (Eastern bloc)	Regional IG
CMF Chemical Manufacturing Federation (UK)	Chemical industry
CMFA Agro-chemical and Speciality Chemicals	Chemical industry
CMG Commission for Marine Geology (ICSU)	Geology
CMI Comité Maritime International	Marine industry
CMM Commission for Marine Meteorology (WHO)	Meteorology
CMPI Commission on Maritime Pollution (IMO)	Marine
CNEXO Centre National pour l'Exploitation des Oceans	Marine
CO₂ Carbon dioxide	Chemical

COADC Committee for Oceanographic Advice to Developing Countries (ICSU)	Oceanography
COB Centre Oceanologique de Bretagne	Oceanography
COBIOTECH Scientific Committee on Biotechnology (ICSU)	Biotechnology
CODATA Committee on Data for Science and Technology (ICSU)	Data
COE Council of Europe	Regional IG
COFI Committee on Fisheries (FAO)	Fish.
COGENE Committee on Genetic Experimentation (ICSU: see **TOWD**)	Biotechnology
COGEODATA Committee on Geological Data (ICSU)	Data
COGER Co-ordinating Group on Environmental Radioactivity (NERC)	Nuclear
COGOEDOC Commission on Geological Documentation (ICSU)	Data/geology
COKS Compendium of Known Substances	Data/chemicals
COLREGS Regulations for Preventing Collisions at Sea, 1976 (IMO)	Legal
COMARE Committee on Medical Aspects of Radiation in the Environment (UK)	Nuclear
COMECON Council of Mutual Economic Assistance (CMEA–Eastern bloc)	Regional IG
COMPASS Comparative Assessment of Environmental Effects of Various Energy Sources (OECD)	Energy
CONCAWE Oil Companies European Organization for Environmental and Health Protection (NL)	Oil industry
CONCOM Council of Nature Conservation Ministers (Australia)	Conservation
COOSRA Canadian Offshore Oilspill Research Organization	Oil industry
COOW Committee for the Oil Industry and Public Water Authorities	Oil/water
COPA Control of Pollution Act (UK)	Legal
CORINE Coastal Erosion Project (EC)	Erosion
COSHH Control of Substances Hazardous to Health	Legal
COSHM Chemicals Operations, Safety and Hygiene in Manufacturing	Chemical industry
COSPAR Committee for Space Research (ICSU)	Space
COST European Committee in the Field of Scientific and Technical Research (EEC)	Regional IG
COSTED Committee on Science and Technology in Developing Countries (ICSU)	Development
COWAR Committee on Water Research (ICSU)	Water
CPA Consumer Protection Agency (USA)	Legal
CPEMREC Circum-Pacific Energy and Minerals Resources Conference	Energy
CPPS Permanent Commission for the South Pacific	Regional IG
CPRE Council for the Protection of Rural England	Conservation
CRISTAL Contract Regarding an Interim Supplement to Tanker Liability for Oil Pollution (Oil Industry) (also **CLC**, **IFC** and **TOVALOP**)	Marine/legal
CSCL Chemical Substances Control Law (Japan)	Legal/chemicals
CSIN Chemical Substances Control Network	Data/chem.
CSMA Chemical Specialities Manufacturers Association (USA)	Chemical
CSSR Committee on Science and Social Relations (ICSU)	Social science
CSTD Committee on Science and Technology for Development (ICSU)	Development
CZMA Coastal Zone Management Act (USA)	Legal/marine
DAFS Department of Agriculture and Fisheries for Scotland	Government
DDE 1,1-dichloro-2,2-bis (p-chlorphenyl) ethylene	Chemical
DDT 1,1,1-trichloro-2,2-bis (p-chlorphenyl) ethylene	Chemical
DEVSIS Development Science Information System (ICSU)	Data/dev.
DIESA (see **UNDIESA**)	Inter-gov.
DIN Deutsches Institute for Normung EV	Standards
DNA Deoxyribonucleic acid	Chemical
DOEM Designated Officials for Environmental Matters (UN)	Inter-gov.
DOMES Deep Ocean Mining Environmental Study (USA)	Ocean/energ.
DTCO Department of Technical Co-operation for Development (UN)	Development
EAGS European Association for Exploration Geophysicists (ICSU)	Geophysics
EAMREA Environmental Impact of Mineral Exploration/Exploitation in Antarctica (ICSU)	Polar
EAP Environmentally Acceptable Position	
EC European Communities (CEC)	Regional IG
ECA Economic Commission for Africa (UN-ESOSOC)	Regional IG
ECAFE Economic Commission for Asia and the Far East (UN-ECOSOC)	Regional IG
ECB Environment Co-ordination Board (UN)	Intergov.

ECDIN Environmental Chemical Data and Information Network (EEC)	Data/chemicals
ECE Economic Commission for Europe (UN-ECOSOC)	Regional IG
ECETOC European Chemical Industry Ecology and Toxicology Centre (also JACC)	Chemical industry
ECLA Economic Commission for Latin America (UN-ECOSOC)	Regional IG
ECMWF European Centre for Medium-range Weather Forecasts	Meteorology
ECOR Engineering Commission on Ocean Resources (ICSU)	Marine
ECOSOC Economic and Social Council (UN)	Intergov.
ECWA Economic Commission for West Africa (UN)	Regional IG
EDB Environmental Defense Fund (USA)	Conservation
EDIA European Carbon Dioxide Association	Chemical industry
EEB European Environmental Bureau	NGO
EEC European Economic Community	Regional IG
EEDB Energy and Economic Data Bank (IAEA)	Data/energy
EEPP European Environmental Policy Programme (IEEP and IIED)	Conservation
EEZ Exclusive Economic Zone (UNCLOS)	Legal
EFCTC European Fluorocarbon Technical Committee	Chemical industry
EFTA European Free Trade Association	Regional
EHCP Environmental Health Criteria Programme (WHO)	Chemical
EHSC Environmental Health and Safety Committee (WHO)	Chemical
EIA Environmental Impact Assessment	Monitoring
EINCECS European Inventory of Commercial Chemical Substances (EEC)	Data/chemicals
EINECS European Inventory of Existing Chemical Substances (EEC)	Data/chemicals
EIS Environmental Impact Statement	
EISCAT European Incoherent Scatter Scientific Association (NERC)	Data
ELB Environment Liaison Group (ICSU)	Conservation
ELC Environmental Liaison Centre (UN)	Conservation
ELINCS European List of New Chemical Substances (EEC)	Data/chemicals
EMEP Monitoring and Evaluation of Long Range Transport of Air Pollutants in Europe (UN-ECOSOC, ECE)	Data/atmosphere
EMIC Environmental Mutagen Information Centre	Data/chemicals
ENDS Environmental Data Services (UK)	Data/journal
ENDS European Nuclear Documentation System	Data/nuclear
ENUWAR Environmental Consequences of Nuclear War (SCOPE of ICSU)	Nuclear
EOIC Ethylene Oxide Industry Council (USA)	Chemical industry
EPA Environmental Protection Agency (USA)	Government
EPCA European Petrochemical Association	Chemical industry
EPIA European Petroleum Industries Association (proposed)	Industry NGO
EPOCH European Programme on Climatology and Natural Hazards	Climate
EPPO European Plant Protection Organization	Botanical
EQUO Environmental Quality Objective	
ERS ESA Remote Sensing Satellite	Satellite
ESA European Space Agency	Data/satellite
ESCAP Economic and Social Commission for Asia and the Pacific (UN-ECOSC)	Regional IG
ESF European Science Foundation (ICSU)	Science general
ESO European Southern Observatory (ICSU)	Astronomy
ESPRIT Strategic Research in the Field of Information Technology (EEC)	Data/IT
ESRC European Science Research Council	Science general
ESRO European Space Research Organization	Space
ETIC Environmental Teratology Information Centre	Data/biology
EURATOM European Atomic Energy Community	Nuclear
EUROTRAC European Experiment on Transport and Transformation of Environmentally Relevant Trace Constituents in the Troposphere over Europe	Atmosphere
EUSIDIC European Association of Information Services	Data
FAGS Federation of Astronomical and Geophysical Data Analysis Services (ICSU)	Data/geophysics
FAO Food and Agriculture Organization (UN)	Intergov.
FAOR Federation of Asian and Oceanian Biochemists (ICSU)	Biochemistry
FAPPS Finnish Air Pollution Prevention Society	Atmosphere
FASAS Federation of Asian Scientific Academies and Societies (ICSU)	
FBA Freshwater Biological Association (NERC)	Water
FCC Food and Chemicals Codex	Data/chemicals

FCID Fachverband der Chemische Industrie Osterreichs	Chemical industry
FCN Federatie der Chemische Nijverheid van Belgie	Chemical industry
FDA Food and Drug Administration (US)	Food
FDIC Food and Drug Industries Council (UK)	Food
FEA Fédération Européenne des Associations d'Aerosols	Chemical industry
FEBS Federation of European Biochemical Societies	Biochemistry
FECS Federation of European Chemical Societies	Chemical industry
FEIQUE Federation Empressarial de la Industria Quimica Espanola	Chemical industry
FGGE First GARP Global Experiment (ICSU)	Climate
FIBEX First International BIOMASS Experiment (ICSU)	Climate
FICB Fédération des Industries Chimiques Belges	Chemical industry
FICI Federation of Irish Chemical Industries	Chemical industry
FICSAS Federation of Institutions Concerned with the Study of the Adriatic Sea	Marine
FICZ Falklands Interim Conservation Zone	Marine
FIFRA Federal Insecticide, Fungicide and Rodenticide Act (USA)	Legal/agro.
FIQV Fonds d'Intervention pour la Qualité de la Vie	Conservation
FMC Federal Maritime Commission (USA)	Marine
FOE Friends of the Earth	Conservation
FOI Freedom of Information Act (USA)	Legal
FRAME Fund for the Replacement of Animals in Medical Experiments	Biology
FRS Fellow of the Royal Society (UK)	Science general
FWQA Federal Water Quality Administration (USA)	Water
GAOCMAO Gulf Areas Oil Companies Mutual Aid Association	Oil industry
GARP Global Atmospheric Research Programme (WMO/ICSU)	Climate
GATE GARP Atlantic Tropical Experiment (WMO/ICSU)	Climate
GATT General Agreement on Tariffs and Trade (UNCTAD)	Economic
GCP Global Change Programme (Unesco/ICSU)	Climate
GDCH Gesellschaft Deutscher Chemiker	Chemical industry
GEBCO General Bathymetric Chart of the Oceans (ICSU)	Cartography/marine
GELTSPAP Group of Experts on Long-term Scientific Policy and Planning (IOC)	Marine
GEMS Global Environment Monitoring System (UNEP)	Data
GEOSAT Geodetic Satellite (US Navy)	Satellite
GESAMP Group of Experts on the Scientific Aspects of Marine Pollution (IMO/FAO/Unesco/WMO/WHO/IAEA/UNEP)	Marine
GET Great Environmental Truth	
GEWEX Global Energy and Water Cycle Experiment of WCRP (WMO/ICSU)	Climate
GFCM General Fisheries Council for the Mediterranean	Fish.
GIAM Global Implications of Applied Microbiology	Microbiology
GIFAP Groupement International des Associations de Fabricants de Pesticides	Agro. industry
GIN Global Information Network (UNCSTD)	Data
GIPME Global Investigation of Pollution in the Marine Environment (IOC)	Marine
GMAG Genetic Manipulation Advisory Group (UK)	Biotechnology
GMDSS Global Maritime Distress and Safety System (IMO)	Satellite
GMO Genetically Modified Organism(s)	Biotechnology
GOOS Global Ozone Observing System (IOC)	Atmosphere
GOS Global Observing System (IOC)	Marine
GRAS Generally Recognized as Safe (USA/FDA)	Food/chemicals
GRID Global Resource Information Database (UNEP)	Data
GRPE Group of Rapporteurs on Atmospheric Pollution and Energy (ECE)	Energy
GSA Geological Society of Africa (ICSU)	Geology
GURC Gulf Universities Research Consortium (KAP)	Marine
HAPEX Hydrological Atmospheric Pilot Experiment (ICSU)	Atmosphere
HAS Hazard Alert System (ILO)	Health and safety
HASAWA Health and Safety at Work Act (UK)	Health and safety
HAZAN Hazard Analysis	Safety
HAZOP Hazard and Operability Study	Safety
HELMEPA Hellenic Marine Environment Protection Association (MAP)	Marine
HOMS Hydrological Operational Multi-purpose Sub-programme (WMO)	Hydrology
HPC Health Protection Commission (CEFIC)	Chemical industry

HSE Health and Safety Executive (UK)	Health and safety
IAA International Astronautical Academy (ICSU)	Space
IABO International Association for Biological Oceanography (ICSU)	Marine
IABS International Association of Biological Standardization (ICSU)	Standards
IAC International Agricultural Centre (Wageningen, NL)	Agro.
IACOMS International Advisory Committee on Marine Services (ICSU)	Marine
IACS International Association of Classification Societies	Marine
IADC International Association of Drilling Contractors	Geology
IAEA International Atomic Energy Agency (UN)	Nuclear
IAEC International Association of Environmental Co-ordinators (IPRE)	
IAEE International Association of Earthquake Engineering (ICSU)	Geology
IAEG International Association of Engineering Geology (ICSU)	Geology
IAFS International Academy of Environmental Safety (Belgium)	
IAF International Astronautical Federation (ICSU)	Space
IAG International Association of Geodesy (ICSU)	Geodesy
IAGA International Association of Geomagnetism and Aeronomy (ICSU)	Geophysics
IAGC International Association on Geochemistry and Cosmochemistry (ICSU)	Geophysics
IAGOD International Association on the Genesis of Ore Deposits (ICSU)	Geology
IAH International Association of Hydrogeologists (ICSU)	Geology
IAHS International Association of Hydrological Sciences (UK)	Water
IAIA International Association for Impact Assessment	
IAITO International Association of Independent Tanker Owners	Marine
IAMAP International Association of Meteorology and Atmospheric Physics (ICSU)	Climate
IAMG International Association of Mathematical Geology (ICSU)	Geology
IAMS International Association of Microbiological Sciences	Microbiology
IAP International Association of Planetology	Astronomy
IAPC International Association for Pollution Control	
IAPO International Association of Physical Oceanography	Marine
IAPP International Association of Plant Physiology (ICSU)	Biology
IAPSO International Association for the Physical Sciences of the Ocean (ICSU)	Marine
IAPT International Association of Plant Taxonomy (ICSU)	Biology
IARC International Agency for Research on Cancer (WHO)	Cancer
IARC International Agricultural Research Centres (ICSU)	Agro.
IAS International Association of Sedimentologists (ICSU)	Geology
IASPEI International Association of Seismology and Physics of the Earth's Interior (ICSU)	Geophys.
IAU International Astronomical Union (ICSU)	Astronomy
IAVCEI International Association of Volcanology and Chemistry of the Earth's Interior (ICSU)	Geophysics
IAWPRC International Association on Water Pollution Research and Control (ICSU)	Water
IAWR International Arbeitsgemeinschaft der Wasserwerke im Rhein Einzugsgebiet (FRG)	Water
IBFSC International Baltic Sea Fisheries Commission	Fish.
IBI International Bureau for Informatics (ICSU)	Data/IT
IBN International Biosciences Networks (ICSU)	
IBP International Biological Programme, 1964–74 (ICSU)	
IBPGR International Board for Plant Genetic Resources (ICSU)	Botanical
IBRD International Bank for Reconstruction and Development (World Bank – see **BIRD**)	Development
ICA International Cartographic Association (ICSU)	Cartography
ICACGP International Commission on Atmospheric Chemistry and Global Pollution (ICSU)	Climate
ICAE International Commission on Atmospheric Electricity (ICSU)	Climate
ICAO International Civil Aviation Organization (UN)	Transport
ICARDA International Centre for Agricultural Research in Dry Areas (ICSU)	Agro.
ICC International Computation Centre (UN)	Data
ICC International Chamber of Commerce	
ICCE International Centre for Conservation Education (UK)	Conservation
ICCE International Commission on Continental Erosion (ICSU)	Geology

ICCL International Commission on Climate (ICSU)	Climate
ICCP International Commission on Cloud Physics (ICSU)	Climate
ICE International Centre for the Environment	Conservation
ICEAM International Committee on Economic and Applied Microbiology (ICSU)	Microbiology
ICEF International Conference on Environment Future	Conservation
ICEF International Federation of Chemical, Energy and General Workers Unions	Unions
ICES International Council for the Exploration of the Sea (Copenhagen)	Marine
ICES International Commission on Erosion and Sedimentation (ICSU)	Sedimentology
ICFTU International Confederation of Free Trade Unions	Unions
ICG International Commission on Geodynamics	Geology
ICGEB International Centre for Genetic Engineering and Biotechnology (ICSU)	Biotechnology
ICGW International Commission on Groundwater (ICSU)	Water
ICHMT International Centre for Mass and Heat Transfer (ICSU)	Energy
ICIE International Centre for Industry and the Environment (ICC)	Industry
ICITA International Co-operative Investigations of the Tropical Atlantic (IOC)	Marine
ICID International Commission on Irrigation and Drainage (ICSU)	Agro.
ICIPE International Centre for Insect Physiology and Ecology (ICSU)	Biotechnology
ICL International Commission on the Lithosphere (ICSU)	Climate
ICLAS International Council on Laboratory Animal Science (ICSU)	Biology
ICMG International Commission for Microbial Genetics (ICSU)	Biotechnology
ICMT International Commission on Mycotoxicology (ICSU)	Biology
ICMUA International Commission on Meteorology of the Upper Atmosphere (ICSU)	Meteorology
ICNAF International Commission for North-West Atlantic Fisheries (FAO)	Fish.
ICO International Carbohydrate Organization (ICSU)	Food
ICOD International Centre for Ocean Development (Canada)	Development
ICOE International Conference on Oil and the Environment	Oil
ICOH International Committee on Occupational Health	Health and safety
ICOME International Commission on Microbial Ecology (ICSU)	Biotechnology
ICOMIA International Council of Marine Industry Association	Marine industry
ICPAE International Commission on Planetary Atmospheres and their Evolution (ICSU)	Astronomy
ICPEMC International Commission for Protection against Environmental Mutagens and Carcinogens	Cancer
ICPM International Commission on Polar Meteorology (ICSU)	Polar
ICRAF International Council for Research in Agroforestry	Forestry
ICRISAT International Crops Research Institute for Semi-arid Tropics (ICSU)	Agro.
ICRO International Cell Research Organization (ICSU)	Biotechnology
ICRP International Commission on Radiological Protection	Nuclear
ICRU International Commission on Radiation Units	Nuclear
ICS International Chamber of Shipping	Marine transport
ICS International Commission on Stratigraphy (ICSU)	Geology
ICSEM International Commission for the Scientific Exploration of the Mediterranean Sea	Marine
ICSI International Commission on Snow and Ice (ICSU)	Climate
ICSPRO Inter-secretariat Committee on Scientific Programmes Relating to Oceanography (FAO/Unesco/WHO/IMO)	Marine
ICSU International Council of Scientific Unions	
ICSW International Commission on Surface Water (ICSU)	Water
ICTA International Centre for Tropical Agriculture (ICSU)	Agro.
ICVA International Council of Voluntary Agencies	NGO
ICWQ International Commission on Water Quality (ICSU)	Water
ICWRS International Commission on Water Resources Systems (ICSU)	Water
ICWU International Chemical Workers Union	Union
IDA International Development Association	Development
IDLH Immediately Dangerous to Life and Health	Health and safety
IDNDR International Decade for Natural Disaster Reduction (ICSU)	Disasters
IDOE International Decade of Ocean Exploration	Marine
IDRC International Development Research Centre (ICSU)	Development

IEA International Energy Agency — Energy
IEA International Epidemiological Association (IPCS) — Epidemiology
IEEP Institute for European Environment Policy (Bonn, FRG) — Conservation
IEO Industry and Environment Office (UNEP) — Industry
IER International Environment Rapporteur (ECE) — Regional IG
IFAD International Fund for Agriculture Development (ICSU) — Agro.
IFC Convention on the Establishment of an International Fund for Compensation for Oil Pollution Damage, 1971 (IMO) (also **CLC**, **CRISTAL** and **TOVALOP**) — Legal/marine
IFE Institute of Freshwater Ecology — Biology
IFIP International Federation for Information Processing (ICSU) — Data
IGBP International Geosphere–Biosphere Programme (ICSU: see **SCGB**) — Climate
IGC International Geological Congress (ICSU) — Geology
IGCP International Geological Correlation Programme (Unesco LUGS) — Geology
IGOSS Intergrated Global Ocean Station System (WMO) — Climate
IGS Institute of Geological Sciences — Geology
IGU International Geographical Union (ICSU) — Geology
IGY International Geophysical Year (ICSU) — Geophysics
IH Institute of Hydrology (NERC) — Water
IHD International Hydrological Decade — Water
IHB International Hydrographic Bureau (IHO) — Climate
IHO International Hydrographic Organization (ICSU) — Climate
IHP International Hydrological Programme (ICSU) — Water
IHR International Hydrographic Review — Water/journal
IIASA International Institute for Applied Systems Analysis (Laxenburg) — Data
IIEA International Institute for Environmental Affairs — Education
IIED International Institute for Environment and Development — Education
IIOE International Indian Ocean Expedition (IOC) — Marine
IISI International Iron and Steel Institute — Industry
IITA International Institute of Tropical Agriculture (ICSU) — Agro.
ILA International Law Association — Legal
ILCA International Livestock Centre for Africa — Agro.
ILMR International Laboratory of Marine Radioactivity (IAEA) — Nuclear
ILO International Labour Organization (UN) — Labour
ILSI International Life Sciences Institute — Science
ILZRO International Lead–Zinc Research Organization — Industry
IMA International Mineralogical Association (ICSU) — Minerology
IMB Institute of Marine Biochemistry (UK) — Marine
IMDG International Maritime Dangerous Goods Code (IMO) — Legal/transport
IMEKO International Measurement Confederation (ICSU) — Standards
IMER Institute of Marine Environmental Research — Marine
IMF International Monetary Fund — Economic
IMI International Meteorological Institute (Stockholm) — Meteorology
IMO International Maritime Organization — Intergov.
IMS International Magnetospheric Study (ICSU) — Meteorology
INA Institute National Agronomique — Agro.
INDIS Industrial Information System (UNIDO) — Data
INFOTERRA International Referral System for Sources of Environmental Information (FAO/UNEP) — Data
INHIGEO Committee on History of Geological Sciences (ICSU) — Geology
INIS International Nuclear Information System (IAEA) — Data
INMARSAT International Maritime Satellite Organization — Satellite
INQUA International Union for Quaternary Research (ICSU) — Geology
INSA International Shipowners Association (Eastern bloc) — Marine transport
INSPEC International Information Services for the Physics and Engineering Communities — Database
INTECOL International Association for Ecology (ICSU) — Ecology
INTELSAT International Telecommunications Satellite Organization — Satellite
INTER-TANKO International Association of Independent Tanker Owners — Marine transport
INTIB Industrial and Technological Information Bank (UNIDO) — Database
IOBC International Organization for Biological Control (ICSU) — Biology
IOC Intergovernmental Oceanographic Commission (Unesco) — Marine
IOC International Ozone Commission (ICSU) — Climate
IOCARIBE Association for the Caribbean and Adjacent Regions (IOC) — Marine

IOCD International Organization for Chemical Sciences in Development (ICSU)   Chemicals
IOCU International Organization of Consumer Unions   Consumer
IODE International Oceanographic Data Exchange (IOC)   Data
IOFC International Ocean Fisheries Commission (FAO)   Fish.
IOI International Ocean Institute   Marine
IOPC International Oil Pollution Compensation Fund (IMO) (also **CLC, CRISTAL, IFC, TOVALOP**)   Legal/marine
IOSDL Institute of Oceanographic Sciences Deacon Laboratory (NERC)   Oceanography
IOSO International Oil Spill Association   Marine
IOTC International Oil Tankers Commission   Marine transport
IOTTSG International Oil Tankers Terminal Safety Group   Marine transport
IOV Institute of Virology (NERC)   Biology
IPA International Palaeontological Association (ICSU)   Palaeonotology
IPAI International Primary Aluminium Institute   Industry
IPCC Intergovernmental Panel on Climate Change (UNEP)   Climate
IPCS International Programme on Chemical Safety (WHO/ILO/UNEP)   Chemicals
IPFC Indo-Pacific Fisheries Council (FAO)   Fish
IPIECA International Petroleum Industry Environmental Conservation Association   Industry NGO
IPMS International Polar Motion Service (ICSU)   Polar
IPRE International Professional Association for Environmental Affairs   Conservation
IPY International Polar Year (ICSU)   Polar
IQSY International Years of the Quiet Sun (ICSU)
IRC International Research Council (pre-ICSU)
IRC International Commission on Radiation (IAEA)   Nuclear
IRCHA Institute National de Recherche Chimique Appliquée   Chemicals
IRCP International Commission on Radiological Protection   Nuclear
IRLG Inter-agency Regulatory Liaison Group (FDA/OSHA/EPA/CPSC)   Legal
IRPA International Radiation Protection Association   Nuclear
IRPTC International Register of Potentially Toxic Chemicals (UNEP)   Chemicals
IRRI International Rice Research Institute   Agro.
IRS International Referral System (UNEP)   Data
ISC International Seismological Centre (ICSU)   Geology
ISCCP International Satellite Cloud Climatology Project (ICSU)   Climate
ISGHO International Study Group on Hydrocarbon Oxidization (ICE) Chemicals
ISGOTT International Safety Guide for Oil Tankers and Terminals   Marine transport
ISHS International Society of Horticultural Science (ICSU)   Agro.
ISI International Statistical Institute (ICSU)   Standards
ISIC International Standard Industrial Classification   Standards
ISLSCP International Satellite Land Surface Climatology Project (WMO/UNEP/ICSU/IAMAP and COSPAR)   Climate
ISMA International Superphosphate Manufacturers Association   Chemical industry
ISO International Organization for Standardization   Standards
ISOMED International Society for Mediterranean Ecology   Marine
ISPA International Society for the Protection of Animals   Fauna
ISSC International Sciences Council (ICSU)   Science general
ISSP International Solar Systems Programme (ICSU)   Energy
ISSS International Society of Soil Science (ICSU)   Agro.
ISTPM Institute Scientifique and Technique des Pêches Maritimes   Fish.
ISY International Space Year (COSPAR/ICSU: proposed for 1992; see **SAFISY**)   Space
ITC International Tar Conference (EC)   Chemicals
ITE Institute of Terrestrial Ecology (NERC)   Ecology
ITIA International Tanker Indemnity Association   Marine transport
ITOPF International Tanker Owners Pollution Federation   Marine transport
ITSSC International Toxic Substances Strategy Committee   Chemicals
ITTO International Tropical Timber Organization (Yokohama)   Forestry
ITU International Telecommunications Union   Tele.
IUAC International Union Against Cancer (UICC)   Cancer
IUAES International Union for Anthropological and Ethnological Sciences (ICSU)   Anthropological
IUAPPA International Union of Air Pollution Prevention Associations   Atmosphere
IUB International Union of Biochemistry (ICSU)   Biochemistry

IUBS International Union of Biological Sciences (ICSU) — Biology
IUCN International Union for the Conservation of Nature and Natural Resources — Conservation
IUFRO International Union of Forestry Research Organizations (ICSU) — Forestry
IUGG International Union of Geodesy and Geophysics (ICSU) — Geodesy
IUGS International Union of Geological Sciences (ICSU) — Geology
IUMS International Union of Microbiological Societies (IUBS/ICSU) — Microbiology
IUPAB International Union of Pure and Applied Biophysics (ICSU) — Biophysics
IUPAC International Union of Pure and Applied Chemistry (ICSU) — Chemistry
IUPAP International Union of Pure and Applied Physics (ICSU) — Physics
IUPsyS International Union of Psychological Science (ICSU) — Psychology
IUTOX International Union of Toxicology (ICSU) — Toxicology
IWC International Waddenzee Commissie — Marine
IWC International Whaling Commission — Marine
IWSA International Water Supply Association (ICSU) — Water

JACC Joint Assessment of Commodity Chemicals (ECETOC) — Chemical industry
JCIA Japanese Chemical Industry Association — Chemical industry
JECFA Joint Expert Committee on Food Additives (FAO/WHO) — Food
JETOC Japanese Chemical Industry Ecology and Toxicology Centre — Chemical industry
JGOFS Joint Global Ocean Flux Study (SCOR/ICSU) — Oceanography
JMPR Joint Meeting on Pesticide Residues (FAO/WHO) — Agro.
JOA Joint Oceanographic Assembly (ICSU/SCOR) — Oceanography
JOC Joint Organizing Committee for GARP (WMO/ICSU) — Climate
JSC Joint Scientific Committee of the WCRP (WMO/ICSU) — Climate

KAP Kuwait Action Plan (UNEP Oceans and Coastal Areas Programme) — Marine
KIWA Keuringsinstituut voor Waterleidingartikelen (NL) — Water
KNCV Koninklijke Nederlandse Chemische Vereniging (NL) — Chemical industry
KNMI Koninklijke Nederlandse Meteorologische Instituut (NL) — Meteorology

LABN Latin American Biosciences Network (IBN of ICSU) — Bioscience
LAFTA Latin America Free Trade Area — Regional IG
LASA Latin American Ship Owners Association — Marine transport
LDC Convention on the Prevention of Marine Pollution by Dumping of Wastes and Other Matter (London Dumping Convention) — Legal/wastes
LEPOR Long-term Expanded Programme for Oceanic Exploration and Research (IOC) — Oceanography
LPGA Liquified Natural Gas Association (USA) — Industry
LPGITA Liquified Petroleum Gas Industry Technical Association — Industry

MAB Man and the Biosphere Programme (Unesco) — Conservation
MAC Maximum Admissible Concentration — Chemical
MACINTER Man–Computer Interaction Research (ICSU/IUPsyS) — Data/IT
MAFF Ministry of Agriculture, Fisheries and Food (UK) — Agro.
MAGIC Model of Acidification of Groundwater in Catchments (IH) — Water
MAMBO Mediterranean Association for Marine Biology and Oceanography — Marine
MAP Middle Atmosphere Programme (ICSU) — Atmosphere
MAP Mediterranean Action Plan (UNEP Oceans and Coastal Areas) — Marine
MAP-MOPP Pilot Project on Marine Pollution Monitoring (IGOSS) — Marine
MARC Monitoring and Assessment Research Centre (UK) — Research
MARPOL International Convention for the Prevention of Pollution from Ships, 1973 *et seq.* (IMO) — Legal/marine
MARPOL-MON Marine Pollution Monitoring System (IGOSS) — Marine
MBA Marine Biological Association (UK) — Marine
MEDI Marine Environment Data and Information Referral System (IOC) — Data/marine
MEDI-CHEM Occupational Health in the Chemical Industry (PCIAOH) — Chemical industry
MEDLARS Medical Literature Analysis and Retrieval System — Data/medical
MEDPOL Co-ordinated Mediterranean Pollution Monitoring and Research Programme (MAP) — Marine
MEMAC Marine Emergency Mutual Aid Centre (KAP) — Marine
MEPC Marine Environment Protection Committee (IMO) — Marine
MERIT Monitor Earth Rotation and Inter-compare the Techniques of Observation and Analysis (ICSU)
MIRCEN Microbial Resource Centres (WHO) — Biology
MIRG Marine Industry Response Group (USA) — Marine transport

MMS Minerals Management Service (USGS) — Geology
MODU Mobile Offshore Drilling Unit — Drilling
MONEX Monsoon Experiment (ICSU; see **WAMEX**) — Climate
MONSEE Monitoring the Sun Earth Environment (ICSU) — Climate
MRC Medical Research Council — Medical
MSC Maritime Safety Committee (IMO) — Marine
mSv Millisievert — Nuclear
MTOE Million tonnes oil equivalent — Energy

NAAQS National Ambient Air Quality Standards (EPA) — Atmosphere
NACA National Agricultural Chemicals Association (USA) — Agro.
NACD National Association of Chemical Distributors (USA) — Chemical industry
NAEP National Agency of Environmental Protection (Denmark) — Conservation
NAFO North-West Atlantic Fisheries Organization — Fish.
NAS National Academy of Science (USA) — Science general
NASA National Aeronautics and Space Administration (USA) — Space
NATO North Atlantic Treaty Organization — Regional
NAWDIC National Association of Waste Disposal Contractors (UK) — Waste
NBS National Bureau of Standards (USA) — Standards
NC Nordic Council — Regional
NCC Nature Conservancy Council (UK) — Conservation
NCI National Cancer Institute (USA) — Cancer
NCTR National Centre for Toxicological Research (UK) — Toxicology
NEAFO North-East Atlantic Fisheries Organization — Fish.
NEPA National Environmental Policy Act (USA) — Legal
NERC Natural Environmental Research Council (UK) — Research
NESHAP National Emission Standards for Hazardous Air Pollutants (EPA) — Atmosphere
NFAIS National Federation of American Information Services — Data
NGO Non-governmental Organization — NGO
NHMRC National Health and Medical Research Council (UK) — Medicine
NIEHS National Institute of Environmental Health Sciences — Science general
NIH National Institute of Health (USA) — Health
NIHMR National Institute for Health and Medical Research (France) — Health
NIMBY 'Not in My Back Yard!' — Conservation
NIOSH National Institute of Occupational Health and Safety (USA) — Health and Safety
NIPH National Institute of Public Health (Bilthoven, NL) — PH
NISCON National Industrial Safety Conference (RoSPA) — Safety
NKI Norges Kjemsike Industrigruppe (Norway) — Chemical industry
NL The Netherlands
NOAA National Oceanic and Atmospheric Administration (USA) — Atmosphere
NODC National Oceanographic Data Center (US) — Data/oceanography
NOFO Norwegian Clean Seas Association for Operation Companies — Oil industry
NORAD Royal Norwegian Agency for International Development — Development
NPC National Ports Council (UK) — Marine transport
NPL National Physical Laboratory (UK) — Physical sciences
NRC National Research Council (of NAS) — Science general
NRDC National Research Development Council (UK) — Science general
NRPB National Radiological Protection Board (UK) — Nuclear
NRSC National Remote Sensing Centre (NERC) — Data
NSF National Science Foundation (USA) — Science general
NTIS National Technical Information Service (USA) — Database
NUSS Nuclear Safety Standards — Nuclear
NUTIS Unit for Thematic Information Systems (NERC) — Data

OAMEX Ocean Atmosphere Materials Exchanges (ICSU) — Atmosphere
OAS Organization of American States — Regional IG
OAU Organization of African Unity — Regional IG
OCAW(IU) Oil, Chemical and Atomic Workers International Union — Union
OCIMF Oil Companies International Marine Forum — Marine transport
OCS Outer Continental Shelf — Legal
ODA Overseas Development Administration (UK) — Development
ODAS Ocean Data Acquisition Systems, Aids and Devices (ICSU) — Data/marine
ODNRI Overseas Development Natural Resources Institute (UK) — Development
ODP Ocean Drilling Programme — Geology
OECD Organization for Economic Co-operation and Development — Regional IG

OECS Organization of Eastern Caribbean States	Regional IG
OEL Occupational Exposure Level	Health and safety
OILPOL International Convention for the Prevention of Pollution of the Sea by Oil, 1978 (IMO)	Legal/marine
OJEC Official Journal of the European Communities (EC)	Legal/journal
OMCI Organisation Intergouvernmentale de la Navigation Maritime (IMO)	Intergov.
OMM Organisation Meteorologique Mondiale (WMO)	Intergov.
OMS Organisation Mondiale de la Santé (WHO)	Intergov.
ONG Organisation non-gouvernementale (NGO)	NGO
ONU Organisation des Nations Unies (UN)	Intergov.
ONUDI Organisation des Nations Unies pour le Developpement Industriel (UNIDO)	Intergov.
OPEC Organization of Petroleum Exporting Countries	Intergov.
OPP Office of Pesticide Programmes (EPA)	Agro.
OPTS Office of Pesticides and Toxic Substances (EPA)	Agro.
OSHA Occupational Health and Safety Administration (USA)	Health and safety
OSIR Oil Spill Intelligence Report (USA)	Data/journal
OST Office of Science and Technology (USA)	Science general
OSW Office of Solid Waste (EPA)	Waste
OTAN Organisation du Traité Atlantique Nord (NATO)	Regional IG
OTC Office of Technical Co-operation (UN)	Intergov.
OTEC Ocean Thermal Energy Conversion	Energy
OTS Office of Toxic Substances (EPA)	Chemicals
PAARS Pan-American Association of Biochemical Societies	Biochemistry
PAC Programme Activity Centre(s) (UNEP)	Management
PAC Programme Advisory Committee (IPCS)	Chemicals
PACT Pollution Abatement Control Technology (ECE/UNEP)	Pollution
PAHO Pan-American Health Organization (WHO)	Regional IG
PANPARCOM Paris Commission	Intergov.
PBR Polybrominated biphenyl	Chemical
PBq Petabequerel	Nuclear
PCA(H) Polycyclic aromatic hydrocarbon	Chemical
PCB Polychlorinated biphenyl	Chemical
PCDD Polychloro-dibenzo-para-dioxin	Chemical
PCDF Polychloro-dibenzofuran	Chemical
PCP Pentachlorophenol	Chemical
PCT Polychlorinated terphenyls	Chemical
PEL Permissible Exposure Levels	Health and safety
PERGSA Red Sea and Gulf of Aden Environment Programme (ALECSO)	Marine
PIACT Programme for the Improvement of Working Conditions and Environment (ILO)	Labour
PICC Professional Institutions Council for Conservation	Conservation
PIM Pacem in Maribus	Marine
PN(A)H Polynuclear aromatic hydrocarbon	Chemical
PNUE Programme des Nations Unies pour l'Environment (UNEP)	Intergov.
POEM Physical Oceanography of the Eastern Mediterranean (SCOR)	Data
POLEX Polar Experiment (ICSU/SCAR)	Polar
ppb Parts per billion	Standards
ppm Parts per million	Standards
PPP Polluter Pays Principle	Economic
PSA Pacific Science Association (ICSU)	Science general
PSFG Permanent Service on Fluctuation of Glaciers (ICSU/SCAR)	Polar
PTSED Pesticide and Toxic Substances Enforcement Division (EPA)	Agro.
PVC Polyvinyl chloride	Chemical
QA Quality Assurance	Management
QC Quality Control	Management
QUANGO Quasi-autonomous Non-governmental Organization	Management
RAC Re-combinant-DNA Advisory Committee (NIH)	Biotechnology
RCEP Royal Commission on Environmental Pollution (UK)	Royal Commission
RCRA Resource Conservation and Recovery Act (USA)	Legal
REC Radiation Equivalent Chemical (numerical value)	Nuclear
RID International Regulations for the Carriage of Goods by Rail (EC)	Transport

RIOS River Inputs to Ocean Systems — Marine
RNA Ribonucleic acid — Biotechnology
ROCC Regional Oil Combating Centre (MAP) — Marine
ROPME Regional Organization for the Protection of the Marine Environment (KAP) — Marine
RoSPA Royal Society for the Prevention of Accidents — Safety
RS Royal Society (UK) — Science general
RSC Royal Society of Chemistry (UK) — Chemistry
RTECS Register of Toxic Effects of Chemical Substances (NIH) — Chemicals

SAC Scientific Advisory Committee (UNEP) — Science general
SACEP South Asia Co-operative Environment Programme (UNEP) — Regional IG
SAEP Senior Advisors on Environmental Problems (UN-ECE) — Regional IG
SAFISY Space Agencies Forum for the International Space Year (ICSU) — Space
SAOIR South African Institute of Oceanographic Research — Marine
SAP Scientific Advisory Panel (FIFRA)
SAREC Swedish Agency for Research Co-operation with Developing Countries — Development
SCAR Scientific Committee on Antarctic Research (ICSU) — Polar
SCEI Swedish Council of Environmental Information — Data
SCF Scientific Committee for Food (EEC) — Food
SCGB Standing Committee for the Geosphere–Biosphere Programme (ICSU) — Climate
SCIBP Special Committee for the International Biological Programme (ICSU) — Biology
SCOPCAS Standing Committee on Oil Pollution Clean-up at Sea (UK) — Marine
SCOPE Scientific Committee on Problems of the Environment (ICSU) — Research
SCOR Scientific Committee on Oceanic Research (ICSU) — Oceanography
SCOSTEP Scientific Committee on Solar-Terrestrial Physics (ICSU: see STEP) — Astronomy
SCOTTIE Society for the Control of Troublesome and Toxic Industrial Emissions (UK) — Atmosphere
SDIA Soap and Detergent Industry Association (UK) — Chemical industry
SECOTOX International Society for Ecotoxicology and Environmental Safety — Toxicology
SEARNG South-East Asia Region Network for Geosciences (ICSU/IBN) — Geology
SEEEE Societe Européenne d'Etudes et d'Essais d'Environment — Conservation
SEG Society of Economic Geologists — Geology
SEPC Service de l'Environnement et la Protection du Consommateur (EEC) — Consumer
SERC Science and Engineering Research Council (UK)
SES Solar Energy Society (ICSU) — Energy
SETAC Society of Environmental Toxicology and Chemistry (UK) — Toxicology
SFR Societé Française de Radioprotection — Nuclear
SGAMD Society for Geology Applied to Mineral Deposits (ICSU) — Geology
SGCI Sweischzerische Gesellschaft fur Chemische Industrie — Chemical industry
SGOMSEC Scientific Group on Methodologies for the Safety Evaluation of Chemicals (ICSU) — Chemical
SI Statutory Instrument — Legal
SID Society for International Development — Development
SIDA Swedish International Development Authority — Development
SIP Solar and Interplanetary Programmes (ICSU) — Space
SIPRI Stockholm International Peace Research Institute — Research
SKI Sveriges Kemiske Industrikontor — Chemical industry
SMBA Scottish Marine Biological Association (NERC) — Marine
SMIC Study of Man's Impact on Climate — Climate
SMRU Sea Mammal Research Unit (NERC) — Marine
SMY Solar Maximum Year (ICSU) — Astronomy
SMYA Solar Maximum Year Analysis (see also **SMY, ICSU**) — Astronomy
SO₂ Sulphur dioxide — Chemical
SOCMA Synthetic Organic Chemicals Manufacturers Association — Chemical industry
SOEC Statistical Office of the European Communities — Standards
SOHO Solar Oscillations and Heliospheric Observatory (NERC) — Astronomy
SOLAS International Convention for Safety of Life at Sea (IMO) — Legal
SPC South Pacific Commission — Regional IG

SPEC South Pacific Bureau for Economic Co-operation	Regional IG
SPI Society of the Plastics Industry (UK)	Industry
SPIB Society of Petroleum Industry Biologists	Biology
SPREP South Pacific Regional Environment Programme	Regional IG
SSSI Site of Special Scientific Interest (NCC)	Conservation
STABLE Stable Antarctic Boundary Layer Experiment (NERC)	Polar
STEL Short-Term Exposure Level	Health and safety
STEP Solar-Terrestrial Energy Programme (ICSU/SCOSTEP)	Energy
STEP Science and Technology for Environmental Protection (NERC)	Conservation
STP-MET Solar-Terrestrial Physics Meteorology (ICSU/SCOSTEP)	Meteorology
SUT Society for Underwater Technology (UK)	Marine
SWCC Second World Climate Conference of WCRP (WMO/ICSU)	Climate
SWMTEP System-wide Medium-term Environment Programme (ILO/ UNEP)	Management
TAC Technical Advisory Committee of CGIAR	Agro.
TAC Total Allowable Catch (EEC)	Fish.
TAPS Trans-Alaska Pipeline System	Energy
TBT Tributyltin	Chemical
TEMA Training, Education and Mutual Assistance in the Marine Sciences (ICSU)	Marine
TCDD 2,3,7,8-Tetrachlorodibenzo-para-dioxin	Chemical
TDI Tolerable Daily Intake	Chemical
TLV Threshold Limit Value	Health and safety
TNC Trans-national Corporation	Industry
TNO Organization for Applied Scientific Research (NL)	Research
TOGA Study of the Interannual Variability of the Tropical Oceans and Global Atmosphere (ICSU/SCOR)	Climate
TOSCA Toxic Substances Control Act (USA)	Legal
TOVALOP Tanker Owners Voluntary Agreement Concerning Liability for Oil Pollution (also **CLC**, **CRISTAL** and **IFC**)	Marine transport
TOWD Toxic Waste Disposal (ICSU/COGENE)	Waste
TWAS Third World Academy of Sciences (ICSU/IBN)	Science general
UAEEC Union of EEC Artisans	Union
UARS Upper Atmosphere Research Satellite (NERC)	Satellite
UCPE Unit of Comparative Plant Ecology (NERC)	Botanical
UES Uniform Emission Standard	Atmosphere
UGAMP UK Universities' Global Atmospheric Modelling Project (NERC)	Climate
UIC Union des Industries Chimique	Chemical industry
UICC Union Internationale Contre le Cancer	Cancer
UKAEA UK Atomic Energy Authority	Nuclear
UKCIS UK Chemical Information Service (CIS)	Data/chemicals
UKREP UK Permanent Representative to the European Communities	
UMC Upper Mantle Committee (ICSU)	Geophysics
UMP Upper Mantle Programme (ICSU)	Geophysics
UN United Nations	Intergov.
UNCHE UN Conference on the Human Environment (Habitat)	Social
UNCHS UN Centre for Human Settlements (Habitat)	Social
UNCITRAL United Nations Commission on International Trade Law	Legal
UNCLOS UN Conference on the Law of the Sea	Legal
UNCSTD UN Conference on Science and Technology for Development	Development
UNCTAD UN Conference on Trade and Development	Trade
UNCTC UN Centre on Transnational Corporations	Industry
UNDIESA UN Department of International Economic and Social Affairs	Econ/social
UNDP UN Development Programme	Development
UNDRO UN Disaster Relief Organization	Disasters
UN-ECE UN Economic Commission for Europe (ECOSOC)	Regional IG
UN-ECOSOC UN Economic and Social Council	Intergov.
UNEP UN Environment Programme	Environment
UNEP-IEO UNEP Industry and Environment Office	Industry
UNEPTA UN Expanded Programme of Technical Assistance	Development
Unesco UN Educational, Scientific and Cultural Organization	Education
UNESOB UN Economic and Social Office in Beirut	Econ/social
UNFDAC UN Fund for Drug Abuse Control	Drugs

UNFPA UN Fund for Population Activities — Demography
UNICE Union des Industries de la Communauté Européenne — Industry NGO
UNIDO UN Industrial Development Organization — Development
UNIDROIT International Institute for the Unification of International Law — Legal
UNIF International Union for Inland Navigation — Union
UNIPEDE International Union of Producers and Distributors of Electrical Energy — Union
UNISIST Joint Project to Study the Feasibility of a World Scientific Information System (Unesco/ICSU) — Data/IT
UNITAR UN Institute for Training and Research — Education
UNRISD UN Research Institute for Social Development — Social
UNRWA UN Relief and Works Agency for Palestinian Refugees — Refugees
UNSAC UN Scientific Advisory Committee
UNSCEAR UN Scientific Committee on the Effects of Atomic Radiation — Nuclear
UNU United Nations University — Education
USCG United States Coast Guard — Marine
USDA United States Department of Agriculture — Agro.
USGS United States Geological Survey — Geology
USNOO United States Naval Oceanographic Office — Marine

VCI Verband der Chemischen Industrie (FRG) — Chemical industry
VLCC Very Large Crude (oil) Carrier — Marine transport
VOC Volatile Organic Compound — Chemical
VOS Voluntary Observing Ships (WMO/WCRP/CCCD) — Climate

WAES Workshop on Alternative Energy Strategies — Energy
WAGBI Wildflowers Association of Great Britain and Northern Ireland — Botanical
WAITRO World Association of Industrial and Technical Research Organizations (ICSU) — Industry
WAMEY West African Monsoon Experiment (ICSU) — Climate
WAP Working Group on Air Pollution (Belgium) — Atmosphere
WARDA West Africa Rice Development Association (ICSU) — Agro.
WASA West African Science Association (ICSU/IBN) — Science general
WATCH Working Group on the Assessment of Toxic Chemicals (UK) — Chemical
WCAP World Climate Applications Programme (ICSU) — Climate
WCDP World Climate Data Programme (ICSU) — Data/climate
WCIP World Climate Impacts Programme (ICSU) — Climate
WCP World Climate Programme (ICSU) — Climate
WCRP World Climate Research Programme (WMO/ICSU) — Climate
WCS World Conservation Strategy (UNEP/IUCN) — Conservation
WDC World Data Centre (ICSU) — Data
WDDES World Digital Database for Environmental Sciences (ICSU) — Data
WECAFC Western Central Atlantic Fishery Commission (FAO) — Fish.
WED World Environment Day — Conservation
WEI World Environment Institute — Education
WERC World Environment and Resources Council — Conservation
WES Wetland Evaluation System — Habitats
WESTPAC Western Pacific Working Group (IOC) — Marine
WFA White Fish Authority (UK) — Fish.
WFP World Food Programme (FAO) — Food
WGMS World Glacier Monitoring Service (ICSU/SCAR) — Polar
WHO World Health Organization — Health
WHOI Woods Hole Oceanographic Institution — Oceanography
WICEM World Industry Conference on Environmental Management — Industry
WITO Working Group on Industrial Toxicological Research (TNO) — Toxicology
WITS World Ionosphere Thermosphere Study (ICSU) — Climate
WMO World Meterological Organization (UN) — Meteorology
WMS World Magnetic Survey (ICSU) — Geodesy
WOCE World Ocean Circulation Experiment (IOC/ICSU/SCOR) — Marine
WOCOL World Coal Study — Energy
WOO World Oceanographic Organization — Marine
WQUIS Water Quality Insurance Syndicate (USA) — Water
WRC Water Research Centre (UK) — Water
WRI World Resources Institute — Conservation
WSO World Safety Organization — Safety

WTC Worst Tolerable Compromise
WWF Worldwide Fund for Nature — Conservation
WWP Working Group on Water Pollution (Belgium) — Water
WWW World Weather Watch (WMO) — Climate

Zn Zinc — Chemical
ZnO Zinc oxide — Chemical

Appendix 4 USEFUL ADDRESSES

1. Intergovernmental agencies
(a) Headquarter addresses
Commission of the European Communities
   (CEC)
(Environment and Consumer Protection
   Services)
rue de la Loi 200
1049 Brussels
Belgium
Tel: +(32 2) 235 1111

Council of Europe (COE)
Information Department
Palais de l'Europe
BP 431 R6
67006 Strasbourg Cedex
France
Tel: +(33) 88 61 49 61

European Free Trade Association
9211 rue de Varembe
CH-1211 Geneva 20
Switzerland
Tel: +(41 22) 749 1111

United Nations
UN Plaza
New York
New York 10017, USA
Tel: +(1 212) 963 1234

United Nations
Palais des Nations
1211 Geneva
Switzerland
Tel: +(41 22) 98 58 50

United Nations Economic and Social Council
   (UN-ECOSOC)
Palais des Nations
1211 Geneva
Switzerland
Tel: +(41 22) 98 58 50

(b) Development agencies
General Agreement on Tariffs and Trade
   (UNCTAD-GATT)
Centre William Rappard
154 rue de Lausanne
1211 Geneva 21, Switzerland
Tel: +(41 22) 73 10 211

Organization for Economic Co-operation and
   Development
2 rue Andre-Pascal
75775 Paris Cedex 16
France
Tel: +(331) 45 24 82 00

UN Conference on Trade and Development
   (UNCTAD)
Palais des Nations
1211 Geneva 10, Switzerland
Tel: +(44 22) 98 58 50

UN Development Programme (UNDP)
One United Nations Plaza
New York
New York 10017, USA
Tel: +(1 212) 963 1234

UN Economic Commission for Europe
Palais des Nations
CH-1211 Geneva 10
Switzerland
Tel: +(44 22) 98 58 50

UN Industrial Development Organization
   (UNIDO)
Vienna International Centre
Wagramer Strasse 5
PO Box 300
A-1400 Vienna
Austria
Tel: +(43 1) 222 2631

(c) Environment
North Atlantic Treaty Organization (NATO)
Committee on the Challenges of Modern
   Society (CCMS)
NATO Information Service
B-1110 Brussels, Belgium
Tel: +(32) 728 4846

United Nations Educational, Scientific and
   Cultural Organization (UNESCO)
7 place de Fontenoy
F-75700 Paris, France
Tel: +(331) 45 68 10 00

United Nations Environment Programme
   (UNEP)
PO Box 30552
Nairobi, Kenya
Tel: +(254) 233 3930

UNEP Industry and Environment Office
Tour Mirabeau
39-43 quai Andre Citroen
39-43 Paris Cedex 15
France
Tel: +(331) 45 78 33 33

(d) Health, chemicals and ecotoxicology
International Agency for Research on Cancer
  (IARC)
150 cours Albert Thomas
69372 Lyon 2
France
Tel: +(33) 78 75 81 81

International Labour Office
4 rue des Morillons
CH-1211 Geneva 22
Switzerland
Tel: +(41 22) 299 6161

UNEP International Register of Potentially
  Toxic Chemicals
Pavillion du Petit Saconnex
16 avenue Jean Tremblay
CH-1209 Geneva
Switzerland
Tel: +(41 22) 798 8400

World Health Organization
20 avenue Appia
CH-1211 Geneva 27
Switzerland
Tel: +(41 22) 91 21 11

(e) Marine safety and pollution
International Maritime Organization (IMO)
Marine Environment Division
4 Albert Embankment
London SE1 7SR
Tel: +(44 71) 735 7611

(f) Food and agriculture
Food and Agriculture Organization (FAO)
via della Terme di Caracalla
00100 Rome, Italy
Tel: +(39 6) 514 1718

World Food Programme
via Christoforo Colombo 426
00145 Rome, Italy
Tel: +(39 6) 57971

(g) Population
UN Centre for Human Settlements (HABITAT)
PO Box 30030
Nairobi, Kenya
Tel: +(254 2) 333930

UN Population Fund (UNFPA)
222 East 42nd Street
New York
New York 10017, USA
Tel: +(1 212) 850 5600

(h) Meterology
World Meteorological Organization (WMO)
41 avenue Giuseppi Motta
PO Box 5
CH-1211 Geneva 20
Switzerland
Tel: +(41 22) 34 64 00

(i) Energy
International Energy Agency
OECD
2 rue André Pascal
75755 Paris Cedex 16
France
Tel: +(331) 45 24 82 00

(j) Nuclear and radiation
International Atomic Energy Agency
Vienna International Centre
Wagramer Strasse 5
PO Box 100
A-1400 Vienna
Austria
Tel: +(43 1) 23600

Nuclear Energy Agency
OECD
2 rue André Pascal
75755 Paris Cedex 16
France
Tel: +(331) 45 24 82 00

UN Scientific Committee on Atomic Radiation
PO Box 475
A-1011 Vienna
Austria
Tel: +(43 1) 23600

National and non-governmental scientific, conservation and other organizations

British Antarctic Survey
High Cross
Madingley Road
Cambridge CB3 0ET
Tel: +(44 223) 61188

Conservation Foundation
Lowther Lodge
Kensington Gore
London SW7 2AR
Tel: +(44 71) 235 1743

Council for Environmental Education
School of Education
University of Reading
London Road
Reading RG1 5AQ
Tel: +(44 734) 875234

Council for the Protection of Rural England
Warwick House
25 Buckingham Palace Road
London SW1
Tel: +(44 71) 976 6433

Countryside Commission (UK)
John Dower House
Crescent Place
Cheltenham
Gloucestershire GL50 3RA
Tel: +(44 242) 521 381

Department of the Environment
Marsham Street
London SW1
Tel: +(44 71) 276 3000

European Environment Bureau (EEB)
rue du Luxembourg 20
1040 Brussels, Belgium
Tel: +(32 2) 514 1250

Forestry Commission
231 Corstorphine Road
Edinburgh EH12 7AT
Tel: +(44 31) 334 0303

Greenpeace
30 Islington Green
London N1
Tel: +(44 71) 354 5100

Friends of the Earth
26–28 Underwood Street
London N1 7JQ
Tel: +(44 71) 490 0290

International Council of Scientific Unions
(ICSU)
51 Boulevard de Montmorency
75016 Paris, France
Tel: +(331) 45 25 03 29

- Committee on Data for Science and
  Technology (CODATA)
- Committee on Science and Technology in
  Developing Countries (COSTED)
- Committee on Water Research (COWAR)
- Scientific Committee on Antarctic
  Research (SCAR)
- Scientific Committee on Biotechnology
  (COBIOTECH)
- Scientific Committee on Oceanic Research
  (SCOR)
- Scientific Committee on Problems of the
  Environment (SCOPE)

ICSU Special Committee for the International
Geosphere-Biosphere Programme (SC-IGBP)
IGBP Secretariat
The Royal Swedish Academy of Sciences
Box 50005
S-104 05 Stockholm, Sweden
Tel: +(46 8) 15 04 30

International Chamber of Commerce
ICC United Kingdom
Centre Point
103 New Oxford Street
London WC1A 1QB
Tel: +(44 71) 240 5558

International Institute for Environment and
  Development (IIED)
3 Endsleigh Street
London WC1H 0DD
Tel: +(44 71) 388 2117

International Union for the Conservation of
  Nature and Natural Resources (IUCN)
avenue du Mont-Blanc
1196 Gland, Switzerland
Tel: +(41 22) 64 71 81

National Academy of Sciences
National Research Council
2101 Constitution Avenue
Washington DC 20418, USA
Tel: +(1 202) 334 2807

National Radiological Protection Board (UK)
Chilton, Didcot
Oxfordshire OX11 0RQ
Tel: +(44 235) 83 61 00

National Trust (UK)
36 Queen Anne's Gate
London SW1H 9AS
Tel: +(44 71) 222 9251

Natural Environmental Research Council
  (NERC)
Polaris House
North Star Avenue
Swindon
Wiltshire SN2 1EU
Tel: +(44 793) 411500

Nature Conservancy Council
Northminster House
Peterborough PE1 1UA
Tel: +(44 733) 40345

Overseas Development Administration
Eland House
Stag Place
London SW1E 5DH
Tel: +(44 71) 273 0216

Royal Society for Nature Conservation (RSNC)
The Green, Nettleham
Lincoln LN2 2NR
Tel: +(44 522) 752326

Royal Society for the Protection of Birds
The Lodge, Sandy
Bedfordshire SG19 2DL
Tel: +(44 767) 80551

Wildfowl and Wetlands Trust
Slimbridge
Gloucestershire GL2 7BT
Tel: +(44 453) 890 333

Worldwide Fund for Nature
11–13 Ockford Road
Godalming
Surrey GU7 1QU
Tel: +(44 483) 426444

Contact addresses for further information

The addresses listed below may be contacted for full information on the contents of bibliographies and databases, together with details on the methods for obtaining or accessing data.

ACCIS (Advisory Committee for the Co-
    ordination of Information Systems)
ACC Secretariat
Room S-3720
United Nations
New York, NY 10017, USA
Tel: +(1 212) 963 1234

ACCIS
Palais de Nations
CH-1211 Geneva 10
Switzerland
Tel: +(41 22) 98 85 91

Belindis
Belgian Information and Dissemination Service
Ministry of Economic Affairs
Rue J. A. de Mott 30
B-1040 Brussels, Belgium
Tel: +(32 2) 233 6737

BLAIZE-LINE and BLAIZE-LINK
British Library
2 Sheraton Street
London W1V 4BH
Tel: +(44 71) 636 1544

CDC (Caribbean Documentation Centre)
PO Box 1113
Port of Spain, Trinidad
Tel: +(500 809) 623 5595

CDC (Conservation for Development Centre)
IUCN, avenue du Mont-Blanc
1196 Gland, Switzerland
Tel: +(41 22) 64 71 81

CEC (see EUROBASES)

CEDOCAR
Centre de Documentation de l'Armament
36 boulevard Victor
F-75996 Paris-Armées, France
Tel: +(331) 45 52 45 34

CERVED
Società di Informatica delle Camere di
    Commercio Italiane
Corso Stato Uniti 14
I-35100 Padova, Italy
Tel: +(39 4) 984 9411

CILEA
Consorzio Inter-universitario Lombardo per
    l'Elaboranzione Automatica
via R Sanzio 4
I-20090 Segrate
Milano, Italy
Tel: +(39 2) 213 2541

CNUCE
Institutio de Centro Nazionale Ricerche
via Santa Maria
I-56100 Pisa, Italy
Tel: +(39 5) 05 93 11

DC
DATA CENTRALEN
Retortvej 6-8
DK-2500 Valby
Denmark
Tel: +(45 1) 46 81 22

DATA STAR
Data Star Marketing
The Plaza Suite
Jermyn Street
London SW1Y 9HJ
Tel: +(44 71) 930 7646

DIALOG
Learned Information/DIALOG
Woodside, Hinksey Hill
Oxford OX1 5AU
Tel: +(44 865) 73 02 75

DIMDI
Deutsches Institut für Medizinische
    Dokumentation & Information
Weisshausstrasse 27
D-5000 Köln 41
Federal Republic of Germany
Tel: +(49 2) 214 7241

ECA, Economic Commission for Africa
PO Box 3001
Addis Ababa, Ethiopia
Tel: +(251 1) 44 72 00

ECLAC, Economic Commission for Latin
America and the Caribbean
PO Box 1113
Port of Spain
Trinidad & Tobago
Tel: +(1 809) 623 5595
Casilla 179-D
Santiago, Chile
Tel: +(56 2) 48 50 51

ESCAP, Economic and Social Commission for
Asia and the Pacific
United Nations Building
Rajdamnern Avenue
Bangkok 10200, Thailand
Tel: +(66 2) 282 9161

ECHO
European Commission Host Organization
BP 2373
L-1023 Luxembourg
Tel: +(35 2) 48 80 41

Executive Telecom
Human Resource Information Network
9585 Valpariso Court
Indianapolis
IN 46268, USA
Tel: +(1 317) 872 2045

ESA-IRS
European Space Agency Information Retrieval
Services
Via Galileo Galilei
1-Frascati, Italy
Tel: +(39 6) 94 18 01

EUROBASES
Commission of the European Communities
200 Rue de la Loi
B-1049 Brussels, Belgium
Tel: +((33 2) 23 50 01

EXIS
Exis Limited
38 Tavistock Street
London WC2E 7DB
Tel: +(44 71) 623 3456

FAO
Food and Agriculture Organization
via della Terme di Caracalla
0100 Rome, Italy
Tel: +(39 6) 57971

FIZ Technik
Ostbahnhofstrasse 13
D-Frankfurt-Main
Federal Republic of Germany
Tel: +(49 69) 430 8225

HSE
Health and Safety Executive
Baynards House
Chepstow Place
London W2 4TF
Tel: +(44 71) 229 3456

IAEA
International Atomic Energy Agency
Vienna International Centre
PO Box 100
1400 Vienna, Austria
Tel: +(43 1) 22 23 60

ICAO
International Civil Aviation Organization
1000 Sherbrooke Street West
Montreal, Quebec H3A 2R2, Canada
Tel: +(1 514) 285 8219

ICJ
International Court of Justice
Peace Palace
2517-KJ The Hague, The Netherlands
Tel: +(31 70) 392 4441

ILO
International Labour Organization
4 Rue route des Morillons
1211 Geneva 22, Switzerland
Tel: +(41 22) 99 61 11

INKADATA
Leopoldshafen 2
D-7514 Eggenstein
Federal Republic of Germany
Tel: +(49 72) 47 82 45 68

IRS-DIALTECH
Department of Trade and Industry
Room 392, Ashdown House
123 Victoria Street
London SW1E 6RB
Tel: +(44 71) 212 5638

ITC International Trade Centre
UNCTAD-GATT
54–56 rue de Montbrillant
CH-1202 Geneva, Switzerland
Tel: +(41 22) 30 01 11

MAB National Committee (UK)
MAB Secretary
(Natural Environment Research Council)
Institute of Terrestrial Ecology
Furzebrook Research Station
Wareham, Dorset BH20 5AS
Tel: +(44 929) 551518

MIK-KIBIK
Mic-Karolinska Institutets Bibliotek Och
  Informationcentral
Box 60201
Solnavaegen 1
Doktorsringen 21C
S-10401 Stockholm, Sweden
Tel: +(46 8) 23 22 70

OECD
Organization for Economic Co-operation and
  Development
2 rue André Pascal
75775 Paris Cedex 16, France
Tel: +(33 1) 45 24 82 00

ORBIT
Pergamon Infoline
12 Vandy Street
London EC2A 2DE
Tel: +(44 71) 377 4650

PAHO
Pan American Health Organization
Apartado postal 37-473
06696 Mexico City
DF Mexico
Tel: +(52 5) 254 2033

QUESTEL
Télésystèmes Questel
83-85 Boulevard Vincent Auriol
F-75013 Paris, France
Tel: +(33 1) 45 82 64 64

STN International
PO Box 2465
D-7500 Karlsruhe 1
Federal Republic of Germany
Tel: +(49 721) 47 82 45 66

Telecom Gold
42 Weston Street
London SE1 3QD
Tel: +(44 71) 403 6777

UNCTAD-GATT
Centre William Rappard
154 rue de Lausanne
1211 Geneva 21, Switzerland
Tel: +(41 22) 731 0211

UN-CTC
UN Centre on Transnational Corporations
United Nations
New York, New York 10017, USA
Tel: +(1 212) 963 1234

UN-DIESA
Department of International Economic and
  Social Affairs
Palais des Nations
1211 Geneva 10, Switzerland
Tel: +(41 22) 98 58 50

UN-DIS
UN Development Information System
Department of International Economic and
  Social Affairs
United Nations
New York, New York 10017, USA
Tel: +(1 212) 963 1234

UNDRO
UN Disaster Relief Co-ordinator
Palais des Nations
1211 Geneva 10, Switzerland
Tel: +(41 22) 31 02 11

UN-ECE, Economic Commission for Europe
Palais des Nations
1211 Geneva 10, Switzerland
Tel: +(41 22) 34 60 10

UNEP-GEMS
Monitoring & Research Centre
The Octagon Building
459A Fulham Road
London SW10 0QX
Tel: +(44 71) 376 1577

UNEP-INFOTERRA
Department of the Environment
2 Marsham Street (Rm P3/008D)
London SW1P 3EB
Tel: +(44 71) 212 5270

UNEP, Geneva
Palais des Nations
1211 Geneva 10, Switzerland
Tel: +(41 22) 98 58 50

UNEP, Nairobi
PO Box 30552
Nairobi, Kenya
Tel: +(254 2) 33 39 30

UNEP, Paris
Industry and Environment Office
Tour Mirabeau
39–43 quai André Citroen
75739 Paris, France
Tel: +(33 1) 45 78 33 33

Unesco
7 place de Fontenoy
75700 Paris, France
Tel: +(33 1) 45 68 10 00

UNIDO
Vienna International Centre
PO Box 300
1400 Vienna, Austria
Tel: +(43 1) 222 2631

UN-RISD
UN Research Institute for Social Development
Palais des Nations
1211 Geneva 10, Switzerland
Tel: +(41 22) 98 58 50

UN-SIS
UN Statistical Office
New York, New York 10017
USA
Tel: +(1 212) 963 1234

WCMC/IUCN
World Conservation Monitoring Centre
219c Huntingdon Road
Cambridge CB3 0DL
Tel: +(44 22) 327 7314

WHO (World Health Organization)
20 avenue Appia
1211 Geneva 27, Switzerland
Tel: +(41 22) 91 21 11

WHO, IARC
International Agency for Research on Cancer
150 Cours Albert Thomas
69372 Lyon Cedex 2, France
Tel: +(33) 78 75 81 81

WMO World Meteorological Organization
Case Postale 5
1211 Geneva 20
Switzerland
Tel: +(41 22) 33 64 00

World Bank
Information Services Division
66 avenue d'Ièna, Paris
Tel: +(33 1) 47 23 54 21

The telephone numbers listed are based upon the international dialling system. Dialling from the UK, 010 is required for access to the international telephone network. This number is, of course, different according to country.

Thus the plus sign indicates that the appropriate international access code according to originating country must be used; the bracketed numbers (xx yy) provide the country code (xx –) and the area code (– yy); the digits following the brackets are the subscribers' numbers. Dialling from within the same country, the 'y' numbers must be preceded by a zero. For example, within the UK, the number to dial for the Department of the Environment from outside the Central London area would be 071 222 5270. A local caller would not need to use 071.

APPENDIX 5 THE FRAMEWORK FOR INTERNATIONAL AND REGIONAL PROGRAMMES

Intergovernmental organizations, conventions and programmes

The primary functions of intergovernmental organizations such as the United Nations, the Organization for Economic Co-operation and Development and the various secretariats set up by these organizations under international treaties and agreements (such as the United Nations Environment Programme) are to gather information from member governments for the purpose of enabling member governments to enact common approaches to problems of international significance in their national legislation. The UN consists of a central political organization and a galaxy of autonomous specialized agencies (FAO, WHO, Unesco, WMO, ILO, etc.) and programme agencies such as UNEP, UNDP, UNPF, UNCTAD-GATT, etc., whose activities are co-ordinated by the UN Economic and Social Council. The UN's difficulties in co-ordinating and controlling the activities of its agencies, exacerbated by political competition and rhetoric, is well-aired in the media. This is at the expense of appreciation of some of the valuable scientific work that is done in its name in the fields of health, the environment, labour relations, child labour, human rights, marine safety, maritime law (Law of the Sea Conventions), population, trading standards, economic development, nuclear safety and global security, most of which are referred to in this book.

Assuming that the UN system will evolve into an organization that will be better able to respond to the global forces with which it is faced, including poverty, the communications explosion, electronic transfers of money, world demographics (population, migration and urbanization), emergent religious and political dogmatism, drugs, Aids, terrorism, disaster relief, the environment, new and more significant roles in global issues will need to be assumed by industry and private sector agencies.

UN Economic and Social Council (ECOSOC)

ECOSOC has five regional commissions:

1. ECE (Economic Commission for Europe, USSR, USA and Canada)
2. ESCAP (Economic and Social Commission for Asia and The Pacific)
   Australia, Bangladesh, China, Fiji, India, Indonesia, Iran, Japan, Korea, Malaysia, New Zealand, Pakistan, Papua New Guinea, the Philippines, Sri Lanka, Thailand
3. CEPAL (European Commission for Latin America)
4. ECA (Economic Commission for Africa)
5. ECWA (Economic Commission for West Africa)

UN Educational, Social and Cultural Organization (Unesco)

Neither the UK nor the USA support Unesco. Both countries withdrew from the Organization on account of Unesco's radical political alignments, its system of political appointees within a top-heavy and financially profligate secretariat, lack of focus in its programme and highly controversial promotion of a 'new world information order', justifying state intervention in the flow of news. Nevertheless, many of Unesco's programme activities in the environment have provided an important focus for the scientific community to study problems which are recognized to be of universal and common interest. Despite politics, materials developed for environmental education and awareness building in schools are both apolitical and of high quality.

Unesco's 'Man and the Biosphere Programme' (MAB), launched in 1971, followed by ICSU's International Biological Programme extending its scientific base to encourage international studies into the interface between ecologically critical areas, combining the natural sciences with economic and social aspects – in other words, man in relation to his environment. Thus MAB is concerned with developing scientific information for application to resources management, conservation, education and training.

Internationally, MAB is operated in co-operation with FAO, WHO, UNEP and WMO, as well as with international non-governmental scientific and conservation bodies such as ICSU and the IUCN. Nationally, MAB programmes are initiated and conducted through national committees in Unesco member states and in the UK, through the Institute of Terrestrial Ecology (ITE of NERC).

The broad scientific and sociological nature of MAB's programmes is exemplified in the Integrated

Project on Arid Lands (IPAL), among others, which is a multidisciplinary project involving specialists in climatology, hydrography, agriculture, geology and biology. In Europe, another MAB project is concerned with establishing a greater compatibility in the Pays d'Enhaut between tourism, agriculture and the local ecology. Overall, it is associated with field research projects in developed countries and the Third World, but especially in relation to tropical and subtropical forest systems, temperate and Mediterranean forest landscapes and savannah and grasslands in temperate and arid areas.

A principal feature of the MAB programme is the establishment of an international network of Biosphere Reserves, representing particular types of ecosystem, which provide the basis for long-term research into ecosystem dynamics. Apart from MAB, Unesco is associated with the oceanographic, geophysical, meteorological and other specialist ecological and environmental activities in its sister agencies.

United Nations Environment Programme (UNEP)

UNEP's funding is in part (some 5%) provided by the regular UN budget, with most of its activity and secretarial costs provided by additional voluntary contributions from national governments. UNEP's overall annual budget is $35 million and programme expenditure is some $5.0 million, mostly drawn from surpluses of income over expenditure from the earlier years of its operations.

UNEP Industry and Environment Office (UNEP/IEO)

The UNEP Industry and Environment Office, based in Paris, provides the basis for dialogue between industry and the UN system. With a staff of but seven people operating on a $1.2 million budget, it seeks collaboration with industry associations to produce technical guidelines and to seek their participation at conferences and seminars.

Scientific Committee on Atomic Radiation (UNSCEAR)

UNSCEAR operates as an independent agency established by the UN General Assembly working in association with UNEP and the International Atomic Energy Agency (IAEA).

Other UN specialist agencies

Apart from Unesco and UNEP, which take a leading role in the development of international environmental programmes, the environment is on the agenda of the International Maritime Organization (marine pollution and safety of life at sea), the World Meteorology Organization (climate and weather), the International Atomic Energy Agency (nuclear power and its alternatives), the World Health Organization (chemical safety and health effects of pollutants), the Food and Agriculture Organization, the International Labour Office, the UN Conference on Trade and Development and the UN Industrial Development Organization.

Regional intergovernment organizations: OECD

The OECD environment programme began in 1970, two years before the Stockholm Conference, with basically research-oriented activities focused upon policy issues relating to the quest for comparative economic advantages which can accrue to its member states. OECD's programmes for the 1990s extend previous work into trans-boundary air pollution and encompass a range of other issues, including chemical safety, industrial accidents, environmental policy evaluation, sustainable economic development and the instruments for expanded co-operation between member states and developing countries.

International Energy Agency

Founded in November 1974, the IEA provides an institutional counterpart to OPEC on behalf of OECD member countries, excluding France, providing a forum for the energy industries in their relations with government (also OECD Nuclear Energy Agency).

Commission of the European Communities

The CEC Comprises 25 Directorates General (DGs); DG11 (Environment, Consumer Protection and Nuclear Safety) is responsible, *inter alia*, for drafting European environmental legislation. 1992 sees the end of the EC's Fourth Environmental Action Programme (1987–92) and the first year of the implementation of the 1987 Single European Act (SEA), in which environmental protection requirements also become a component of other EC policies (Articles 130 R, S and T), e.g. the Common Agricultural (CAP) and Regional, Social and Transport policies.

The Single European Act enables the EC to propose and adopt binding legislation upon member states as well as permitting more stringent legislation to be adopted by them, provided it is not protectionist. It extends the Commission's powers from its current tasks of ensuring the implementation of EC Directives by member states, identifying approaches to regulating chemical substances, rights of public access to information and to examine the employment potential of environmental investment. The 'Polluter Pays Principle' is included within the Act as a Recommendation along with other mechanisms to impose taxes and levies on polluters within national legislative programmes.

A key aspect of the EC environmental programme is measurement, verification, certification, information technology and early-warning systems, and the establishment of the necessary mechanisms for data sharing and maintaining community awareness of the costs and impact of neglect. Specific priorities are ocean and fresh water pollution, atmospheric pollution and the 'greenhouse effect', waste management, chemical evaluation, biotechnology, nuclear and radiation monitoring and safety and the protection of nature and natural resources with additional reference to an EC strategy for the protection of tropical forests. A European Environment Agency is proposed for 1992. All twelve states are bidding to act as host and Cambridge in the UK is a likely choice.

The environmental effects of 1992 are discussed in IEEP's 'Environmental Policy and 1992' report to the UK Department of the Environment. It asserts that 'not all effects are immediately obvious and [that] no single dramatic change should necessarily be expected'. Nevertheless, it is worth reiterating the main points concerning the additional prosperity anticipated with the completion of the internal market and its implications for transport, energy, the working environment and air pollution (CO_2 specifically).

Summary of EC environmental legislation

The hierarchy of EC statutory instruments are as follows:

1. *Regulations:* are binding and directly applicable in all member states.
2. *Directives:* must be implemented within the legislation of member states within the given time limits.
3. *Decisions:* are binding upon individuals, member states and legal entities.
4. *Recommendations and resolutions:* non-binding.

The basic range of topics covered are listed below.

Regulations

ACE (Action by the Community Relating to the Environment) establishes funding of 24 million ECUs for demonstration projects on clean technology, environmental monitoring, habitat restoration and maintenance, etc. (1892/84).

CITES (Convention on Trade in Endangered Species) extends the trade prohibition provisions of the convention and introduces a uniform system of documentation (3626/82).

Cetaceans: prohibits import of whale parts or products for commercial purposes (348/81).

Environmentally Sensitive Areas (ESA): Council Regulation EEC No. 797/85.

Directives

There are some 100 EC directives concerned with control and monitoring the implementation of environmental policy and legislation in member states. These are broadly classified below by topic giving titles of the principal items:

Air pollution
Air pollution Framework Directive
Sulphur Dioxide and Suspended Particulates (80/779/EEC)
Nitrogen Dioxide Emissions (85/205/EEC)
Motor vehicle pollution (83/351/EEC)
Chlorofluorocarbons (82/795/EEC)
Lead in air (62/884/EEC)

Industrial plants
Framework Directive (84/360/EEC)

Energy, fuels and transport
Sulphur content of gas oil (75/716/EEC)
Lead in petrol (85/210/EEC)

Conservation and special protection areas
Conservation of Wild Birds (79/409/EEC)
Environmental Impact Assessment (EIA) (85/337/EEC)
Seal pups and products (85/444/EEC)

Chemical controls
Testing of Chemicals (67/548/EEC *et seq.*)
Industrial Action and Emergency Response ('Seseo Directive', 82/501/EEC)
Asbestos (87/217/EEC)
Marketing Dangerous Substances (76/769/EEC)
Labelling of Dangerous Chemicals
Directive on the Safe Handling of Benzene
Harmonized Controls (79/631/EEC)
Systematic evaluation

Waste
Framework for Waste (75/442/EEC)
Waste Oils (75/439//EEC)
Polychlorinated biphenyls (PCBs) and polychlorinated terphenyls (PCTs) (76/403/EEC)
Toxic and Dangerous Waste (78/319/EEC)
Trans-frontier Shipment (84/631/EEC)
Sewage Sludge (86/278/EEC)
New Municipal Waste Incineration Plants (89/369/EEC)
Existing Muncipal Waste Incineration Plants (89/429/EEC)
EC Network for Environmental Technology Transfer (NETT): information exchange on clean technologies, cost-effective pollution abatement and waste-treatment methods.

Water quality
Detergents (73/404/EEC)
Surface Water for Drinking (75/440/EEC)
Bathing Water (76/160/EEC)
Dangerous Substances (76/464/EEC)
Freshwater Fish (78/659/EEC)
Shellfish Waters (79/923/EEC)
Sampling of Surface Water for Drinking (76/869/EEC)
Protection of Groundwater Against Pollution Caused by Certain Dangerous Substances (80/68/EEC)
Drinking Water (80/778/EEC)
Mercury (82/176/EEC)
Cadmium (83/513/EEC)
Hexachlorocyclohexane (84/491/EEC)
Enabling Directive (86/280/EEC)

Decisions
Convention for the Protection of the Rhine against Chemical Pollution, Berne, 1963 and annexes (77/586/EEC; 82/460 and 85/336); adopting the foregoing
Information Exchange on Fresh Water Quality (86/574/EEC)
Paris Convention on marine pollution from land-based sources (75/737/EEC) and subsequent annexes related to mercury and cadmium (85/613/EEC); adopting
Barcelona Convention for the Protection of the Mediterranean Sea from Pollution and Subsequent Protocols relating to Dumping from Ships and Aircraft (77/585/EEC); emergency response (81/420/EEC); pollution from land-based sources (83/101/EEC) and specially protected areas (84/132/EEC)
CORINE (Co-ordination of Information on the Environment): made under the EIA Directive as a four-year pilot project to collect information on biotopes, atmospheric pollution, resources of the Mediterranean (85/338/EEC)
Berne Convention: approving the convention to have regard for conservation of habitats in planning and development policies (82/72/EEC)
Bonn Convention: approving the convention on the protection of endangered species of migratory birds and to provide information to UNEP (82/461/EEC)
Canberra Convention: approving the convention and collecting data (81/691/EEC)
Convention on Long-Range Trans-boundary Air Pollution: adopting the convention (81/462/EEC)
Information System on Oil Pollution from the Sea (86/85/EEC)
EMEP: co-operative programme of monitoring and evaluating long-range transmission of air pollutants in Europe (86/277/EEC)
CORINAIR: European Inventory of Atmospheric Emissions
Information exchange on air-polluting substances, adding heavy metals, NO_x, CO_2 and ozone (82/459/EEC)

Recommendations
'Polluter Pays Principle' (PPP). The application of PPP should not make any distinction between

pollution affecting member states' own or other countries (trans-boundary implications) (75/436/Euratom, ECSC, EEC)

Pollution Control Cost Evaluation: cost evaluation methods and harmonization of information collection for purposes of direct inter-state comparability (79/3/EEC).

Council of Europe

The Council of Europe (COE) executive committee consists of European Ministers of Foreign Affairs. COE's European Committee for the Conservation of Nature and Natural Resources (CDPE), set up in 1962, has established a legislation framework for the management of natural habitats, species protection and natural resources and promotes harmonization of nature-conservation policies, including the relationship between nature and agriculture, hedgerow conservation and protection of endangered species under the CITES Convention. Conventions, agreements and programmes with which COE is associated or has initiated are:

Berne Convention on the Conservation of European Wildlife and Habitats, 1979
European Convention for the Protection of International Watercourses against Pollution (draft)
Charter on Invertebrates, 1986
European Information Centre for Nature Conservation
Biogenetic Reserves; COE's Network of Biogenetic Reserves (Biotopes of European significance);
European Campaign for the Countryside European Diploma for well-protected sites

COE acts as a bridge between EC and other European countries on questions of farming and agriculture orientation, farming and wildlife and in other areas where co-operation can improve the quality of life.

European Free Trade Association

The EFTA environment programme tends to operate in association with the EC as well as the Council of Europe but mainly providing a focus on EC environmental activities for its member states.

North Atlantic Treaty Organization

The Committee on the Challenges of Modern Society (CCMS) was set up in 1969 on the initiative of President Nixon to extend the defence remit of NATO member states into promoting the uses of science and technology for improving the quality of life. CCMS develops pilot scientific studies which complement the work of specialist international organizations in health, meteorology, marine pollution, energy conservation, alternative energy, waste disposal, air pollution and the environmental aspects of defence activities, including effects on flora and fauna.

Basic framework of legislation and responsibility in the UK

Government departments responsible for environmental legislation
Department of Trade and Industry
Department of the Environment
Department of Energy
Ministry of Agriculture, Fisheries and Food (MAFFs)
Department of Agriculture and Fisheries, Scotland (DAFs)

Principal UK legislation relating to the environment and protection of species
National Parks and Access to the Countryside Act, 1949
Prevention of Oil Pollution Act, 1971
Town and Country Planning Act, 1971 (1972, Scotland)
Control of Pollution Act (COPA), 1974
Health and Safety at Work, etc. Act, 1974
Wildlife and Countryside Act, 1981
The Control of Trade in Endangered Species (Enforcement) Regulations, 1985

Statutory and policy agencies
National Forests Authority
National River Authority
Controlled Waste Inspectorate (DoE)
Health and Safety Commission
Industrial Air Pollution Inspectorate (DoE)
Inspectorate of Pollution (HMIP – proposed in new Bill)

Developments within the Environmental Protection Bill and proposals for an 'Integrated Pollution Control (IPC)' system administered by HMIP will regulate emissions from industrial plant as they affect air, water and land, rather than treating separately under different control agencies. The implementation of the Bill would co-ordinate the provisions of various environmentally related Acts of Parliament, and the often-conflicting activities of control agencies, within the IPC system. Greater direct responsibilities are being proposed for local authorities.

Provisions of the Bill
Formal operating licences to be obtained by chemical manufacturers, smelting works, oil refineries, etc. in England and Wales, detailing industrial processes for inspection and regulation (affecting some 3,500 enterprises)
Right of public access to licence details
Division of the NCC into regional agencies and combining the work of the NCC and Countryside Commission in Wales and Scotland
Prison sentences and unlimited fines for serious pollution offences
Waste controls including radioactive substances; licensing systems and responsibilities extending to final disposal; local councils as regulating authorities; recycling; import bans on hazardous cargoes; public registers of radioactive waste; no exemptions for public agencies
Disposal of hazardous chemicals. New storage and disposal regulations
Dumping at sea. Licences required for all vessels to dump in the UK sector of the North Sea
Defining 'statutory nuisances', including noise and gaseous emissions
Litter and waste recycling. Increased local authority responsibility for public lands and urban cleanliness; fines
Genetically modified organisms (GMOs)
Authorization for proposed uses of GMOs
Straw and stubble burning (under MAFFS)
Chemical controls. Mechanisms for assessing the effects on human health of industrial chemicals

Appendix 6 SELECT BIBLIOGRAPHY AND REFERENCES

Acknowledgement has been given to organizations which have provided data and information making possible the publication of this book. In addition, reference has been made to the following.

Darwin, C., *On the Origin of Species*, John Murray, London, 1859

Ehrlich, Paul R. and Ehrlich, Anne H., *Population, Resources, Environment*, W. H. Freeman, San Francisco, 1970

European Community Environmental Legislation series

GESAMP, *The State of the Marine Environment*, UNEP Regional Seas Reports and Studies No. 115, UNEP, 1990

Haigh, Nigel and Baldock, David, *Environmental Policy and 1992*, IEEP, 1989

IEEP, *The Organisation of Nature Conservation in Selected EC Countries*, October 1987

International Commission on International Development Issues, *North–South: A Programme for Survival* (The Brandt Commission Report), Pan Books, London, 1980

IUCN, *World Conservation Strategy*, 1980

IUCN, *African Wildlife Laws*, Environmental Policy and Law Occasional Paper No. 3, undated

Malthus, T. R., *Essay on the Principle of Population*, Macmillan, London, 1803 (9th edition, 1826)

McKeown, T., *The Modern Rise of Population*, Edward Arnold, London, 1976

McKibben, Bill, *The End of Nature*, Viking/Random House, New York, 1989

NRPB, *Living with Radiation*, 1989

NRPB, *Board Statement of Radon in Homes*, National Radiological Protection Board, Vol. 1, No. 1, 1990

NRPB, *Radioactive Waste Management in the UK*, March 1990

OECD, *State of the Environment, 1985*, OECD, Paris, 1985

OECD, *Energy Technologies for Reducing Emissions of Greenhouse Gases*, Proceedings of an Experts Seminar 12–14 April 1989, International Energy Agency, Paris, 1989

Perutz, M. F., 'Is Britain Befouled?' *New York Review of Books*, 23 November 1989

Prather, Michael J. et al., *An Assessment of the Impact on Stratispheric Chemistry and Ozone Caused by the Launch of the Space Shuttle and Titan IV*, Report to Congress from the Upper Atmosphere Program, NASA, 1990

Proceedings of Seminar on Pesticides in Agriculture, EC–EFTA Meeting, University of Agricultural Sciences, Uppsala, Sweden, 14–15 November 1989

Report of the 1985 Conference on the Assessment of the Role of Carbon Dioxide and of Other Greenhouse Gases in the Climate Variations and Associated Impacts (The Villach Report), 1985

Social Trends 19, Central Statistical Office, HMSO, London, 1989

UNEP, *Radiation: Doses, Effects, Risks*, 1985

UNEP, *Environmental Data Report*, Monitoring and Research Centre and World Resources Institute, Bakewell Scientific Editions, 1989/90

UNSCEAR, *Sources, Effects and Risks of Ionising Radiation*, Report to the United Nations General Assembly, New York, 1988

USGS, *Our Changing Planet: The FY 1991 US Global Change Research Program*, A Report by the Committee on Earth Sciences, 1990

Vonnegut, Kurt, *Galapagos*, Jonathan Cape, London, 1985

World Commission on Environment and Development, *Our Common Future* (The Brundtland Report), Oxford University Press, Oxford, 1987

Meetings and conferences

11–15 June 1990: International Conference on the Role of Polar Regions in Global Change, University of Alaska, Fairbanks, Alaska

15–19 July 1990: CODATA '90, 12th International Codata Conference, Columbus, Ohio

September 1990: Conservation and Management of Rivers, Nature Conservancy Council, York (Dr P. J. Boon, NCC)

September 1990: 'Clean Technology' (David Pounder, Department of the Environment, Marsham Street, London SW1P 3PY)

29 October–7 November 1990: Second World Climate Conference, WMO, Geneva

March 1991: 'Environmental Control in the Steel Industry', International Iron and Steel Institute (IISI), Brussels

1992: World Climate Conference (proposed)

1992: 'Twenty Years after Stockholm', Brazil

1992: World Parks Conference

INDEX